A Lion for Love

A LION FOR LOVE

A CRITICAL BIOGRAPHY OF

STENDHAL

BY

ROBERT ALTER

IN COLLABORATION WITH CAROL COSMAN

Harvard University Press

CAMBRIDGE, MASSACHUSETTS

1986

Published by arrangement with Basic Books, Inc.

Library of Congress Cataloging-in-Publication Data

Alter, Robert.
   A lion for love.

   Reprint. Originally published: New York : Basic
Books, © 1979.
      Includes index.
      1. Stendhal, 1783–1842. 2. Novelists,
French—19th century—Biography. I. Cosman,
Carol. II. Title.
[PQ2436.A5   1986]   848'.309 [B]   86-11984
ISBN 0-674-53575-8

For Tom and Marilyn

two of the Happy Few

To speak of Stendhal means each time to be condemned to the impression that you have said nothing, that he has eluded you, that everything remains to be said. One must resign oneself, then, to restoring him to the unpredictable wonder of his own sudden utterance.

JEAN-PIERRE RICHARD,
Littérature et sensation

Enfin Dominique regarde *love as a* lion terrible *only at forty seven.*

STENDHAL, in the margin of
Promenades dans Rome

CONTENTS

[ix]

CONTENTS

Part Three
The Free Lance

Part Four
The Consul

PREFACE

STENDHAL has elicited so much intelligent attention and industrious research that a few words are in order about the need for a new biography. There is now a substantial international body of first-rate criticism of Stendhal's fiction. Some of the more relevant French studies will be cited in the course of this life, and to touch on only a few of the leading items of Stendhal criticism written in English, one might mention the graceful and perceptive discussions by Robert Martin Adams, Victor Brombert, Harry Levin, and Michael Wood. English biographical accounts of Stendhal, however, are by no means in the same class as these critical studies. When I began preliminary work on this book in 1973, no full-scale English biography had appeared since Matthew Josephson's large, well-meaning, lumbering, and often inaccurate 1946 volume. Since then, biographies by Joanna Richardson and Gita May have been published: both make dutiful use of the available scholarship, but each in different ways strikes me as lacking a fresh, or, indeed, a coherent, critical perception of Stendhal, and each falls short of the complexities of its subject.

In France, an enormous amount of biographical research has been done: nineteenth-century hotel registries, municipal records, diplomatic archives, and unpublished memoirs and letters have been scrutinized to ascertain every possible geographical displacement, every passing acquaintance in Stendhal's life. And yet, perhaps because in France they order these matters so differently, there is no single book that, by Anglo-American standards, could be considered a satisfying literary biography. Henri Martineau's nine-hundred-page opus (1952–53), the fruit of a lifetime of research, is impressive in clarifying many factual matters but often debatable or deficient in its interpretative views. Martineau's more lasting contributions, in fact, are his three invaluable guidebooks to Stendhal's movements, acquaintances, and writings, respectively, *Le Calendrier de Stendhal*, *Petit Dictionnaire stendhalien*, and *L'Oeuvre de Stendhal*. Perhaps the most subtle inquiries into Stendhal's life are those conducted by Paul Arbelet over half a century ago, but they deal only with the youth and early manhood, and later research has uncovered important material unavailable to Arbelet. Victor Del Litto, Martineau's successor as dean of Stendhal studies, has done admirable work as a bibliographer, editor, and intellectual historian, but his 1965 life, however sensible, is of very modest proportions, virtually intended as a means of setting the context for the display of documents and illustrations.

Stendhal is such a complicated, elusive, and compelling figure, the connections between his life and work are so multifarious and at times ambiguous, that what was needed, I came to feel, was a biography in which the narrative and interpretative strands would be constantly intertwined. Interpretation in my understanding did not imply the presumption of psychoanalytic conjecture, but I tried to find ways of talking about Stendhal's life that would tactfully direct readers toward its psychological dimensions, at least at the most appropriate junctures.

This study is intended, moreover, as a critical biography where no proper one exists. Though the facts of Stendhal's life—his relations with women, his involvement in the historical movements of his age, the long wayward course of his ambition—are in themselves fascinating, his life is more than a matter of historical gossip because, after all, he is the man who wrote *La Chartreuse de Parme* and *Le Rouge et le Noir*. I have sought to give some concrete sense of how the major fiction emerged from the experience of the author, without, however, assuming that this implied a search for "models" of the fictional characters in Stendhal's life or that the work could be reductively explained by the life. Seeing the shifting correspondences between life and work meant for me not only attending to themes, values, and psychological patterns in the fiction but also some close analysis of how in details of style and technique Stendhal managed to create a form of the novel so distinctively his own.

I would not have undertaken this large task of research and synthesis without the steadily perceptive collaboration of my wife, Carol Cosman. We read all of the primary texts, and many of the secondary ones, in parallel. Occasionally, we had formal evaluative sessions on our readings, but more often Stendhal's motives and habits and literary craft simply insinuated themselves as subjects of discussion over breakfast coffee or dinner dishes and at odd times in between. He became a thoroughly agreeable ghostly addition to our family during the past five years—a test of domestic experience, perhaps, in which other writers would not have worn so well. The specific planning of each chapter and all the actual writing were done by me, as were the translations of all French texts. My wife then went over the draft of each chapter, raising occasional but invariably helpful objections about anything from the choice of a facile adjective to the dubious attribution of a motive or the absence of a particular historical context.

PREFACE

The finished versions of each chapter were read by our friends Tom Schmidt and Marilyn Fabe, who served energetically and shrewdly as our ideal general readers. The manuscript as a whole was then read by Will and Louise Clubb, who were equally admirable as our ideal professional readers. The first three chapters were also examined by Marc Blanchard, who made a number of helpful suggestions, and the book has benefited from the comments of still another alert reader, Chana Kronfeld.

I have kept footnotes to a readable minimum, citing only those sources that seemed strictly necessary and wherever possible giving references to Stendhal's works after the quotations in parenthesis by chapter number or by date in the case of the correspondence and the journal. For the fiction, journal, letters, and autobiographical writings, the French text used was that of Henri Martineau's Pléiade editions. Otherwise, I have used the more recent Del Litto–Abravenel version in the Éditions Rencontre, except for a few odd texts covered only in the old Divan volumes of the complete works. Titles of Stendhal's books are given in French because some of them sound odd in English (e.g., *Memoirs of an Egotist*) while others are known by more than one English title (e.g., *The Red and the Black,* which is, alas, *Scarlet and Black* in the Penguin Edition). Most of the titles, in any case, should be quite intelligible to the English reader.

Monetary figures are cited in the francs of Stendhal's time. To get some rough idea of what these sums mean, the reader, keeping in mind the misleading aspects of all such equivalences, can figure that one franc during this period might more or less equal two 1979 U.S. dollars or one 1979 English pound.

On the subject of dollars, I am grateful to the John Simon Guggenheim Memorial Foundation and to the Humanities Research Council of the University of California at Berkeley for their generous support of this project. I also would like to thank the Committee on Research at Berkeley for covering typing costs and other incidental research expenses. I am indebted to Elisabeth Giansiracusa for her patient and intelligent research assistance and to Florence Myer for typing the manuscript with the same care and precision with which she has done all my books since I came to Berkeley. Professor Victor Del Litto showed great kindness in making illustrations available from his collection. But I suppose this book owes its greatest debt of gratitude to Stendhal himself, who managed, as few of us do, to be so abundant and intense and various in his character and in his writing that, as Robert Martin Adams once aptly remarked, we shall never be done discussing him.

Berkeley
January 1979

A Lion for Love

ROMAN PRELUDE

ON A SUNDAY IN ROME, April 6, 1834, the French consul at Civitavecchia, a portly, red-faced man of fifty-one, the coarseness of his features oddly contrasted by his careful elegance, was in the midst of one of his frequent extended flights to the capital city from his dull provincial post. Making his way through the bustling street, he heard screams from the doorway of the Trattoria dell'Aurora. He hurried in the direction of the disturbance: on the ground lay the body of a young woman just murdered.

Later in his room, he noted in the margin of *Promenades dans Rome*, one of eight books he had published: "Sunday 6 April 34. Young girl murdered near me. I run up, she is in the middle of the street, at her head a little pool of blood a foot in diameter. That is what M. Victor Hugo calls bathed in blood." The same day, in another marginal note in *Promenades dans Rome*, he would make the description still more specific, observing that there was foam floating in the middle of the pool of blood. But the second note joins the concern for clinical precision with a quiet sense of deep disturbance: "While I was reading Letronne on the cosmology of the Church Fathers—the world is made like a chest with two covers, etc.—I was telling myself: what good is it to learn such absurdities when a young girl is murdered two steps from me. . . ?"

Both the odd lucidity of notation and the peculiar junction of attitudes are thoroughly characteristic of the distinctive stance as writer and observer that Henri Beyle had learned to define for himself. Hardly a violent man, though in his self-conscious way rather a passionate one, he runs to witness the manifestation of violent passion. (This was one of the strongest attractions of Italy for him, as he was soon to make abundantly clear in *Les Chroniques italiennes,* his reworking of an obscure collection he had discovered of lurid Renaissance tales of passion, jealousy, and implacable revenge.) To witness, however, clearly did not mean to gape and exclaim, but to observe with scientific exactitude; and as his journals, letters, and marginalia from late adolescence onward demonstrate, he had turned his life, outwardly a casual round of worldly hedonism, into a daily regimen of disciplined observation.

The act of observing was for him closely bound with the act of literary criticism, with the distance he needed to set between himself and the fashionable writers of his time, because seeing clearly meant finding a transparently adequate language for what one saw, free of the exaggeration and false pathos of emphatic literary cliché. This seeming dilettante, in other words, was above all a relentlessly professional writer, of the sort that figures like Flaubert and Henry James would a generation or two later make familiar in European literary culture—the kind of writer who is constantly working on the mixed materials of his daily experience in order to sharpen the instruments of his vocation as a novelist. At the same time, the discipline of observation may well have provided a defense against the excesses of his own emotions, as one might infer here from the careful focus on the diameter of the pool of blood even as the murder of an unknown girl makes him ponder the futility of historical knowledge and abstract speculation.

To make oneself a vehement champion of Romanticism but, unlike M. Victor Hugo, a cool clinician as well, was an unusual stance to assume, especially in France during those uneasy years of the Bourbon Restoration and the July Monarchy (1815–48), when writers were drawn both to the defiant rebelliousness and to the transcendental aspirations of the new European literary movement. The combination of Romantic fervor and critical detachment might explain much about the one masterpiece that Henri Beyle, under his preferred pseudonym, Stendhal, had already produced, *Le Rouge et le Noir,* including why so relatively few of his contemporaries had recognized the originality and imaginative authority of that novel when it appeared in 1830. This subtle, precarious tension of identities had taken decades of experience in the world and with himself to evolve to the point where it could translate itself into accomplished fiction—Stendhal's first, artistically uncertain novel, *Armance,* was not written till he was forty-three. Geographically, the field of evolution of this complex self stretches from Moscow to Italy; professionally, from Napoleon's military bureaucracy to free-lance journalism; emotionally, from binges of rhapsodic passion to the verge of suicide, with a good deal of high and low farce in between. The aspiring writer, impelled by the consciousness of his vocation but gravely misguided about how to realize it, embraced the spirit of his age yet somehow held himself apart from it. The long process through which he learned to do both comfortably is one of the great nineteenth-century stories of a life lived with a growing strength of self-awareness. That strength, once fully attained, would make a new poised complexity of imagination available to the European novel.

Although the importance of Stendhal's achievement has been generally recognized since the last decades of the nineteenth century, the special role he played in the development of the novel as a serious art may still not be fully appreciated. Writing as rapidly and as variously as he did, Stendhal seems worlds away from the painstaking devotion to the cult of writing that would characterize Flaubert and his followers in sundry languages who are associated with the creation of the modern art-novel. But in one crucial respect Stendhal initiated the tradition of the novel which was to be carried on by writers as different from him as Flaubert, Turgenev, Tolstoy, Henry James, Arnold Bennett, Conrad, Joyce, and Gide. For however casual his manner, he was deeply committed to the most exacting ideal of fidelity to experience in fiction, which in turn dictated an adversary stance to many of the prevalent conventions of the novel, an innovative subtlety in the management of narrative point of view and other techniques, and a style strenuously resistant to effusion, cliché, and all merely ornamental effects. It is in Stendhal's work that the novel is embarked on a course of self-discovery through the rejection of the temptations abounding in the popular practice of the genre—a rejection that implies an ultimately experimental relation to the making of fictions. His movement toward the creation of this quiet revolution in literary consciousness was at first slow and uncertain. There were many disparate elements in his own intellectual and emotional history that led him toward this point, but in order to understand the whole process, we shall have to begin now to follow it from its proper beginning.

The main path back to the beginning, however, is marked by an extended act of retrospection which the mature Stendhal was to undertake two and a half years after the April Sunday in Rome on which we have already encountered him. It is in the brilliant but at times subtly distortive mirror of his own self-reflection that we must try to perceive his origins.

Part One

The Young Man from the Provinces

If Beyle was never able to forgive his childhood,
Stendhal never stopped loving it.

> Jean-Paul Weber, *Stendhal:*
> *les structures thématiques*
> *de l'oeuvre et du destin*

I

GRENOBLE

(Aetat. 1–16)

"I AM GOING to be fifty years old," Stendhal tells us at the beginning of his autobiography, *La Vie de Henry Brulard*. "It is more than time for me to know myself. What have I been, what am I, in truth I would find it most difficult to say." In truth, he was almost fifty-three when he actually conceived the autobiographical project on the Hill of the Janiculum, looking out over the archaeologically layered panorama of Rome. But the invention of a date more than three years off the historical mark can be forgiven as the artistic smoothing of a ragged edge of fact for the edification of the posthumous audience to which the book was directed. In this way, the hero of the autobiography—for despite retrospective self-judgment, he is clearly that—appears at the very outset as a man precisely on the brink of the grand climacteric, the fiftieth year, like Don Quixote, one of the fictional heroes who deeply engaged Stendhal from childhood onward, but with all his foolhardy forays now behind him, reaching for a perhaps elusive autumnal lucidity.

The interweaving of fact and invention for the double purpose of revelation and concealment was a lifelong habit of Stendhal's, this self-consciously guarded man capable of great candor who surrounded himself with a cloud of pseudonyms (the list runs to more than two hundred) in his publications, correspondence, and social intercourse; who began his literary career as a nonchalant plagiarist; and who finally discovered in the novel the ideal form for the deployment of invented versions of himself, making the ambiguities of inventing a self the distinctive subject of his novels. For him, as for few other novelists of his age, fiction became a form of self-knowledge.

"I would rather be taken," one of his contemporaries remembers his remarking, "for a chameleon than for an ox," upon which the memoirist aptly observes: "He made a studied effort all his life to disguise himself and to pass for an ungraspable, *conjectural* figure."[1] The chameleon response, of course, was primarily a strategy of Stendhal's social life, but it is characteristic of him that his imaginative life as a writer was at once directly continuous with and impressively superior to his quirky, endearing, exasperating existence among the men and women of his time.

Henry Brulard presents itself as a rigorous effort at candid recollection. Stendhal is careful to note possible confusions between actual experiences and subsequent remembered images of them; he freely admits that he cannot absolutely guarantee the accuracy of the facts, only the emotional tenor of his response to them as the subject of the experience; in his effort to reconstitute experienced scenes with geometric clarity, he provides dozens of actual sketches and diagrams as insets in the text. He repeatedly takes pains to expose even the most socially unacceptable of his own motives and desires or, what may be more difficult, the most ridiculous of them; and maintaining the rapid, seemingly casual, unemphatic prose that he elevated to a first principle of integrity everywhere in his writing, he skirts the primrose paths of self-inflating rhetoric down which other Romantic autobiographers were so easily led.

All this makes *La Vie de Henry Brulard* an enormously appealing autobiographical narrative and in several ways a uniquely revealing one as well: it remains the central, indispensable source of knowledge for the first seventeen years of Stendhal's life. Its factual inaccuracies, hunted down by squadrons of determined scholars over the last three generations, seem minor and mostly trivial; the meticulous rendering of the writer's sensibility is finely convincing and jibes perfectly with everything we know about Stendhal both from his own writing elsewhere and from the comments of his contemporaries. And yet the chameleon habit of selecting a self-image nicely adjusted to the surroundings and, here, in the act of

---

1. Louis Desroches, "Souvenirs anecdotiques sur M. de Stendhal," reprinted in Pierre Jourda, *Stendhal raconté par ceux qui l'ont vu* (Paris, 1927), p. 163.

recollection, of subtly adjusting the surroundings to the selected self-image, is at work throughout the book, is ultimately responsible for its peculiar imaginative wholeness.

Stendhal, always obsessed with the idea of persecution by the authorities (both the papal authorities and Metternich's secret police actually had dossiers on him as a suspect liberal), chose to "disguise" the autobiography on the manuscript title page by describing it as "The Life of Henry Brulard . . . Novel Imitating *The Vicar of Wakefield*," and one might well think of it as a plausible fiction of origins built up from carefully recollected documentary materials, what in postliterate America would be called a first-person "nonfiction novel." *Henry Brulard*, for all the care of its diagrams and for all the minute details of family circumstance it conveys, is Stendhal's Portrait of the Artist as a Young Man. The incidents remembered, the traits of character brought forth, and, above all, the lineaments of the family figures around the young Brulard/Beyle, are those that will lead to the author of *Le Rouge et le Noir*, the disaffected liberal critic of post-Napoleonic society, and the artist so aristocratically sure of his uncompromising solitary way that he was content, or so he often claimed, to wait for the readers of 1880 or 1935. *Henry Brulard*, then, provides the only circumstantial access we have to Stendhal's formative years, and an illuminating one at that, but the real Beyle, the real Henri, behind the images refracted through its prism remains ultimately *conjectural*, as the memoirist said of the adult Stendhal.

Marie-Henri Beyle was born in Grenoble on January 23, 1783, graced with a perfectly timed historical entrance to become the chronicler (as the subtitle of *Le Rouge et le Noir* would one day announce) of the nineteenth century: his early childhood memories were intertwined with the career of the Revolution in Grenoble; his coming of age was just at the turn of the century, as Bonaparte assumed the first consulship and began the great thrusts of conquest to the south and the east; his mature years as a devotee of art and love and as a social observer began with Napoleon's fall and the restoration of the Bourbons; his final return to the civil service as a consul in Italy was made possible by the July Revolution of 1830.

The first surviving child of Chérubin-Joseph Beyle and Henriette Gagnon, he had two sisters, Pauline (born in 1786), whom he saw as an ally and later cultivated as a protégée, and Zénaïde-Caroline (born in 1788), whom he detested as a talebearing accomplice of parental authority and for whom subsequently he would never evince much affection.

Chérubin Beyle is particularly hard to make out through the warp of his son's retrospective feelings toward him. He was a prosperous attorney, with an appointment to the provincial parliament, whose family had been firmly established in Grenoble and environs for nearly two centuries. He seems to have had certain aristocratic pretensions, and during the revolutionary period, he remained loyal to the nobility and to the Church, allegiances that confirmed him in the eyes of his son as a villain and tyrant. Henri would recall his father as a man narrowly preoccupied with money, although Chérubin's subsequent behavior suggests that he was more essentially an obsessed hobbyist using the profit motive as an excuse to give free rein to his quixoticism: he became progressively involved in grandiose agricultural schemes, in which he actually sought to interest his son, and by the end of his life, in 1819, he had succeeded in losing the better part of his son's patrimony, something Henri, who aspired only to a carefree life of modest independence, would never forgive him. There was apparently a good deal of snobbery in Chérubin Beyle, enough to make him raise his son in social isolation—"under a bell jar" is the image Stendhal uses—for fear that contact with the common herd would contaminate the boy. This durance vile of early childhood undoubtedly helped make Henri Beyle painfully shy and uncertain in his social relations for many years afterward, but it also provided him with an unforgettable model of the essential bourgeois vice of snobbery, which was the key to the social psychology of an upwardly mobile France after the Restoration of 1815.

Stendhal's hatred of his father, still smoldering in 1835, is one of the leading themes of *Henry Brulard*, and the hostility can be attributed in large part to the fact that the father is set in the constricting third corner of an Oedipal triangle drawn with a schematic boldness that the most orthodox Freudian might well admire. Henri was at the vulnerable age of seven when his mother died in childbirth, and with her death, as he retrospectively noted, all the joy of his childhood ended. He remembers her as a gracefully lovely woman in the flower of her youth, and in a famous passage, he recalls the frankly erotic nature of his attachment to her:

> I wanted to cover my mother with kisses, and that there not be any clothing. She loved me passionately and often would embrace me, and I would return her kisses with such ardor that she was often forced to leave. I detested my father when he came to interrupt our kisses. I always wanted to give them to her on the breast. [*Brulard*, chap. 3]

Psychoanalytic exegetes of Stendhal have found this so explicit an account of incestuous desire as to be not quite credible, and so have conjectured that it is a screen-memory for other unconfrontable desires or guilts. More literal followers of Freud have taken it as a cue to read all Stendhal's fiction as a single-minded pursuit of the lost, poignantly longed-for mother. What is clear about the passage is its utility as an image in a personal mythology that would enable Stendhal to render in narrative the full poignancy of what he habitually called "the pursuit of happiness" together with the obstacles that society sets in the way of that pursuit. The erotically welcoming woman remained the focus of all his visions of bliss, including those linked with the most sublime moments of art and nature, and in his novels, one of the two recurring faces of womanhood is that of the grace-granting affectionate mother, as the career of Fabrice in *La Chartreuse de Parme*, constantly guided and supported by older women, bears witness.

The father provides the strong link between this private mythology and the larger social context. He is not only the resented sexual competitor—Henri gloated over the information later conveyed to him by the family maid that his mother had been physically repelled by her husband—but the embodiment of all the institutional forces that are inimical to the fulfillment of uninhibited desire: class loyalties and prejudice, political repression, subservience to religious and social restrictions, devotion to material gain. All this freight of negative association is more than the figure of poor Chérubin Beyle, whatever his real faults, can bear. Stendhal dwells on his father's ugliness and wrinkled features, and as far as one can surmise, he was in fact not very pleasant to behold: the only presumed portrait of him that has survived gives him a rather beady-eyed, suspicious look, his thin lips pursed in an enigmatic expression, perhaps disdainful, perhaps afraid. But Stendhal made Chérubin's unappealing exterior a token of his role as an unfeeling, hypocritical monster, and that identity seems less than plausible.

After his wife's funeral, Chérubin Beyle had his son's bed moved into his own bedroom, hardly the gesture of an uncaring father; and whether out of guilt or devotion or a mingling of the two, he kept Henriette Gagnon's room closed as a kind of perpetual shrine. (Stendhal tries to undercut the seriousness of Chérubin's long years of mourning for his wife by weaving around him conjectures of amorous involvements, most strategically with Aunt Séraphie, the younger sister of Henri's mother, who was Chérubin's chief minister in instituting a grim reign of piety in the household; but there is scant evidence to support the conjectures.) Chérubin Beyle appears to have been one of those parents doomed to express their love for their children only in ways that will be vehemently misconstrued. He and Séraphie would take the boy for walks in the country, pointing out the beauties of the Alpine landscape around Grenoble, but these attempts *to give me pleasure*, as Stendhal recalled with italic irony, were taken as sheer hypocrisy—because the company of father and aunt seemed so odious, because the boy could not believe in his father's affection, because he could not concede any genuine capacity for the appreciation of nature in the straitlaced attorney. When Henri at the age of sixteen set out for Paris, Chérubin's eyes, by his son's own account, were filled with tears, but even such a testimony of unaffected feeling could only sharpen the image of resentment long harbored by the boy: "The only impression that his tears made on me was that I found him quite ugly."

In the parentally imposed isolation that marked the years immediately after his mother's death, young Henri sought companionship from two adults, his grandfather Henri Gagnon (to whom we shall return) and his grandfather's valet, a young man named Lambert. From the age of seven till ten, these two figures were, as he notes, the two branches of his sociability: the grandfather was his "serious and respectable comrade," while Lambert was his friend and confidant (*Brulard*, chap. 14). Lambert, an intelligent and enterprising fellow, seeking to better himself, had taken up the cultivation of silkworms. One day in June 1793, while climbing to pick mulberry leaves, Lambert fell and was brought back to the house on a ladder, with a severe concussion. Attended by Dr. Gagnon "like a son," he lingered for three days, crying out piercingly in his delirium. Lambert's death, confirming the loneliness that had begun for Henri with the loss of his mother, left the child with a bleak sense of bereavement, the real beginning of an adult's disillusioned perception of human existence: "The pain of Lambert's death was pain as I have experienced it all the rest of my life, a dry, considered pain, without tears, without consolation." The mature Stendhal recalls seeing an Italian painting of the face of St. John watching "his friend and God being crucified," a scene of sacred suffering that brought back in a rush the powerful sensation of the loss of Lambert, experienced a quarter of a century earlier. The seven-year-old Henri had been unable to cry over his mother's death; a year after Lambert's demise, he suddenly began to sob violently—as though the first, primal loss had somehow at last found a voice in his continued contemplation of the later bereavement. Sharply rebuked for the outburst by his Aunt Séraphie, he ran off to the kitchen, muttering to himself defensively in response to this new evidence of persecution, "*infame! infame!* contemptible tyrant!"

The condition of embattled isolation, then, may have been objectively grounded, but it is necessary for Stendhal to imagine his father (together with his father's allies) as more morally ugly than he could actually have been in order to justify the purity of his own stance of rebellion. Most of the crucial incidents that he recalls from his childhood are ones that in fact set him in dramatic opposition to the adults around him. His two earliest memories are of having bitten the cheek of a certain Mme Pison du Galland, a cousin, in response to a request for a kiss, and of having accidentally dropped a knife out a window, barely missing a Mme Chenevaz, one of the most censorious women of the town.[2] On both occasions, he was declared a wretch who gave evidence of having the most monstrous character, the detested Séraphie of course leading the chorus of denunciation. Most of the subsequent incidents reported in *Henry Brulard* follow this same pattern, though, as we shall see, the insistent presence of revolutionary political activity in Grenoble after 1789 provided a special channel for the child's impulse to put himself in opposition to his family.

The ogrefied version of Chérubin Beyle was important to his son in another way, for it helped him define another axis of his private mythology—the division by temperament, character-type, cultural mood, ethos, and climate between north and south, France and Italy or Spain. The idea of the south as the land of passion is of course a collective European fantasy—indeed, one recent anthropological critic of Stendhal has tried to link this orientation toward the south in *Henry Brulard* with the European myth of Egypt as a bourn of sensual, sun-warmed bliss, noting, among other clues, that Grandfather Gagnon shows young Henri an illustrated travel book on Egypt and Africa.[3] Such myths may be dubious guides to the complexities of geocultural reality, but they can provide a writer the means of thematically organizing his own experience and then working his experience into fiction as, say, the instance of Thomas Mann, like Stendhal enamored of north-south oppositions, graphically demonstrates.

In placing the Gagnons vis-à-vis the Beyles, Stendhal turned the Family Romance—"Could I not have been the son of a great prince?" he ponders in *Henry Brulard* (chap. 26)—into a perspective for imagining the possibilities of culture. He was scarcely willing to grant his affiliation with the purse-proud bourgeois Beyles. He was, he felt, all Gagnon, and the Gagnons, he believed (probably with some reason), were not natives of Dauphiné but traced their origins to Italy, to "lands where," in a favorite

2. Jean-Paul Weber, with an eccentrically anti-Freudian view of the unconscious, has made these two incidents, together with a third, in which the child Henri sees a fatally wounded workman carried upstairs, the universal key to Stendhal's psychology and thematics. His readings are repeatedly ingenious, occasionally brilliant, and always monomaniacal. See *Stendhal: les structures thématiques de l'oeuvre et du destin* (Paris, 1969).

3. Gilbert Durand, "*Henry Brulard* et l'Egypte," in *Stendhal et les problèmes de l'autobiographie*, ed. Victor Del Litto (Grenoble, 1976).

phrase of Stendhal's, "the orange tree grows." (The phrase, one suspects, may have been borrowed from the famous song Goethe assigns to Mignon in *Wilhelm Meister*.) After his mother's death, he perpetuated the identification with the Gagnons in the long hours he spent with his grandfather, Henri Gagnon, a physician, a disciple of Voltaire and the values of the Enlightenment, and an exemplar for young Henri of literate good taste. Henri Gagnon's easygoing ways contrasted with the severity of the Beyles, but he finally disappointed the boy by his pliancy, which made him unwilling to stand up to his son-in-law and to his daughter Séraphie. Henri Gagnon's sister Elisabeth, on the other hand, persisted in Henri Beyle's memory as the perfect pattern of what he fancied to be the *Espagnolisme*, the noble Hispanic character, of the Gagnons—a nature that exhibited not only spontaneous passion and sensitivity but above all a heroic energy of will, precisely the resource that the French, in their entrapment in petty prudential calculation and social conformism, seemed to him to have irreparably lost. When at the age of seventeen Henri crossed the Alps into Italy with Bonaparte's armies, he thought he had discovered at last the land where the hidden roots of his nature lay. Afterward, he nurtured the dream of coming back to live in Italy, eventually fulfilling it with predictably mixed results; and in the instructions he left before his death that "Arrigo Beyle, Milanese" be inscribed on his gravestone, he was making his final affirmation of where he stood between the dour Dauphiné character of the Beyles and the southern temperament of the Gagnons.

In point of historical fact, Grenoble at the end of the eighteenth century must have been in many ways a rather charming place. It had the reputation of being a lively, quite worldly town, especially for a provincial outpost. The main part of the city clustered in a large oval on the north bank of the winding Isère River, which was spanned by several stone bridges. The shuttered, gray facades of the tile-roofed houses, four and five stories high, were grouped around a series of small cobbled plazas. Extending out from the *hôtel de ville*, the aristocratic mansion that had been turned into the municipality building, was a gracious public park with a promenade of stately chestnut trees. Renaissance church spires thrust up over the orange-red rooftops, and still higher, the massive outjuttings of the Alps, surrounding the city, were visible from almost every point. Henri Beyle could not have been entirely impervious to all this—as a loyal *Grenoblois* despite himself, he would never forgive Paris its lack of mountains—but the image he chooses to convey of his native city in his autobiography suggests nothing of its charm, insisting instead on its oppressiveness, its cultural and physical staleness. It was, quite simply, a place from which to escape.

Young Henri's rebellion against the paternal world seemed to him to receive public confirmation in the Revolution and its militant aftermath. Jacobin activism, impinging on the Beyles, visibly sharpened the hostility between father and son, while Henri found in politics a way of critically seeing the family constellation and, conversely, managed to feel through the immediate pressures of familial tensions the dynamics of political conflict. This habit of bracketing private distress and public upheaval probably encouraged a certain simplification and schematization in his vision of both realms, but in his fiction, it would at times provide him with a valuable means of dramatically defining both the historical and the familial scene with something of their intricate interrelation. A few key incidents of Henri's juvenile career as a would-be revolutionary are worth particularly close attention for what they reveal both of his character and of his way of recapturing his own early experience.

The Reign of Terror, when it reached Grenoble in the spring of 1793, was notably mild, perhaps because the aristocracy of the region was on the whole rather conciliatory toward the revolutionary party in comparison with its counterpart elsewhere. As a result, the Terror provides a background for rather touching farce, not incipient tragedy, in the disturbances of the Beyle household. On April 21, André Amar and Jean-François-Marie Merino, district representatives to the Convention in Paris, arrived in Grenoble with instructions to purge the town of counterrevolutionary elements. Five days later, they published a list of 152 "notoriously suspect" individuals who were to be arrested for their presumed disloyalty to the Republic. The list included the names of Chérubin Beyle and of the Abbé Raillane, the tutor Stendhal would anachronistically label a "Jesuit" and remember as oppressively tyrannical. Raillane fled into the mountains, to the immense delight of his ten-year-old pupil. Chérubin Beyle, on the other hand, merely went around the corner with his family and took up residence in the home of his father-in-law, Dr. Gagnon, being duly careful not to show himself in public. He was in fact arrested three times during the next year and a half and may have been imprisoned in all for as much as eleven months, but even so there is no evidence of his having suffered any great or irreparable privations. The most palpable impact of the Terror on the Beyles was psychological, the two older generations of the family living for many months in dread that they might be barbarically victimized at any moment by the local revolutionary powers.

Henri, by contrast, was enraptured at the sight of revolutionary dragoons marching through town on their way to the Italian front, delighted when, as repeatedly occurred, one of the troops was quartered at the Beyle house. The mumbled curses of his father in the background, always vigorously seconded by his domineering Aunt Séraphie, must have been a piquant counterpoint for him to his own joy over the triumph of the revolutionary forces, his eagerness to imagine himself marching in their ranks. Before long, the Beyles would be hiding fugitive priests in their home, and Henri's revulsion from their gluttonous eating habits, their appalling *commonness*, perfectly expresses the conjunction in him, even at this early age, of passionate republican principles and a thoroughly aristocratic sensibility.

The overthrow and execution of the king seem to have encouraged the boy's dreams of rebellion against the parental regime, and he began to act on them, both directly and by subterfuge. The news that Louis XVI had been guillotined on January 21, 1793, produced in the boy what he would unabashedly describe some forty years later as "one of the most intense movements of joy that I have experienced in my life" (*Brulard*, chap. 10). During the months to come, Henri would attempt on at least three separate occasions to raise the revolutionary tricolor at home in defiance of what he conceived as familial and particularly paternal tyranny.

When the list of notoriously suspect figures was promulgated, Chérubin Beyle suggested to his family that his name had been included by André Amar only because Amar, who also practiced law in Grenoble, wanted to eliminate a professional rival. Henri responded to his father with scathing directness: "Amar put you on his list as notoriously *suspect* of not loving the Republic, but it seems to me *certain* that you do not love it" (*Brulard*, chap. 11). The statement—at least as he chooses to recall it four decades later—takes the form of a concise, witty rejoinder, in the polished eighteenth-century manner much admired by Grandfather Gagnon. Henri's most successful act of republican rebellion, according to his own retrospective claim, was purely in the verbal realm—the elegant turning of a defiant phrase. The elder Beyle reddened with anger at the child's impudence; he was peremptorily sent to his room and later isolated in chilly silence at the dinner table, but he had succeeded in striking a perfect republican pose. When some months later, however, he tried to move from words to acts, he ignominiously tripped himself up on his own youthful ineptitude, and in a way that cut him off from his family in a direction he had not foreseen.

Sometime in 1794, the Jacobin Society of Grenoble founded an organization for children from the ages of eight to eighteen called the Battalion of Hope. The children were to learn how to bear arms and parade, would maintain order at patriotic celebrations, and in general were to be indoctrinated with revolutionary values. Parents were not strictly obliged to send their children to the meetings of the Battalion, and of course, Chérubin Beyle made sure that his son kept clear of all contact with this instrument of godlessness. A prominent figure in the republican movement of Grenoble was a certain Antoine Gardon-Desvial, a priest who had recently renounced his orders and who was often spoken of in the Beyle home as one of the most dreaded of the local Jacobins. Young Henri thought that Gardon was the director of the Battalion of Hope, though actually the former priest had nothing to do with it. In any case, his name was calculated to strike fear into the hearts of the Beyles and Gagnons, and Henri used it in an attempt to break out of what he called his "cage" and to join the republican ranks openly.

The boy forged a note addressed to his grandfather—this is during the period when the Beyles were taking refuge with Dr. Gagnon—signed with the name "Gardon." In the note, Citizen Gagnon was ordered to see to it that his grandson appeared at St. André Church (which had been sequestered by the Jacobins) to be enlisted in the Battalion of Hope. The note was affixed to the space between the double doors of the Gagnon residence, and when it was discovered by the family, it threw them into a state of total consternation, just as Henri had hoped. Unfortunately for him, however, a young commoner named Isidore Tourte was then present at Dr. Gagnon's, a diminutive hunchback with gogglelike spectacles who had, in Stendhal's words, "insinuated himself into the house as a subordinate creature, taking offense at nothing, subtly flattering everybody" (*Brulard*, chap. 12). Tourte had much less cause to be alarmed by the name of Gardon than did the Beyles and Gagnons, so he could examine the horrid document coolly, and requesting to see a sample of Henri's handwriting, he quickly uncovered the ruse.

Henri, his flimsy deception revealed, was sent off to wait by himself in his grandfather's natural history study, while the family convened to decide on an appropriate punishment. Stendhal's narrative pauses for three paragraphs to describe Henri in the study, and this of course effectively builds suspense before the moment when he is summoned back to the living room to hear his judgment pronounced. The child, obviously distraught by the whole affair, kneads a ball out of soft red clay and begins to toss it up and down nervously. Having pitched it particularly high up toward the lofty ceiling, he discovers to his dismay that the plummeting ball has grazed his grandfather's precious map of Dauphiné, leaving a long red streak. Strangely, the child seems at least as upset over this accident as over the exposure of his forgery. "I am offending," he thinks, "my sole protector." Called back at that very moment to face the family, Henri is full of high resolve to play the part of a noble Roman, proclaiming duty and patriotism as his chief motives, but in the actual confrontation, he finds himself helplessly yielding, softened (*attendri*), and he attributes this weakness to his consciousness of guilt at having defaced his grandfather's cherished map.

The pattern of grand expectation and woeful performance here is one that will be repeated in Henri Beyle's life and even more emphatically in his novels: the protagonist of the action self-consciously adopts a role from the books he has read, but when the moment of action comes, he is forced to recognize an unbridgeable gap between his real nature and the part he would like to play. Stendhal, to be sure, commenting on this particular failure of intention four decades after the fact, tries to minimize the gap by a finesse of terminology: "I unfortunately lost my proud position through my weakness of disposition [*ma faiblesse de coeur*], not of character." In other words, Stendhal chooses to imagine a kind of ideal self, his "character," which remains fixed from his earliest years onward and which is finally in perfect consonance with the high vocation inspired by literature that he repeatedly sets as his goal in the real world of doings and undoings.

One may still wonder why guilt toward his grandfather should be presented here as the critically disabling force or why Stendhal's account of the episode lingers as it does over the accident with the red clay ball. It was, one should emphasize, in this affair of the forged note that young Henri was first clearly disabused of the faith he had placed in his beloved grandfather. Waiting in the study, the child could not yet know that his grandfather would side with the family against him, but he had already seen the old man's face turn pale with fear at the sight of a note signed "Gardon," and that same blanched countenance is the one visual detail he notes when he returns to confront the assembled family. Dr. Gagnon emerges from the episode a coward and a weakling in the child's eyes, and Henri is quick to recognize that it is not only a fear of political terror but also cowardice on the plane of simple personal relations: the old man's fear of his daughter, Séraphie. The harsh father, it seemed to him, had of course always stood against him, and now the gentle grandfather in his sudden transparent weakness had equally abandoned him. The whole episode, with its peculiar shift of focus from Chérubin Beyle to Henri Gagnon, strikingly confirms the acute isolation of the child.

The boy's dream of joining the revolutionary ranks, entangled as it was with ambivalent feelings of filial resentment and perhaps guilt as well, was frustrated but far from stifled. The sequestered St. André Church continued to loom in his imagination as some forbidden and alluring realm. One chilly evening, probably during the cold months of 1794–95, he hurried out of his house as darkness was falling, under the pretext of going to join his great-aunt Elisabeth, his sole remaining ally in the family, who was visiting with a cousin, Mme Colomb. Instead of walking directly to Mme Colomb's, he slipped off to St. André Church, where a meeting of the Jacobin Society was in progress. Once again, Henri coaches himself to play a heroic Roman role, imagining as he approaches the church that one day he will be another Cincinnatus or Camillus, a valorous savior of his people by the might of his sword. As he moves through the shadows, he is tensely alert for spies of the enemy, the dreaded Séraphie.

The reality of a republican meeting was quite another matter. Having actually crossed the threshold of St. André, Henri found himself in a crowded room filled with a motley variety of shabbily dressed, malodorous members of the lower class carrying on an unruly general discussion with frequent interruptions of the speakers. From the crowd of plebeians, the fifty-three-year-old Stendhal, in recalling the episode, singles out only one group: "I discovered there many women of the lowest class . . . badly dressed women" (*Brulard*, chap. 15). Ruefully, the boy remembers his grandfather's gay mockery of the common people's coarseness, and he is compelled to recognize how close his own attitude is to his grandfather's: "I found these people whom I had wanted to love horribly vulgar." As Stendhal tells us several times in *Henry Brulard*, there is a continual split in his consciousness between democratic principle and aristocratic propensity. He is eager to defend the rights of the people, but in actual intercourse with the masses, he repeatedly finds them to be not *le peuple*, that sloganized ideal of republican rhetoric, but *canaille*—rabble, scum.

Back at his grandfather's, after having received a gentle but firm warning from Aunt Elisabeth not to try such tricks again lest his father find out, Henri soon pushes aside his distaste for the filthiness of the Jacobins at the account of some new republican military victory that strikes the family with trepidation. Stendhal retrospectively confesses, however, that it would have taken but a few well-placed words of mockery spoken by his grandfather at the time to have made him a firm convert to the aristocratic party.

The part of the Roman that Henri had sought to play at the Jacobin meeting was, in all its literary stereotypes to which he had been exposed, a manly part—the steely grip of patriotic virtue on the hilt of a sword. But most curiously, Stendhal explains his squeamish response to the unkempt republicans in physiological terms, borrowing, he tells us, the language of the eighteenth-century physiological theorist, Cabanis: "My skin is far too delicate, it is a woman's skin" (a refined woman, one must assume). The seemingly casual illustration he offers in parentheses to prove this assertion actually bears directly on the situation of the youthful self aspiring to Roman heroism that he has just described: the writer, a veteran of the Napoleonic campaigns and an officer in the diplomatic corps, confesses that he can scarcely hold his saber an hour without getting blisters.[4]

Henry Brulard was written, like most of Stendhal's books, as a brilliant, rapid improvisation, and though its overall scheme is chronological, the links between episodes and the principles of selection often seem governed by some movement of association. Just as he has concluded the account of his surreptitious visit to the Jacobin Society, Stendhal tells of his sudden involvement around the same period with the visual arts and immediately proceeds to muse for the next several paragraphs over a landscape that hung in the studio of his drawing master, M. Le Roy. The large, dark painting represented a steep mountain at the foot of which ran a broad, clear brook lined with trees. What especially caught the eye of the pre-adolescent, however, was a group of three gaily bathing nudes that formed the only bright area in the big canvas. These naked female figures at play in an idyllic setting blended perfectly with the elegant eroticism of the novels that Henri had been filching from his grandfather's study. "The landscape . . . became my ideal of happiness. It was a mixture of tenderness and sweet sensuality. To bathe like that with lovely women!"

The bathing nudes are a neatly symmetrical antithesis of the lower-class women at the Jacobin meeting. Outside the artist's atelier, in the real world of flesh and mud, the women encountered were shoddy and repugnant. *Saleté*, filth, is the verbal keynote of the whole St. André episode, and coming immediately after it, the bathing nudes in the painted landscape constitute an imaginative act of purification. Henri's stirred erotic longings transport him in fantasy inside the frame of the painting as he

---

4. Stendhal's emphasis on having a woman's skin—it is asserted twice in close sequence—has the effect, by invoking Cabanis's notion of physiological determinants for moral qualities, of excusing the would-be republican's recoil from the common people, for it reduces his social fastidiousness to a reflex of his physical makeup. At the same time, the insistent identification with a woman's physical delicacy surely reflects something of Stendhal's self-consciousness about his coarse features and heavy-set physique: except for the lively intensity of his eyes (which his better portraits manage to catch), this subtle intellectual had the physiognomy of a butcher. To think of his skin as a woman's, then, was a gratifying fantasy, for through it he could project the fineness of his sensibility onto at least one limited aspect of his physical being.

fancies himself splashing with the lovely naked women in the limpid brook, thus joining an act of cleansing with delicate sensual delight.

What emerges from the juxtaposition of scenes is a piquant but problematic hiatus between women in fact and women in art. Within the artwork—and Stendhal pointedly relates painting to fiction in order to convey his response to the landscape—the desired female figure can be sexually exciting yet ennobled, purified of the imperfections and the pungent effluvia of physical existence that are evident in her real-life counterparts. The split is one that will recur in several of Stendhal's fictional protagonists—on the most clinical level, in Octave de Malivert, the sexually impotent hero of his first novel, *Armance*. It also will exert an abiding influence on his own lifelong pursuit of love, for, despite the real anguish of his often unrequited passions, he sometimes seems to have been drawn to women precisely because they were unattainable. From a distance, in some cases for years, he could plan his elaborate campaigns of amorous attack, he could garland the elusive loved one with festoons of ideal qualities. And even in his technically successful love affairs, he seems to have particularly relished the moments when erotic reality most closely resembled the images of it adumbrated for him in art. At the end of this episode in *Henry Brulard*, he pleasurably recalls how in 1805, at Marseilles, he watched Mélanie Guilbert, the "extraordinarily well-made" young actress who was then his mistress, bathing in the Huveaune in the shadow of tall trees, the alluring mirage of M. Le Roy's canvas become flesh.

Yet literature was the most powerful art medium for the young Beyle from as early as the age of seven or eight, and even as an adult amateur of the arts, he would retain a pronounced tendency to see the music and painting to which he became passionately devoted in ultimately literary terms. Much of the literature he read, moreover, at this precocious age had a potent erotic tenor, imparting to him a whole set of sad, absurd, or amusing illusions about the nature of women and the role he should play with them, illusions he would wonderfully use and see through as a novelist but nevertheless continue to carry with him as a private person to the verge of apoplectic old age. In his grandfather's library, he secretly perused fashionable erotic novels of the eighteenth century with titles like *Félicia ou mes fredaines—Felicia or My Frolics* (this was the book he recalled in looking at M. Le Roy's painting) and *Vie, faiblesse et repentir d'une femme—Life, Follies and Repentance of a Woman*. As a complement to this pornography of the flesh, there was one work of fiction that he used repeatedly as emotional pornography, Rousseau's *La Nouvelle Héloïse*, which led him to fantasies of love's producing an endless round of exalted and rhapsodic feelings, just as Félicia and her fictional sisters encouraged fantasies of unending carnal delight. The mature Stendhal would have some misgivings about his early enthusiasm for *La Nouvelle Héloïse*, especially deploring its inflated style: in *Le Rouge et le Noir*, Julien Sorel, who cynically dismisses all novels as the contrivances of rogues to get ahead in the world, memorizes *La Nouvelle Héloïse* (as Stendhal himself had done) and then lifts passages from it to recite to the women he tries to seduce. Nevertheless, Stendhal, writing in 1835, can still claim that reading Rousseau's novel and identifying with its inexhaustibly scrupulous hero, Saint-Preux, instilled in him a permanent sense of moral probity. The contradictory way he formulates this is characteristic: "I could still, after this reading performed with tears and in transports of love of virtue, commit the acts of a scoundrel, but I would feel I was a scoundrel" (*Brulard*, chap. 20).

As a matter of fact, at about this time, the pubescent Henri was engrossed in another fictional introduction to erotic life that could well serve as a scoundrel's primer, Choderlos de Laclos's *Les Liaisons dangereuses*. Laclos, a general in the French army, had been stationed in Grenoble from 1769 to 1775, and local rumor had it that this brilliantly cynical novel of relentless erotic egotism was explicitly based on Grenoble. Stendhal, in any case, firmly believed that as a boy he had known the real-life model for Mme de Merteuil, the novel's high priestess of sexual cynicism, and so Laclos's compelling fictional inventions were reinforced for the child by a sense that he could actually glimpse around him the real figures who had lived these careers of coldly calculating sensuality. Valmont, then, the epistolary confidant of Mme de Merteuil and her male rival in sexual conquest, became a model for the boy. This touchingly virginal adolescent, as Stendhal wrily notes of his earlier self, would arrive in Paris from the provinces determined somehow to be at once both Saint-Preux and Valmont. The contradictory aspirations are ones that, in varying proportions, will persist in most of Henri Beyle's relations with women. Though there were some women who were a simple sexual convenience for him and others who presented him with enormously complicated emotional problems (and sometimes little else), one should not make any facile assumptions about a madonna/whore split in Stendhal's imagination of women. On the contrary, there is continual and unpredictable interaction between the Valmont and the Saint-Preux in him—or, to adopt the alternative set of literary archetypes he later used, between the Don Juan and the Werther in him—and what makes him such a fascinating amorist as well as such a probing psychologist of love is that he rarely played one role toward a particular woman without an impulse to switch to, or rather to combine it with, the other.

On the Valmont side, young Henri had before his eyes a personal model in addition to the literary ones, and that was his uncle Romain Gagnon. The three children of Dr. Henri Gagnon, Henriette, Séraphie, and Romain, present a wildly disparate sequence of moral characters. Romain has the distinct look of a pampered son raised at the emotional expense of his two sisters, one of whom becomes a submissive wife, the other a pietistic spinster. A lawyer by profession, all he seems to have acquired of his father's Enlightenment literary tastes was a fondness for novels of amorous intrigue, an activity to which, beyond mere reading, he devoted himself with greater zeal than to his official occupation, at least as far as his young nephew could see. In a provincial town like Grenoble, where gossip was always rife, he had an honestly earned reputation as a seducer, and, what equally impressed his nephew, he was a splendidly elegant dresser—and one who could often attribute a ruffled silk shirt or a fine embroidered suit to the largesse of an affluent mistress. In 1790, he married and established residence in the village of Les Échelles in Savoy, some seven hours by coach from Grenoble, and most of Henri's memories of his uncle are from Romain's excursions to Grenoble during the mid-1790s to find relief from the quiet of country life and perhaps to see his old mistresses.

More important, however, for the boy's sentimental education were his stays with his uncle in Savoy. One of the finely intimated moments of beatitude in *Henry Brulard* is an account of a visit with Romain Gagnon and his young wife at Les Échelles. Stendhal is reticent, as he is repeatedly elsewhere both in his journals and in his public writing, about violating the subtle perfection of the experience with so gross and inadequate an instrument as language, but the visit to Les Échelles is clearly felt as a delicate prefiguration of the landscape of happiness he will later know in northern Italy. Before cutting short the effusion, he characterizes his stay in the Savoyard countryside, only a few hundred feet from an Alpine stream, as a "sojourn in heaven." Les Échelles is clearly an anti-Grenoble for him, just as Italy would become an anti-France and just as Romain Gagnon, dandy and sexual intriguer, was clearly a quintessential anti-Beyle. The conjunction of a lovely bucolic setting, limpid water, and, as we shall see, erotic titillation, takes us back to M. Le Roy's canvas and forward to later Stendhalian landscapes of bliss. Henri's tall attractive aunt by marriage, Camille Poncet, both by the direct appeal of her physical presence and, no doubt, through her charged association with Uncle Romain, became, in his own words, "an object of the most ardent desire"—particularly, he recalls, after he glimpsed two inches of exposed thigh as she climbed down from a covered wagon. (Surprisingly, he has a similar response to an inadvertently exposed leg of his other, detested, aunt Séraphie—with a little start, we realize that she was a young woman, not an old harridan. But it is surely at least as plausible that the preadolescent should dream of "supplanting" his father, whom he imagined to be Séraphie's lover, as that he should secretly long to usurp the sexual prerogatives of his envied and admired uncle.)

A male child's first oblique sightings of what he conceives to be the paradise of the flesh are, of course, the banal stuff of any boyhood. What is remarkable in the case of Henri Beyle, at least as he recalls his childhood from the vantage point of late middle life, is how the alluring glimpse of the desirable female is regularly orchestrated into a harmonious natural setting, linked with a sense of openness, freshness, spontaneity, all of which together constitute the perfect antithesis to his restricting bourgeois family situation. As one follows these "privileged moments" onward through Stendhal's letters, journals, and novels, one begins to notice a tight ring of associations: erotic pleasure-nature (by preference, hilly or mountainous and with lakes or streams)-painting-music. If one of the terms of the ring of associations is not explicitly present, it generally seems to be implied, or at least ultimately implicated. This early memory of the visit to Les Échelles has deep reverberations throughout Stendhal's imaginative world because it illustrates so vividly how the "pursuit of happiness" was not the quest of an abstract state of contentment, as it tended to be in the Enlightenment writers from whom he took the phrase, but was the attempt to recover or reenact a concrete, sensuously apprehended experience of plenitude for which every medium of achieved art was at once a potential catalyst and a kind of metaphor. One of the qualities that most strikingly distinguishes Stendhal among nineteenth-century novelists is precisely his being impelled, as Walter Benjamin said so aptly of Proust, by "a dual will to happiness, a dialectics of happiness: a hymnic and an elegiac form."[5] Even in these novels, where the materialistic and political oppressiveness, the chicanery, the emptiness of nineteenth-century society constantly vex the heroes, there is a reaching for the still moment of beatitude insulated from the vexatious world: it is probably the repeated realization of such moments that, more than anything else, gives *La Chartreuse de Parme* the unique tenor it has among the novels of the age.

If, as is clear in the idyllic episode at Les Échelles, one focus of the young Henri's will to happiness was nature, the other was the ultimate realm of artifice, the theater. This, too, is an oscillation between complementary opposites that would continue in later life: the rapture he experi-

5. Walter Benjamin, *Illuminations* (New York, 1968), p. 206.

enced in the lake country of northern Italy can be matched only by his exaltation during the nightly opera performances at La Scala in Milan. As a boy, his first visits to the local theater, just a few hundred feet from his doorstep in the center of Grenoble, were in the company of Romain Gagnon. The fact that the place was dingy, badly lit, ill-smelling, in no way diminished its magic for him. (Even before that, he was an avid reader of plays, and he claims to have fixed on the idea of writing comedies like Molière as early as the age of seven—a lofty ambition with the impressive power to misdirect most of his literary energies for nearly three decades.) By the season of 1797–98, Henri was old enough to go off by himself to the theater, where he regularly watched performances from a standing-room place in the pit.

It is hardly surprising that his free-floating desire, some of whose passing excitations we have noted, should now firmly attach iteslf to a particular object—a nineteen-year-old actress named Virginie Kubly. The passion he nurtured for her was wonderfully, hopelessly quixotic. He went to see her perform night after night in flimflam melodramas and operettas (it was here, Stendhal himself observes, that his ardent love for music began); he trembled, grew faint when he heard her name pronounced; he became indignant if anyone mentioned her in a way that implied the slightest disrespect; and of course, he never exchanged a word with her. The only time he remembers encountering her offstage was a chance near-meeting one morning in the municipal park a block from the theater. Suddenly noticing her as he was walking alone at one end of the *allée* of chestnut trees, he immediately took flight, terror-struck—a historic retreat which the fifty-three-year-old Stendhal would try to fix for posterity with one of his more elaborate drawings, labeling *H* for the spot where he was so vulnerably exposed to the devastating presence of *K*, Mlle Kubly, over by the wall toward the river side of the park. "This," he concludes, "is one of the most distinguishing features of my character, the way I've always been (even the day before yesterday). The happiness of seeing her close up, five or six steps away, was too much, it burned me [*brûlait*—one notices the play on the pseudonym, Brulard], and I fled this burn [*brûlure*], this very real pain" (*Brulard*, chap. 25). Virginie Kubly left Grenoble in April 1798, together with her actor-husband of whose existence Henri was unaware, and went on to a long, undistinguished career with provincial touring companies, moving permanently outside the orbit of her young admirer in Grenoble.

This whole attachment, of course, is the sort of moony adolescent's first infatuation that would be trivial for anyone else but which Henri Beyle, quite characteristically, persisted in working on, brooding or musing over, until the image of the woman and the whole emotional substance of the nonrelation were absorbed into his permanent imaginative apparatus for experiencing and dramatizing the world. His rather comical posture of the desperate aspirant to love vis-à-vis Virginie Kubly looks from one angle like an early rehearsal for the role he would play over a period of years, first with Alexandrine Daru, the wife of his cousin and patron, Pierre Daru, and afterward, in Italy, with the relentlessly unresponsive Matilde Dembowski, through whom he contrived to be driven to the brink of suicide. Though the paths of the young actress and the adolescent had barely crossed, Stendhal set aside a prominent place for Virginie in his private pantheon of beloved women: when, at the beginning of *Henri Brulard*, he describes himself tracing in the sand on the shore of Lake Albano the initials of the women who dominated his passional life, Virginie Kubly stands unambiguously at the head of the chronologically ordered list.

This timid aspirant to love was also, however, a future literary intellectual, and we cannot neglect his avidness for books and knowledge during the Grenoble years, an appetite that easily kept pace with his hunger for romance. Altogether, Henri Beyle, boy and man, was an extraordinary compound of superrational intellectuality and extravagant emotionalism. When he learned how to establish coherent connection between those two sides of himself, as he did for the first time in his first truly original book, the anecdotal treatise, *De l'Amour* (1822), he had become a mature writer with a distinctive voice.

Till the age of thirteen, Henri was educated at home by tutors, in accordance with his father's determined regime of isolation. The tutor who would loom largest in his memory was the Abbé Raillane, a man whom he considered totally devoid of humanity or moral decency and who was engaged by his father, he acidly observes, because Chérubin Beyle's vanity was flattered by the idea that the Abbé Raillane had previously given instruction in the home of the Périers, the richest family of the district. (Stendhal would assign the same snobbery to M. de Rênal in *Le Rouge et le Noir*.) What little is known about the Abbé Raillane's work as an educator outside the Beyle home does not readily corroborate this image of him as a morally destructive scoundrel,[6] but he was

---

6. A bizarre episode, however, that Stendhal reports (*Brulard*, chap. 8) of the Abbé Raillane suggests that, whatever his probity or lack thereof, he was a man obsessed with his own interests to a point where he could scarcely consider the sensibilities of his pupils. Seized by a mania for raising canaries, the abbé hung a large cage in which he kept some thirty canaries at the head of Henri's bed—inevitably, the cage became both malodorous and noisy. The boy was understandably distressed by this ornithological invasion, but Chérubin Beyle apparently did not see fit to object.

obviously a stern taskmaster to the boy—in a surviving portrait, he in fact looks coldly contained, square-jawed, taut-featured, a man of iron—and with his predecessor, the "dour pedant" M. Joubert, and his successor, the sadly uncomprehending master of rote-learning M. Durand, he helped instill in Henri a certain cynicism about formal education. The boy, to impress his masters, committed the Latin Bible to memory (another feat he would pass on to his engaging hypocrite, Julien Sorel), and he acquired a reasonable degree of literacy in Latin, though he appears not to have derived a great deal more from his Roman authors than the images of heroic patriotism that we have already seen in operation. Some Stendhal scholars have tried to make much of the influence of his teachers at the École Centrale, where he was enrolled from 1796 to 1799, and their effect, as we shall presently see, was by no means negligible, but there is finally something of the passionate autodidact about Henri Beyle: he clings most tenaciously to the books and ideas he has made his own in the privacy of his own course of readings, laboriously, grandiosely shaping out of them a "philosophy" that he hopes will guide his life and give him the intellectual leverage to become a great writer.

Perhaps the most noteworthy aspect of his early literary enthusiasms—he excludes *Félicia* and its like from this category as "books to be read with one hand only"—is how European rather than French they are. Among French authors, besides Rousseau and, with serious reservations, Molière, he concedes a certain grudging respect for Corneille, a fondness for La Fontaine, and, by his late teens, a permanent addiction to Saint-Simon. But the two Continental writers he read as a boy in real transports of delight were Ariosto and Cervantes. What clearly drew him most powerfully in any book was the sense it could give him of release from the cage of familial existence: pointedly, he remembers Aunt Séraphie scowling at him reprovingly as he burst into laughter while reading *Don Quixote*. The taste for Ariosto would eventually fade, but Cervantes, perhaps because he offered the kind of imaginative escape that also incorporated a shrewdly critical return to reality, remained a lifelong love, which more than three decades later would be translated into one of the supreme nineteenth-century adaptations of the Cervantine formula for the novel, *Le Rouge et le Noir*.

Sometime during 1798, though Stendhal remembers it as being two years earlier, he discovered, through the uncle of a friend, Pierre Le Tourneur's translation of Shakespeare; and about Shakespeare, he says quite simply and sweepingly, "I felt reborn in reading him." It is hard to guess how much of Shakespeare's poetic power could have been conveyed to the boy in this eighteenth-century French version—he would not acquire a reading knowledge of either English or Italian, his two great windows on European culture beyond France, till his twenties—but the passionate intensity of Shakespeare's heroes and heroines, the uninhibited scope and variety of mankind represented in the plays, inflamed his imagination, gave him a great and compelling alternative to Racine, the paragon of convention-bound French neoclassical drama vaunted to him by his family. When in 1824 he wrote *Racine et Shakespeare*, his famous polemic on behalf of the literary values of Romanticism, he was being perfectly faithful, as he notes in *Henry Brulard*, to the reading experience of his boyhood.

Henri Beyle's Shakespeare, however, is at once Romantic and, in a peculiar way, neoclassical. Shakespeare deeply appeals to Stendhal because of the untrammeled freedom he enjoys, at least from a French viewpoint, in the handling of dramatic and poetic form, and he appears to have been the one writer able regularly to induce in Stendhal that state of aesthetic bliss which certain vocal music could give him ("In my life I have passionately loved only Cimarosa, Mozart, and Shakespeare," he wrote in *Souvenirs d'égotisme*.) At the same time, Stendhal's Shakespeare, like Samuel Johnson's, is above all a poet admirable for his "just representations of general nature," that is, for his grasp of timeless psychological truths. Stendhal would go so far as to equate the imitation of Shakespeare with the imitation of nature, the implied opposite to nature being, of course, rigidified French literary convention, as in the preeminent instance of Racine. The love of Shakespeare was still another case of Henri Beyle's discovering a real spiritual homeland—observe the force of his metaphor of rebirth to describe the effect of the English poet on him—in what he could feel as the most profound antithesis to the values of his Grenoble hearth and home.

The last three years of adolescence in his native town were in any case a time of progressive liberation, and there is no doubt that his enrollment in the École Centrale provided the single most important avenue of liberation. Here again, the chronology of Beyle's life coincided with a fortuitous moment of history to the benefit of his eventual growth as a writer. The principal architect of this educational scheme was Destutt de Tracy, a geometer and an antimetaphysical proponent of philosophic sensationalism, then engaged in the writing of his *Elements of Ideology*, a book which, a decade later, would become a sacred text for Henri Beyle. The curricular innovation of the Écoles Centrales was in their giving a place of honor to science and mathematics as well as to classical literature; in their inclusion of subjects like drawing, history, and modern languages and literatures; and in their attempt to instruct senior students in "general grammar," a subject that Destutt de Tracy hoped would provide the key to clear definitions and logical thought. Dr. Henri Gagnon, as one of the leading champions of Enlightenment in Grenoble, was appropriately chosen as a member of the founding board of overseers of the local École Centrale, and so when the school opened its doors in November 1796, the family had no choice but to enroll Henri. Six years later, with Bonaparte in power and the republican program a thing of the past, the whole enterprise was dismantled: thus, Henri Beyle was a member of what proved to be the only student generation produced by the Écoles Centrales.

Socially, of course, the cloistered Henri's sudden entrance into the society of other boys was a great shock, though, to begin with, a more unpleasant shock than he had expected. He had dreamed of comrades: instead, he found fiercely selfish competitors, many of them already careeristic hypocrites at fourteen or fifteen. (One can assume that Stendhal was still remembering his classmates at the École Centrale when he came to describe the viper's nest of the Besançon seminary in *Le Rouge et le Noir*.) It is hard to know how much of this response was an accurate assessment of his classmates, and how much the overreaction of a child who had led a completely insulated existence, cultivating flamboyant romantic fantasies in the privacy of his reading. Henri at fourteen or fifteen must have been a prickly, sensitive, inflammable sort, uncertain of what behavior he should expect of his fellows, nervously anxious to vindicate the heroic image of himself that he had culled from his books.

Toward the end of his first academic year at the École Centrale, we actually discover him in a duel with one of his classmates. The oddness of the incident points up the extravagance of his feisty pride, for the resort to arms was hardly a usual thing among French high-school students, even in 1797. In drawing class, Henri became involved in a scuffle over places with a certain Marc-François Ordu, who pulled his chair out from under him. Ordu being almost a foot taller, the young Beyle was terrified of getting a drubbing, so the two agreed to duel with pistols. There followed an hour-and-a-half procession of excited, half-scared schoolboys, trailing after the grimly determined combatants across town to a ditch at the city's outskirts. The pistols were readied; the duelists paced off their distance, Henri concentrating on a small piece of trapezoid rock in order not to lose his nerve, and then the guns, perhaps never really loaded by the seconds, failed to go off. The two boys grudgingly accepted a formal reconciliation, a conclusion that afterward pained Henri's martial conscience in a way that would still make him wince thirty-eight years later: "It wounded all my 'Hispanic' daydreams. How could one dare admire the Cid after not having fought? How could one think of the heroes of Ariosto?" (*Brulard*, chap. 32).

By the spring of 1798, however, Henri had succeeded in establishing a number of intimate friendships. Perhaps the most important for him at this time was his relationship with a brother and sister, François and Victorine Bigillion, at whose apartment he became a regular visitor soon after the departure from Grenoble of Virginie Kubly in April 1798. François, Victorine, and Rémy Bigillion, aged sixteen, fifteen, and fourteen, respectively, had come from their country home, accompanied only by a servant, to live in Grenoble in order to continue their schooling there. This adolescent ménage must have seemed an island of exhilarating independence for Henri, so long hedged in and harassed by his family. One gets the impression that François Bigillion was a quiet, loyal boy, by no means brilliant but levelheaded and alert, who shared both Henri's Jacobin sympathies and his enthusiasm for Rousseau. Victorine, presiding as hostess in the adolescent household, seems to have played a gently wise, perhaps vaguely maternal role vis-à-vis the extravagant, self-dramatizing young Beyle: when, for example, he would recount to her the horrors of his Aunt Séraphie (who had died the previous year, to the unabashed delight of her nephew), Victorine would express disbelief and chide him, saying that he had a bad character. Though he was quite alive to her physical attractiveness, their relationship never seems to have become even a serious flirtation. Victorine was, without intervention of romantic fantasy, Henri Beyle's first woman friend. For once, he discovered that social intercourse could be relaxed, playful, unproblematic, and this sense of a carefree idyll is perfectly caught in the faintly absurd bucolic image Stendhal chooses to describe his time with the Bigillions: "We lived then like young rabbits playing in a wood all the while nibbling the wild thyme" (*Brulard*, chap. 27).

Outside the cozy circle of the Bigillions, Henri drew close to several schoolmates who would remain his confidential friends into his twenties, in some cases all his life. Fortuné Mante was to be Beyle's intimate companion in Paris around 1804 and, the following year, his partner in an abortive business venture. Félix Faure, the most reserved and the gloomiest of the group of friends, was a confidant of Henri Beyle till 1814, remaining in Grenoble as a government functionary, but his adherence to the restored Bourbons brought about an eventual estrangement between him and Beyle. Jean-Antoine Plana, born in Turin and thus Henri's first Italian friend, was to go on to a distinguished career as a mathematician at the university of his native town, enjoying Henri Beyle's lifelong admiration and trust. In terms of intellectual interests, the real kindred spirit among these early friends was Louis Crozet. In Paris, after 1803, the two young men would avidly read together and discuss Tracy, Helvétius, Montesquieu, Shakespeare, and Adam Smith, and they actually wrote in collaboration a series of exercises in psychological analysis of character; later, in the early years of the Restoration, Crozet was to aid in the publication and defense of Stendhal's first two books. Eventually, Crozet, settled in his native Dauphiné as a supervisor of bridges and public works, would succumb intellectually to the narrowness and aridity of provincial life, and Beyle also felt that Crozet's wife had driven the two apart. Finally, one of the most important Grenoble friends in regard to the role he would later play in Stendhal's career was his cousin Romain Colomb. He is barely accorded mention in *Henry Brulard*, perhaps because Stendhal tended to take him for granted and to view this solid, faithful, rather stiff and undistinguished younger relative with a certain condescension. During the novelist's later career in Italy, Colomb, then working in Paris as a civil service accountant, would act as Stendhal's unofficial literary agent, and after Beyle's death, he became his devoted literary executor, preserving the writings and supervising the first publication of a collected works.

It was with Colomb, Mante, and two or three other friends that Henri undertook, in the late autumn of 1798, one of the most anomalous of his boyhood escapades—a pistol attack on the Tree of Fraternity, which had been erected by the Jacobin authorities in the Place Grenette, not far from Henri Gagnon's house. The adult Stendhal could not recall exactly what had motivated the boys, except for some general feeling of rancor. The young conspirators succeeded in riddling with bullets the placard on which was inscribed "Death to Royalty, Constitution of the Year III"; then they made a terrified retreat over back alleys and up staircases. This is surely a peculiar act for so ferocious a republican as Henri Beyle to be involved in, and some scholars have ascribed it to his presumed resentment at his grandfather's having been removed from the local jury of instruction and the school's board of overseers. It may be more plausible, though, to view the whole affair chiefly as an impulse to strike out against a symbol of authority, whatever its political provenance; and the incitement of participating in a whole band of conspirators—in marked contrast to Henri's solitary acts of rebellion three or four years earlier—could easily have led him to forget momentarily such secondary considerations as formal ideological principles. This was, above all, a daring adventure, and a prerequisite to its enactment was placing oneself in the danger-fraught opposition. But the overriding need to resist and ultimately to break free from the bonds of provincial life would soon find a more legitimate outlet.

During his three years at the École Centrale, Henri showed increasing signs of distinction in several different areas. There is little convincing evidence that he had any real zeal for his formal studies or for the way most of his teachers presented them, but he appears to have come to realize that excelling in school was an indispensable key to his future plans. At the beginning of his second academic year, he received honorable mention in the prize competition for drawing and for mathematics. The following spring, he won a prize in drawing, for which he was awarded the Abbé Dubos's *Reflections on Poetry and Painting*, a book that he read with enjoyment and that may have planted the seeds of his own subsequent ideas on the interrelation of the arts and the influence of climatic differences on artistic temperament. In September 1798, the beginning of his last full school year, he won first prize in belles lettres, and a year later, just before his departure for Paris, first prize in mathematics with special distinction.

In all this, it is not really clear how much of lasting intellectual utility Henri Beyle derived from his teachers at the École Centrale. His early devotion to an idea of literature transcending national boundaries must have been at least reinforced by the literature curriculum, but he has little praise for J. G. Dubois-Fontanelle, his instructor in this subject. His serious interest in painting would not be aroused until he had lived in Italy. More generally, one may infer, the philosophical sensualism and the geometric spirit imparted in the classes in logic and general grammar could well have helped fix one of his basic modes of thinking.

Peculiarly enough, it was mathematics that became Henri's great passion during his last year in Grenoble. Finding his instructor at the École Centrale intellectually wanting, he, with several of his friends, turned for private lessons to Louis-Gabriel Gros, a young man of real mathematical gifts and a zealous republican besides. Stendhal warmly describes him in *Henry Brulard* as a model teacher and a man of perfect integrity. There was a strong utilitarian motive in the boy's attachment to mathematics, for he realized that if he could prove himself as a promising mathematician, he could earn the privilege of leaving the town he detested—the very thought of Grenoble, he said, gave him indigestion—in order to go to Paris to enroll in the École Polytechnique. Once he actually arrived in the capital city, he immediately jettisoned his mathematical interests, which suggests that his intrinsic love of the subject must have been somewhat limited in scope or, at any rate, feeble when placed in competition with his literary, theatrical, and amorous enthusiasms. Paul Arbelet, the finely perceptive French biographer of Stendhal's early years, puts it with characteristic elegance: "Through the numbers and formulas, Beyle glimpsed the dreamed-of city, freedom at last attained, glory and books, love and women. It was quite enough to make him a passionate mathematician." [7] To translate this into the crudely pragmatic terms in which the sixteen-year-old Henri Beyle also must have sometimes conceived the matter, when he set off at last for Paris on October 30, 1799, supposedly on his way to a career in engineering, it was his excellence in mathematics that had purchased him his coach ticket to independence.

Yet, as Arbelet goes on to say, there was also a disinterested side to his involvement in mathematics, that austere language which "seduced him with its cold and lucid beauty." He would leave the actual apparatus of mathematics behind him, but the alluring *idea* of mathematics persisted as an underlying direction in his future intellectual development. Setting foot in Paris for the first time as the rawest of youths, acutely self-conscious of his total social ignorance, his awkward provincial accent, his ugliness, quixotically determined to make himself into a great poet, he would cling to his discovery of mathematics as a mode of discourse in which hypocrisy was impossible, and over the years, perhaps to his own surprise, he would invent an approximation of that uncompromising truthfulness in narrative prose.

7. *La Jeunesse de Stendhal* (Paris, 1919), p. 287.

II

PARIS

(Aetat. 16–17)

MANY NOTEWORTHY NOVELS of the eighteenth and nineteenth centuries, including three of the five Stendhal himself wrote, are bound—in consonance with a basic direction of European social history during this period—to the centripetal movement of a naive young protagonist impelled from the provinces to the metropolis, where illusory visions of advancement and adventure crash against the shoals of real urban existence. This pattern of lost illusions, inherited in part from the older picaresque novels, is often informed by a kind of briskly energetic cynicism: once the hero disabuses himself of his adolescent dreams about the world, once he recognizes the necessity to play society's game of prudent hypocrisy and harsh competitiveness, he will manage to get pretty much what he wants, though what he wants may have to be imagined with a sober awareness of the moral ambiguities of desire that he did not initially possess.

The shock of disappointment, however, that young Henri Beyle felt upon his arrival in Paris in November 1799 was at least in part of a different order. It was not merely that the capital city was unable to yield to him immediately all he wanted of it but that he ultimately suspected, after a first acquaintance, that it might not really have all that he wanted.

(Faithful to this early intuition, he would later create a series of heroes who are relentless in their worldliness yet secretly devoted to an ideal of happiness that has nothing to do with society or worldly success.) With a certain symbolic appropriateness, Henri Beyle arrived in the capital the day after the coup d'état of the 18 of Brumaire (November 9, 1799), in which the Directorate was overthrown and General Bonaparte made himself chief of state. It was, quite literally, the exact beginning of the Napoleonic Era, but for the moment political horizons were outside the field of vision of the dazed adolescent.

The general impression Paris seems to have made on this sixteen-year-old from Grenoble was one of pervasive bleakness. A rainy, grimy winter was approaching, nothing like the Alpine winters of his native region. The skies were gray, the streets were full of mud, the horizon was dully bare without the mountains he had known all his life. Even the Parisian cuisine seemed to him flat and uninteresting.

Actually, Paris in 1799 was a place of visible public exuberance, teeming activity, and shocking contrasts. A decade of Republican corruption had enriched a swarm of jobbers and contractors without ameliorating the destitution of the general populace. The contrasting extremes were evident in the very look of the streets. One contemporary visitor, walking all the way from the Odéon to the Louvre, passed only eight coaches and one private carriage on the way, but in front of the fashionable theaters and cafés, there was an unending carnival of nouveau riche ostentation, fancy carriages of every conceivable style, some of them ornamented with gold and precious stones, crowding in on one another in noisy confusion. The social situation, like the political one, was at a moment of unstable transition. Many of the old aristocracy had fled Paris after the Revolution; some would return in the months after the coup d'état, while others lay low in their grand residences in the Faubourg St. Germain dreaming of conspiracies—quite like the ousted Jacobins on the Left—against the "Corsican tyrant" who had just made himself first consul. Popular sentiment, on the other hand, tended to favor Bonaparte. People felt a sense of relief in his assumption of power after all the murderous intrigues of the sundry Republican regimes, hoping (though with a certain cynical wariness) that he would bring order and even honesty to French government. Before long, his military triumphs were to make him an adulated hero.

Meanwhile, the end of the Republican era was marked by a celebratory mood among the Parisian populace. Contemporary reports stress the constant hubbub in the streets, the bustling cafés and restaurants, the ubiquity of musical entertainment, and, above all, the dance craze—*dansomanie* was the inelegant coinage of the period—that swept the city. The waltz, considered by some an indecent dance, had been imported from Germany just two years before. Women, following the Greco-Roman mode of the last years of the Republic, wore diaphanous tunics with the most daring décolletage in which, as a contemporary phrase put it, they could "trot out their charms" (*faire galoper leurs attraits*). An evocation of the life of the streets in the *Journal des Débats* from the spring of 1800 sums up this pulsating Parisian variety with rhapsodic emphasis: "See what wealth, what brightness, what freshness, how many pretty women one unlike the next, how many young men all like each other . . . luxury, nature, day, night, women, whores, vice, decency, everything is confused." It must have been an overwhelming, tantalizing confusion for a shy adolescent from the provinces, concupiscent more by principle than by temperament, harboring splendid visions of what he might do in such a sphere, having absolutely no idea of how to become part of it, and therefore depressed both with himself and with this whole unfamiliar urban scene.

Altogether, Beyle's greatest initial disappointment with Paris was in his relations with its inhabitants. The future writer had vaguely dreamed of discovering in the metropolis a society of kindred spirits in which his literary talents would be encouraged and would flourish, and at the same time—the link between the two fantasies was unclear—a profusion of sumptuous women waiting to be rescued from distress by a young hero like himself. Instead, quite predictably, the sense of isolation he had known through so much of his childhood was at first made sharper than ever before by his move to the capital. Parting company with several of his Grenoble classmates who had come up to Paris at this time to enter the École Polytechnique, he abandoned all thought of preparing for entrance exams and soon took up residence in a little garret off the Quinconce des Invalides, where he hoped to prepare himself for a brilliant career of letters. He had, then, no social or institutional framework in which he could orient himself, no regular circle of human connections. (Though one can assume that he called on the Darus, his grandfather's aristocratic cousins, soon after his arrival, he seems to have had no regular contact with them during his first weeks in the city.) He walked the streets surrounded by "so many busy people rushing past in fine carriages by my side, known to no one, having nothing to do" (*Brulard*, chap. 36). During his second stay in Paris, three years later, he would show the first signs of being able to sustain disciplined intellectual activity, but during this difficult initial period in the metropolis, his chief occupation seems to have been daydreaming: "I was a passionate dreamer in the streets of Paris, sky-gazing and always on the point of being run over by a gig" (*Brulard*, chap. 37). Adrift in Paris, having for the moment no way of penetrating its social and intellectual life, Beyle summed up his response of "somewhat foolish astonishment" (as he himself retrospectively calls it) in the famous formula which he would repeatedly apply in life and fiction to society, nature, war, and love, as they all failed to correspond to the magnificent proportions that a virginal imagination had attributed to them: "*Quoi! n'est-ce que ça?* What! Is that all Paris amounts to?" (*Brulard*, chap. 46).

The sour edge of disappointment soon had physical consequences, at least according to Stendhal's own interpretation, which seems on the verge of saying that the young provincial "somatized," as a later age would put it, his emotional upset. In any case, within a few weeks of his arrival he became seriously ill, a fact worth noting both because of the immediate practical results of the illness and because it marks the beginning of a life-long struggle with chronic ailments which repeatedly incapacitated him but which never managed to inhibit his avidness for writing, romantic intrigue, society, and travel. On this occasion, he suffered from some sort of pleurisy accompanied by a stomach disorder and a high fever (perhaps, one might guess, a particularly virulent flu). Probably more dangerous than the disease itself, whatever it may have been, was the fact that he fell into the hands of an old army surgeon, a "notable charlatan" who specialized in curing École Polytechnique students of the clap and who prescribed for him sinister-looking black medicines and otherwise left him alone in his little room with its "single window, seven or eight feet high, like a prison" (*Brulard*, chap. 36).

Word of Beyle's plight somehow reached his elderly, wealthy cousin, Noël Daru, who suddenly appeared in his wretched digs, had him whisked out of bed, barely conscious of what was happening, and transported to the recently acquired Daru family mansion. One of the leading physicians of Paris was summoned to attend to the boy, and within a few weeks, he was recovered, though no doubt still pale and weakened and having lost much of his hair through the illness; from this time, he would wear a toupee, one prominent item in the panoply of cosmetic accoutrements he gradually acquired to compensate for what he felt were the inadequacies of his appearance. Meanwhile, circumstances had thrown him on the mercies and good offices of the Darus, and, however ungraciously he assumed the role, it was as their protégé that he made his entrance into society and professional life.

The Darus on the whole behaved toward this distant provincial cousin with sympathy, patience, and considerable generosity. He on his part felt rather estranged from them, finding them altogether too much concerned with getting ahead in the world in a prudential French manner that offended his flamboyant "Hispanic" notions of heroic achievement. Both Noël and his oldest son, Pierre, were high-ranking bureaucrats. The father, by this time long retired, had used the advantageous connections of his position as provincial intendant of Languedoc to amass a very considerable fortune before the Revolution. In 1784, he purchased for his son a position as provincial commissioner of war. Although Pierre had some temporary difficulties with the Terror, including a brief period of imprisonment, he managed to continue his career in the military bureaucracy through the 1790s, occupying the post of chief paymaster, then secretary general of the ministry of war by the age of thirty-three, around the time his young cousin Beyle arrived in Paris. Eventually, at the height of the Empire, he would become intendant general of the Grand Army and a count of the Empire.

Stendhal recalls little of Noël Daru beyond his large nose, his crossed eyes, and his rather pretentious manner. Mme Daru, on the other hand, a shriveled little old lady in 1800, is singled out as the embodiment of the character traits that would achieve their most energetic expression in the son Pierre: a rigorously self-interested prudence that precluded any spontaneity of feeling, a decency and politeness devoid of what Stendhal, for once succumbing to Romantic jargon, called "celestial fire." The young would-be poet, in other words, discovered in the Daru household essentially the values he thought he was escaping when he left Grenoble.

Pierre Daru was away in Switzerland with the army when Beyle was brought to the family home to recuperate from his illness. Within a few weeks, however, he returned to resume full-time work at the ministry of war in Paris, and it was he of all the Darus who was to play the most important role in Henri's life. A word is in order about what "full-time work" implied for Pierre Daru since that will suggest a principal reason for the chasm that separated the two cousins, however much Henri would continue to be the object of Pierre's benefactions. The future Count Daru was, as Napoleon himself later put it, " a lion for work," exhibiting all the qualities of ferocity and restless strength that the metaphor suggests. He worked at a relentless pace for long hours, frequently returning to his office after dinner to continue at his desk late into the night. A formidably effective administrator, he made merciless demands both on himself and on the men under him. Stendhal—who elsewhere once suggested that no one should ever work more than six hours daily—remembers Daru at the family table after his long days at the ministry of war, red-eyed, tense and impatient with fatigue, talking constantly of his work. Very soon, Pierre Daru, acting out of the best intentions according to his own bureaucratic lights, tried to get his idle young cousin a start in the world by giving him a job as a clerk in his office.

The result, of course, was unmitigated misery for Beyle, tolerable only because the ordeal proved to have a duration of barely three months. It was as though his soaring ambitions had been realized in a gross and humiliating parody—instead of becoming a great writer, he was launched on a career as a lowly scrivener. The first letter he was given to copy he reproduced not only in an abominable scrawl (his handwriting never improved much) but with the indicative pronoun *cela*, "that," egregiously misspelled as *cella* (a slip Julien repeats with M. de la Mole in *Le Rouge et le Noir*). Pierre Daru's sarcastic response cut directly into the rawest nerve of the adolescent's vanity: "So this is the man of letters, the brilliant *humanist* who disputes the merit of Racine and carried off all the prizes in Grenoble!" (*Brulard*, chap. 41). The jibe about Racine may have actually been made sometime after this initiatory incident of the misspelled *cela*, for once Beyle began to work regularly in the office, he engaged in heated debates with a fellow clerk over the relative merits of Racine and Shakespeare, exchanges that were undoubtedly overheard by other staff workers and contributed to making the provincial newcomer an object of satire. Surrounded by these narrow, uncomprehending French souls, Beyle was lonelier than ever, so much so that when he looked out the window and saw the lindens blossoming in his first Parisian spring, he was moved to imagine that in the suddenly resplendent trees he had at last discovered his first friends in the great city.

There could not have been, however, a great deal of time in Pierre Daru's ministry of war either for gazing out the window or for conducting literary discussions, as the prevailing atmosphere seems to have been that of a frantically incessant Dickensian workhouse. "M. Daru," Stendhal concedes, "was my benefactor in the sense that he employed me in preference to many others, but"—he goes on to say, vividly recalling his own misery and the psychological tenor of this devotion to work—"I spent many a rainy day, with a headache from the overheated stove, writing from ten in the morning till one after midnight, and that under the eyes of a furious man constantly in anger because he was *always afraid*. . . . He was mortally afraid of Napoleon, and I was mortally afraid of him" (*Brulard*, chap. 42).

It would be hard to imagine from this account that Pierre Daru was also a man of letters—a writer considerable enough in stature for Sainte-Beuve, two generations later, to devote three articles to him in *Causeries de lundi*, more than to Stendhal himself. Though one might have hoped for some literary affinities between the two cousins, Daru was precisely the sort of writer with whom Henri Beyle could have no intellectual traffic, a man of the cultural establishment in a country where that entity is palpable as an official, institutionalized group. He wrote suitably decorous poetry on a variety of edifying historical, political, and philosophical topics; translated the classics; attempted two plays; and just before his death produced a versification of La Place's astronomy(!). Inevitably, after the Restoration he was made by royal decree a member of the Académie Française. But the concept of being a writer with official affiliations, his diplomas, as it were, hung out like a dentist's, guided Daru's literary career from the beginning. Under his name on the title page of his 1804 translation of Horace, the following is proudly inscribed: "Of the Institute of Boulogne; of the Philotechnical Society; of the Society of Arts, Letters, and Science of Paris; and of the Academies of Montpellier, Aix-la-Chapelle, and Dijon." His young cousin, by contrast, would define himself as a writer by demolishing the pretensions, the inflated rhetoric, and the gestures of cultural piety that were the passwords to success, or so he suspected, in the French literary establishment of his age.

There was, however, one member of the Daru household in whom Henri Beyle immediately felt a strong sympathy of character, and that was Pierre's younger brother Martial, aged twenty-six in 1800. Like Pierre, Martial Daru worked in the military bureaucracy, but he had begun his career as an artillery lieutenant, and he served repeatedly in Bonaparte's expeditionary forces, so that he impresses one more as a career officer than as an administrator. With the added glamour of his military panache and his foreign exploits, he presented altogether a more brilliant version of the figure that had been previously embodied for Beyle in his uncle Romain Gagnon. An elegant man of the world, something of a gambler and a Don Juan who actually kept a tally of the beautiful women he had conquered, Martial seemed the perfect realization of one identity Henri had dreamed of achieving ever since his surreptitious early reading of *Félicia* and *Les Liaisons dangereuses*. Martial was, moreover, unstintingly generous toward his young cousin, encouraging him to be a disciple or junior colleague with no hint of condescension or impatience at his provincial ungainliness.

Martial inspired Henri with the prospect of a military career, and within a few months, he would welcome Beyle in Milan as a comrade-at-arms. The friendship was to continue after Beyle's return to Paris, and

later, beginning in 1806, Henri served under Martial in the military intendancy at Brunswick. As Stendhal, still grateful after three decades
summed up his sense of his cousin in *Souvenirs d'égotisme*, Martial
Daru was "the best man in the world, my master who taught me, in Milan
in 1800, in Brunswick in 1807, the little I know in the art of conducting
myself with women" (chap. 2). But Daru's own career as an erotic adven-
turer had a rather pathetic epilogue: he died in 1829, debilitated, according to Stendhal, because he had been dosing himself with supposedly aph-
rodisiac potions. In any event, one wonders whether the model of Cousin
Martial may not have helped foster in Henri Beyle a delusive ideal of mas-
culine aggressiveness and cool audacity that ultimately caused him considerable pain and frustration through much of his life. Paul Arbelet argues
this case with characteristic aptness: "Beyle was forcing his nature while
Martial was following his. He did not succeed in making himself a Don
Juan, but he lost the merit of delicacy, which suited his temperament." [1]

Before long, Henri would make his first, awkward attempts to emulate
Martial, but during this initial six-month stay in Paris, his aspirations to
become an accomplished seducer were confined to the overheated recesses
of his imagination, while his actions were all timidity and hesitation.
There were, in fact, temptation and—though he was too inexperienced to
realize it—ample sexual opportunity close at hand. Just beneath Beyle's
room in the Daru house, Noël Daru's niece by marriage, Magdeleine
Rebuffel, rented an apartment for herself and her twelve-year-old daughter, Adèle. It was a proper Parisian ménage. M. Rebuffel, a well-to-do
businessman, maintained a separate residence with his mistress and business
associate (who in turn seems to have kept him emotionally busy with
angry scenes and perhaps infidelities) and took care to call punctually on
his wife and daughter for a quarter of an hour each day. Mme Rebuffel,
on her part, a pretty and agreeable woman, used her freedom to the fullest
advantage. One of her former lovers was none other than Romain
Gagnon, who had reported to his nephew the little trick he had used to
seduce her once in Lyon, praising her shapely leg and asking her to lift it
up on a trunk so that he could admire it the better. On one occasion, he
was caught in the act with Mme Rebuffel by her husband. The association
with Uncle Romain (if in fact the boy already knew the story in 1800)
must have surely heightened Henri's sexual interest in Mme Rebuffel, but
of course, he had no way of guessing yet—within two years he would
find out—how readily this mature woman would welcome his advances.

1. *La Jeunesse de Stendhal*, vol. 2, p.35.

Meanwhile, he also took considerable notice of Adèle, who at twelve was already coquettish and vivaciously playful, a decided possibility for the future. By March, Beyle was on comfortable terms with his downstairs female neighbors, frequenting Mme Rebuffel's salon, dancing—no doubt the scandalous waltz—with Adèle. Faithful as he would so often be to the objects of his erotic interest, however hypothetical, he was to return to both Magdeleine and Adèle Rebuffel after his expedition in Italy.

Bonaparte at the head of his army had just invaded Lombardy. Both Pierre and Martial Daru were dispatched to Italy as administrative officers. After three tedious, frustrating, and lonely months scribbling letters in the ministry of war, Beyle found himself on his way to the front. Within a few months, through the good offices of his influential cousin, he would be transformed into a second lieutenant of the dragoons, complete with a splendid green jacket and a formidable black-crested helmet. To be sure, at this point he could scarcely handle a sword, and he did not know how to ride a horse at all. When he first actually climbed onto a military mount in Switzerland on the way to the front, the creature galloped off with him into a clump of willow trees, and he had to be rescued by his captain's orderly. (This humbling ordeal of equitation is a comic rite of passage which he would keenly recall and to which he would repeatedly submit his fictional heroes.)

But such practical difficulties in no way dampened his enthusiasm when he set out from Paris on May 7 to join the army. Adulthood seemed to be opening to him the brilliant vistas he had contemplated so long and so fervently in his reading. With his sword and horse and the prospect of an officer's appointment, he was not only on the point of becoming another Cid, but his route to the fields of glory, as though arranged by a providential destiny, took him through the very places where *La Nouvelle Héloïse* had been conceived. The first thing he did on his arrival in Geneva was to make a reverent pilgrimage to the house in which Rousseau had been born. Then, after the sorry incident of the runaway mount and after having received some lessons in horsemanship from his patient captain (whom he had been quite prepared to challenge to a duel!), he proceeded to Rolle, intoxicated with *La Nouvelle Héloïse*, which he was rereading as he went. At Rolle, he conceived the idea of going on to nearby Vevey, Rousseau's longtime place of residence. In this general state of exaltation, as he looked down a Swiss hillside at the gleaming expanse of Lake Leman below, he suddenly heard the peal of church bells. A constellation of fortuitous circumstances gave him the gift of a privileged moment like the ones he had known as a child at Les Échelles in Savoy. A book read, the "ravishing music" of bells, a lovely mountain landscape with blue water below, formed a perfect whole—the exact antithesis to the jumbled world of dissonant fragments that had been his frustrated experience of Paris—and a moment of elevated sensation, of pure aesthetic bliss, that had nothing to do with his schemes of success and amorous conquest. Thirty-six years after the fact, recalling this moment as he writes *Henry Brulard*, Stendhal again feels his heart pounding with excitement, and rising from his desk, he despairs of the ability of language to convey such an experience without the falsification of effusive rhetoric. "That, it seems to me, was my closest approach to *perfect happiness*. For such a moment it is worth the trouble of having lived" (*Brulard*, chap. 44).

Though Stendhal, perhaps despite himself, may have been the secret devotee of an ideal of contentment beyond the strife of worldly affairs, he was too powerfully drawn to the world to rest more than an instant, literally or figuratively, in the tranquil perfection of the mountaintop. Within a few days, he would be making his way on the treacherous twisting paths, along the sheerest precipices, of the Great St. Bernard Pass (he could still hardly take his mastery of his horse for granted) down into Italy—"Is that all the St. Bernard amounts to?" he would, predictably, ask at the end of the passage—and in a week, he would come under fire for the first time. Till then, Italy had been a place he had known from Ariosto and had fabulated into a magical, passionate "land where the orange tree grows." Now, at the ripe age of seventeen, he was about to plunge into an Italy where there were real armies in battle and flesh-and-blood women to desire and—if he could manage it—pursue, where he would encounter music and art of a sensual power quite beyond the purview of his Grenoble boyhood. Italy also held in store for this quixotic young man a new set of pratfalls, but whatever his misadventures, after his stay in Milan in 1800–01, he would have a new, permanently compelling vision of what he might do with his life.

III

ITALY

(Aetat. 17–18)

BEYLE CROSSED INTO ITALY in the last days of May 1800. On May 30, he saw fire for the first time in the shelling of the fort at the village of Bard. It was, he wrily observed, the loss of a virginity that had weighed on him more heavily than the sexual one. Curiously, though not really surprisingly, what he stressed in this first actual encounter with war, at least as he pondered the experience retrospectively, was a stance of aesthetic contemplation. He observes in *Henry Brulard* (chap. 46), with italic emphasis, that the battle was an evident manifestation of *the sublime*—though a bit too close for comfort to danger and thus not to be enjoyed without an admixture of self-protective apprehension. Perhaps the actual feelings of the seventeen-year-old were barely controlled fright more than anything else: his horse kept rearing at the thunder of the cannonades, and the novice equestrian had all he could do to follow his captain's instructions about holding the reins lightly.

In any case, Beyle's acquaintance with warfare during his whole first military venture was chiefly from a distance. He could not have taken part in the decisive battle of Marengo on June 15, as he sometimes afterward remembered, for he was then in Milan. He may have later participated in the battles of Mincio and Castelfranco and comported himself with bravery, as certificates signed by his commanding officer attest, but some scholars have questioned whether these documents reflect dependable fact or merely the desire of a well-disposed superior to further the young man's career. What is clear is that this first campaign confronted him with no searing images of the terrible carnage of war—an experience to be reserved for his tours of duty in Austria and in Russia—and that his main military obligation was to serve in an army of occupation under relatively peaceful circumstances. The bloody reality of war, then, had little occasion to interfere with his sense of the French conquest of Italy as a festive occurrence.

Beyle's real ceremony of induction into Italy was not the guns of Bard but the footlights of Novara, a town some twenty miles west of Milan on the line of march from the St. Bernard. (In *Brulard*, Stendhal places the crucial event at Ivrea, still farther to the west, but a letter to his sister Pauline in 1808, when the memory was a quarter of a century fresher, more plausibly identifies the town as Novara.) The newly conquered town was in a state of turmoil, its frightened inhabitants forced to quarter French soldiers, while small bands of the invaders roamed the streets looting. Despite the paternal warnings of his captain that it was foolhardy for Beyle to venture out at night in these risky circumstances, dressed as a civilian, armed with a saber he could barely balance, the young amateur of the theater could not resist the temptation of going to see his first real Italian opera. The production by a provincial company could not have been very grand. The female lead, as he could plainly see, was missing a front tooth, though that did not prevent him from becoming instantly, if fleetingly, infatuated with her in the same kind of reflex of amorous reverence for the stage he had exhibited two years earlier in his devotion to Virginie Kubly. The piece performed on that evening of June 1 was Cimarosa's sprightly opera buffa, *Il Matrimonio Segreto*. The effect on the seventeen-year-old was overwhelming, one of those moments in his life that constituted, as it were, a euphoric complementary opposite to a traumatic experience, when a state of perfect rapture was so deeply felt that it was permanently imprinted on his imagination as a haunting ideal of happiness. Having crossed the St. Bernard and having been exposed to fire suddenly seemed crude and insignificant to him. "I experienced something like my enthusiasm over the church above Rolle, but much purer and much more vivid. . . . My life was renewed, and all my disappointment with Paris was buried forever" (*Brulard*, chap. 46). It was this evening, he goes on to say, that destroyed the last vestiges of Grenoble in him: here, one might infer,

at the opera in provincial Lombardy, he had discovered the perfectly realized realm of *Espagnolisme* that he had dreamed about since childhood. At
this moment, he felt there was nothing so worthy as music to which he
could devote his life.

It is likely enough that almost any opera would have had the same
effect, but Cimarosa's work was peculiarly suited to induce in Beyle this
condition of euphoria. The music of *Il Matrimonio Segreto* is wonderfully
playful, abounding in witty inventiveness; the dramatic action develops
with a minimum of recitative through a rapid variety of melodious arias,
duets, trios, and ensemble pieces. The overall impression on Beyle must
have been of comic action liberated into a state of pure floating grace as
song. From this evening, Cimarosa would forever be "the divine Cimarosa" in the French writer's private mythology. The blessed union of language and music in opera would lead him to a certain impatience with
mere instrumental music, and when he eventually achieved mastery in his
own artistic medium, he would find ways of intimating in the narrative
prose of his two greatest novels the endlessly delighting sense of consummate melodious play he had first felt in Cimarosa.

The plot, moreover, of the first Italian opera Beyle attended, though a
conventional farrago of young lovers, mistaken relationships, and interfer-
ing elders, had some prominent elements that might have resonated in a
gratifying way with his sense of his own family situation. The household
in *Il Matrimonio Segreto* is presided over by Geronimo, a widowed father
who is the comic embodiment of the most eminently bourgeois vices: he
is purse-proud, absurdly conscious of his own importance as a prosperous
merchant, and utterly mesmerized by the prospect of attaching a title of
nobility to his family through the marriage of his daughter. (He is also,
symbolically and farcically, half-deaf.) His associate in the management of
this motherless family, and the other main satiric target in the opera beside
the noble suitor, is Geronimo's widowed sister, Fidalma, who takes an
amorous interest in the handsome young man secretly married to her
brother's younger daughter. It is of course unnecessary to conclude that
the young Beyle simply saw his father and his Aunt Séraphie in Geronimo
and Fidalma, but the analogy between the two pairs must have surely
heightened his pleasure in the comedy, and perhaps what may have confirmed his sense of Cimarosa's "divinity" was his glimpsing in the opera
how the oppressive figures of real experience could be beautifully stylized,
distanced, and transformed into comic art.

Around June 10, Beyle arrived in Milan, where he was to remain until
he received his appointment as a second lieutenant of the dragoons toward

the end of October. Riding into town on a bright spring morning, he came upon his cousin Martial in the Corsia del Giardino, resplendent in the blue frock coat and broad-brimmed hat of an adjutant general. Martial, a little anxious that the young Beyle might have been lost in action, greeted him warmly and immediately took him in tow, getting him settled in at the Casa d'Adda, a requisitioned mansion where both men were to be quartered. Beyle was dazzled by the place with its magnificent staircase and its sumptuous salon looking out on the main avenue. It was the first time he had been so moved by architecture, and, indeed, there was little in Milan during this first stay that failed to delight him. The world of harmonious play that Cimarosa's music had opened up for him at Novara seemed to have its natural capital here in Milan.

La Scala was of course the heart of Milan for him, but the passionate, exuberant, unselfconsciously aesthetic attitude toward life that he felt in the splendors of the opera house he could also see in the grand mansions of the city and in its cathedral; in the beautiful Lombard women, who seemed—and in some cases actually were—so much more natural and accessible than Parisian women; in the vivid life of the cafés; in the ferment of cultural activity that made cosmopolitan Milan, with its poets, painters, and composers, the intellectual center of Italy.

Milan in 1800 was just in the first flowering of its modern urban vitality, and perhaps one of the things that excited the young Beyle was the new élan that manifested itself in so many aspects of the city. Through most of the eighteenth century, Milan had been little more than a placid provincial town. At the time of the French conquests, and largely because of them, it was rapidly transformed into a dynamic urban center. In the nine years following Bonaparte's first entrance into the city, the population rose from 128,000 to 142,000. A good part of the increase was due to political refugees from Rome, Venice, Piedmont, and elsewhere in Italy and abroad, and these newcomers gave Milan its new variegated metropolitan character at the same time that they helped make the city a focus for nascent Italian national sentiment.

If Paris disheartened the young man from Grenoble with the rigidity of its elaborate hierarchies, Milan presented a buzzing panorama of innovation. Important reforms in education, for women as well as for men, were under way. A spate of short-lived journals reflected the fervent political atmosphere of the city. The new republican spirit—and this must have especially appealed to Beyle—was boldly translated into the aesthetic realm. The ornate fashions of the aristocratic eighteenth century yielded to an elegant "Greco-Roman" simplicity in both attire and interior decors.

High-waisted white cotton dresses were much in evidence, often subtly set off by a scarf or shawl in subdued colors like russet and olive green. The men tended to frock coats of long, simple lines in dark greens and blues. In the salons Beyle visited, he would have found a cognate version of this classicizing republicanism: the sumptuous tapestries of the eighteenth century had been removed, stressing the sharp linearity of paneled walls, and a new quality of controlled richness was evident in many details of decor. The outward face of the city was also being lifted: avenues were being widened, the facades of buildings were being renovated, new structures were going up. This was manifestly a city being reshaped by the pulsating spirit of the new century, a spirit whose first stirrings had been felt in 1789 but whose destined master, so it seemed to many, was the triumphant young general of the French armies.

If the political excitement and the sense of historical élan touched Beyle, he clearly must have been moved even more by the passionate quality of Milanese cultural life. Theater was particularly active in Milan, and especially since a good many of the contemporary Italian playwrights were Milanese, sharp debates about new plays, often entangled with political issues, were a prominent feature of the local cultural climate. But overshadowing all other cultural and, indeed, social institutions of the city was La Scala. This, too, was a relatively new fashion adopted especially by the younger generation: going to the opera became a daily obligation, one so compelling that only on Friday evening, when La Scala was closed, could the fashionable homes hold their salons. Otherwise, one went to the opera each evening to see acquaintances and to be seen and, not surprisingly, as much attention was devoted to socializing and sometimes even to business transactions as to the performance. For Beyle, fresh from his initiation at Novara, a society revolving around a luminous opera stage must have seemed like an ideal of sublimity fulfilled in social practice. In any case, it is safe to assume that his rapture over this first encounter with Milan had a good deal to do both with his own visits to La Scala and with his sense of its extraordinary importance in the life of the city.

Nearly forty years later, in writing the opening chapter of *La Chartreuse de Parme*, Stendhal would recall these euphoric months in Milan, displacing them back to Bonaparte's first occupation of the city in 1796. The festive entrance of that youthful army in tatters is a perfect introduction to some of the novel's major themes, though one may question whether the French were really so universally greeted as welcome liberators from the Austrian yoke and whether, as the novel suggests, there was really such dancing in the streets, French soldiers rocking Italian babies to sleep, the homes of rich and poor flung open to the conquering troops. There were, to be sure, Milanese enthusiasts who saw the establishment of the Cisalpine Republic as a genuine realization of Italian national aspirations, but there were others who resented the French as foreign interlopers no better than the Austrians. Paul Arbelet's astringent comment on Beyle's vision of turn-of-the-century Milan, though it may err on the side of uncompromising skepticism, surely has considerable justice: "Beyle has left us an image of Milan at once false and charming. It is a lover's memory, wholly compacted of his illusions." [1]

What the lover was actually doing with the object of his affections is a little hard to ascertain from the concluding pages of *Henry Brulard*, for the autobiographical narrative breaks down at this point into a series of superlative affirmations: "it was the most beautiful time of my life"; "it was an interval of mad and complete happiness . . . five or six months of heavenly, perfect happiness." One likely reason, in fact, for Stendhal's abandoning his autobiography at precisely this juncture is his inability, or unwillingness, to violate the happiness of his first encounter with Milan by making it the subject of narrative and analysis.

Professionally, there could have been no great excitements for him during this time. He worked as a clerk under Louis Joinville, commissioner of war in Milan and Pierre Daru's subordinate. Joinville seems to have made some effort to treat him as a protégé, perhaps partly because of his connection with Daru, but Beyle, predictably, found occasion to provoke a quarrel with Joinville. In any case, his duties at the commissariat left him ample enough time to take in the pleasures of the city. These he was as yet not equipped to enjoy very seriously: he was, after all, still a shy adolescent, as ignorant of the intricacies of social life as he was of the Italian language, awkward in the salons to which he was introduced, encumbered everywhere by the extravagant armor of his quixotic defensiveness. But his youthful incapacity may have been closely connected with his sense of euphoria, for, precisely because he remained largely an observer in this Milanese wonderworld he was discovering, it presented itself as a realm of untarnished, unlimited *possibility*, showering his senses with promises of fulfillment that he fervently believed would be kept before long.

As for Beyle's particular ambition to win the affections and enjoy the favors of women, during these months in Milan he had at least one more

1. Arbelet, vol. 2, p. 119.

passing infatuation, underwent his technical sexual initiation, and was overtaken by the first of his great haunting loves, the plausible enough consequence of his determination (as a reader of Rousseau rather than Laclos) to be haunted by love. The infatuation, in the fall of 1800, was with a certain Mme Martin, about whom little is known and who seems to have been a rather trivial episode in the young Beyle's life except for the fact that she was the ostensible reason for his second duel, an affair of honor scarcely less absurd than his first with his schoolmate at the École Centrale. In this case, his opponent was Alexandre Petiet, one year his senior, a former student of the École Polytechnique (which Beyle had chosen not to enter), and at the time a lieutenant in the artillery. One might also note, in connection with what looks like an emerging pattern of entanglements with authority figures or with those closely affiliated to them, that Petiet's father was former minister of war and just then French minister extraordinary to the Cisalpine Republic. Predictably enough, while the two belligerent adolescents were clashing swords over the lady that both made claim to, her affections were actually engaged elsewhere. Beyle came out of the affair with a flesh wound on the foot, which incapacitated him for a week or so and no doubt left him with the consoling feeling that, after his failure actually to fight the redoubtable Ordu in Grenoble, he now had visibly exposed himself to danger in the field of honor. Curiously, the one future point of contact between Petiet's life and Beyle's would again be through their shared interest in a woman, though in this case it was fortunately not a simultaneous interest. In 1808, Petiet was to marry Adèle Rebuffel, Beyle's young Parisian friend, but long before then, as we shall see, Beyle would seek a relationship with her that was distinctly nonmarital in character.

Sometime during these months, Beyle had his first sexual experience, with a Milanese whore. Later he could not recall exactly when, with whom, or what he felt about it, but if one looks to his writing for an echo of his response to this encounter, the most likely place would be in a sexual episode in *Lamiel*, his last, unfinished novel. The forthright adolescent heroine of that book, wanting to know what is this thing "love" so vaunted in fiction and so warned against by her elders, hires a strapping young peasant to disembarrass her of her virginity. After the completion of the transaction, Lamiel—probably quite like Henri Beyle after his own sexual initiation—recites the famous Stendhalian formula: "*Ce n'est que ça?* Is that all love amounts to?"

The emotional effects of Beyle's initiation to sex may have been negligible, but the physical consequences were somewhat more durable. He contracted a venereal infection, to which the usual remedy of mercury was applied, and the remedy itself, together with the local discomfort and the concomitant headaches, fever, and stomach disorder, made a good many of his subsequent days in Italy acutely uncomfortable. Whether the infection was gonorrhea or syphilis is difficult to determine. Henri Martineau, the most exhaustive and factually authoritative of Stendhal's biographers, inclines to the graver of the two diseases, suggesting that various chronic complaints Stendhal suffered from later were the symptoms of tertiary syphilis and that his fatal stroke may be attributed to the ravaging effects of the cardiovascular variety of the disease.[2] Comparing what is known of Stendhal's symptoms in 1800 and later with the textbook description of the several stages of syphilis, one may grant it as a distinctly possible diagnosis but by no means a completely convincing one, and it is perhaps too tempting an inference to draw precisely because it accords so well with the myth of the tragically tainted genius that we have come to cherish in connection with many of the creative heroes of nineteenth-century culture. In any case, that myth is irrelevant to Stendhal since, if in fact he had syphilis, it was clearly not neurosyphilis, with its attendant mental disorders, such as violent rages, delusions, and loss of memory. Regardless of what he may have contracted from a Milanese prostitute in 1800, Stendhal remained lucid, indeed, mentally hale and energetic throughout his career, until his final apoplexy (he was dictating a new story on the morning of the day he died); and so perhaps the simpler working hypothesis is that his first sexual encounter resulted only in an ordinary case of the clap.

By contrast, Beyle's initial contact with an enticing young Milanese woman named Angela Pietragrua had secondary and tertiary stages clearly manifested in his emotional life for the next fifteen years, and as late as 1835, when he begins pondering the idea of *Henry Brulard* by tracing in the dust with his walking stick the initials of the women he has loved, her memory vaguely troubles and stirs him. Angela Pietragrua, who was about twenty-three at the time of Bonaparte's second entrance into Milan, had married a clerk in the bureau of weights and measures when she was sixteen and already had a five-year-old son. Neither matrimony nor maternity, however, imposed any appreciable restraints on her: she was just the sort of Milanese woman who in 1796, and again in 1800, gave certain French officers all the welcome that a soldier's heart could desire. Henri Beyle was introduced to her by Louis Joinville, whose mistress she then

2. *Le Coeur de Stendhal* (Paris, 1952–53), vol. 1, p. 138.

was, and one may speculate that the evident appeal of her womanly charms was at least heightened for him by her intimate association with his immediate superior in the military bureaucracy. The one presumed portrait of Angela that has come down to us tends to confirm Beyle's characterization of her, in an 1804 notation, as "brunette, stately, voluptuous"—the face in the portrait has ripe, full features, just a hint of a sensual pout in the lower lip, and a hard intensity in the expression of the eyes that might be construed as passionate, or perhaps as the reflection of wary calculation.

Retrospectively, in the second chapter of *Brulard*, Stendhal would summarize her as "sublime strumpet in the Italian style," but in 1800–01, she seemed to him altogether unapproachable; or at any rate, he could not quite imagine what should be his first step of approach. For the time being, then, he admired her silently and from afar, attending her salon from time to time during these first months in Milan, afterward seeing her occasionally during his returns to Milan in his remaining year of service in Italy, and once running into her by chance while he was stationed at Brescia. Across the chasm of unrequited, indeed unspoken, love, Beyle brooded over her brilliantly (later he would develop a theory of the psychology of love to explain the dynamics of this process), transforming her into a shimmering image of ideal femininity. During the next eleven years, until he returned to Milan and in fact became Angela Pietragrua's lover, he had two extended liaisons and an abundance of transient ones, in addition to three or so serious emotional involvements that were never translated into actual affairs; but he is elegantly precise when he says of this period at the end of *Brulard* that it was "eleven years not of faithfulness but of a kind of constancy."

What he brought away, then, from his first sojourn in Italy was above all two experiences of a passionate spectator—his recollection of the euphoria inspired by the opera and the vision of the perfect promise of bliss that he associated with the alluring Angela. In due time, he would return to recover one experience and to attempt to realize the other, but what is more important, he would eventually weave both into the imaginative fabric of his fiction, the one as mood and style, the other as a probing perception of male psychology and female character.

On October 23, 1800, through the efforts of Pierre Daru, Beyle received his official appointment as a second lieutenant in the Sixth Dragoons. As we have already had occasion to note, his zeal for winning glory through a military career had given way to his aesthetic and amatory interests almost from the moment he set foot on Italian soil, and he had little satisfaction, apart, perhaps, from the dashing uniform, in his new role as an officer. Toward the end of November, he joined his company, first at Romanengo, then at Bagnolo, small Lombard towns about a day's journey to the east of Milan. Clearly, he felt exiled from Milan, and his sense of his surroundings is aptly reflected in a letter to his sister Pauline dated December 7, in which he describes Bagnolo as "a miserable little Cisalpine village three leagues from Brescia." Vegetating in the Italian provinces as part of an army of occupation, he was quickly overcome by a sensation he would have least expected when he set out from Paris—boredom.

His health, too, whether as a result of the venereal disease or of another kind of infection he had contracted and was unable to shake off, was uncertain throughout this period. The journal which he began to keep in April 1801 is filled with references to the recurring fevers he suffered and to the various medications with which he dosed himself. A shrewd physician, whose opinion is noted in the journal entry for December 10, 1801, was inclined to see the malady as psychosomatic: he detected in Beyle "certain symptoms of nostalgia and melancholy" and informed him that his "chronic complaint was boredom." Boredom, ennui, would remain a haunting presence to be escaped through much of Beyle's life, and he would inflict that condition as a primary motivator on a number of his fictional heroes. This keen apprehension of the tedium of everyday life as a gray menace that has to be conjured away, outmaneuvered, or transcended by some compelling occupation of the imagination or some bold reaching for adventure, is one of the things that makes Stendhal so profoundly a man of the nineteenth century. For the moment, however, one must think of him chiefly as an adolescent whose flushed expectations of a brilliant career at arms had suddenly collapsed into the dull routine of military life in the boondocks. Whether his debilitating fevers were actually caused by his emotional state, as the army doctor proposed, we cannot know, but it seems plausible enough to assume at least that his resistance to whatever it was that he had contracted was appreciably lowered by his downcast mood.

On February 1, 1801, General C.I.F. Michaud, commander of the Third Cisalpine Division, selected Beyle as his aide-de-camp. The young officer had been recommended to the general by Louis Joinville, and both Joinville and Michaud seem to have labored under the illusion that by advancing Beyle they would win the favor of Pierre Daru. As it turned out, Daru was furious over the appointment, which violated military protocol—Beyle had neither the rank of first lieutenant nor the requisite campaign experience to be an aide-de-camp—and also bypassed Daru's own plans for his young cousin, which were to promote him in the hierarchy of the military commissariat once he had put in a decent amount of time at field duty. During the next few months, Daru persisted in his complaints about Beyle's assignment, and around mid-September, Michaud yielded, issuing the order for Beyle to rejoin his regiment in the dragoons. The order arrived, as chance would have it, when he was on another of his stopovers in Milan, so once again he could experience a kind of exile. He paid a last shy farewell visit to Angela Pietragrua, whom he was not to see again for a decade, and headed down to the district of Turin, where his unit was stationed first in one small town and then another. By now, he had been suffering recurrent bouts of fever for many months, and in late October, he was actually bedridden for a week and a half. He applied for convalescent leave, clearly intending to return to France in order not merely to recuperate but also to leave the army altogether and to devote himself to a career of letters.

During this whole protracted period of illness and inaction, Beyle begins to develop a social mien and to conceive a spate of specific projects which suggest that he is already in the process of putting behind him the adolescent dreaminess and timid ineptitude that had been so transparent on his arrival in Paris, only a year before. He notes in his journal (May 15, 1801) an overheard comment about him made by General Michaud to one of his junior officers: "I am quite fond of this little Beyle fellow; he is full of wit . . . but he is too candid and too brusque." The blindly headstrong qualities we have observed earlier were at least being modulated into tactless self-assertiveness, and the young aide-de-camp clearly must have been learning how to exercise in conversation his gifts of lively, quick observation. Beyle would always be inclined to prefer the display of wit to the deployment of tact when a choice had to be made between the two, but what Michaud's perception at this early moment catches nicely is that there was something endearing rather than offensive in this recklessness about the requirements of social discretion or professional prudence. Michaud maintained his liking for the young man from Grenoble after they had parted company. When the two were both in Paris in 1803–04, Beyle was a not infrequent visitor at his home, and the general tried, futilely, to persuade his former aide to resume his interrupted army career.

Meanwhile, Beyle's head, between fits of fever and melancholy, was simmering with schemes for launching himself in the world of art, letters, and manly achievement. He hired a fencing master, then soon dismissed him, and did the same, much more briefly, with an instructor of clarinet.

(Though he had become, as he noted, a *mélomane,* an aficionado of music, none of his efforts to acquire technical training in music was to make any headway.) He of course also engaged a tutor in Italian, and here he actually made some progress, though he would never have any great facility with languages except for his native one. Characteristically, before he could have possessed more than the rudiments of Italian, he plunged into the translation of *Zelinda e Lindoro,* a comedy by Goldoni, completing it within a few weeks in the spring of 1801. This literary effort happily did not trouble the world until it was exhumed by Stendhal's tireless editors in the twentieth century, but he himself seems to have conceived of it as a kind of transitional manuscript, already in part an adaptation and something out of which he might go on to shape an original play.

He had actually written almost three acts of a projected five-act comedy of his own before leaving Grenoble two years earlier. An airless prose piece called *Selmours* about young lovers who are separated by seemingly insuperable obstacles and a hero who imprudently tries to please everyone, it is the work of a tyro who cannot yet see his way beyond the pasteboard horizon of stale stage conventions. Now in Italy, Beyle sketched out scenarios for two other comedies in the same vein, *Le Ménage à la mode* and *Les Quiproquo.* At the same time, aspiring to higher things, he conceived the notion of writing a verse tragedy on Ariodant, a hero from his beloved Ariosto, and another on nothing less than the figure of Ulysses. Like so many of his projects for the theater, all these Molièresque and Cornelian plans fortunately would not be carried beyond the realm of bright ideas.

While mulling over his sundry dramatic schemes, Beyle, no doubt spurred on by the model of his regimental peers, was actually exploring something of the realm of sexual worldliness in which he planned to set his comedies. If during his stay in Milan his activity as a lover had been split between an inaccessible object of yearning and paid professionals, there are indications that in subsequent months he began to take advantage of local female hospitality in the style of a true dragoon. At one of his provincial posts, there were even rumors of a brief affair with an Italian noblewoman. One notes in his journal a cultivated hardness of tone on the subject of erotic opportunity—Arbelet shrewdly calls it "pretensions to insolence" [3]—as though, even in the privacy of a diary, he had to demonstrate that he was a worthy disciple of his Uncle Romain and his Cousin Martial. Thus, in the entry for May 2, 1801, he sizes up a Lombard beauty

3. Arbelet, vol. 2, p. 194.

with the cool calculation of an experienced seducer: "Mme Nota is judged here to be the prettiest woman in town, and in truth she's not at all bad; they say she has an income of 60,000 *lira;* she has a *cavaliere servente,* a handsome fellow, who spends a lot on her; she is therefore unassailable." In his next sentence, the eighteen-year-old diarist maintains this stance of tough sexual savvy, though the substance of what he says about two local noblewomen suggests a certain continuity with the nervous fastidiousness of the boy who had recoiled from the filthy demeanor of the plebeian women at St. André Church: "We could have screwed two countesses who were staying near us, but they were 28 or 30, with a dirty appearance that was repulsive." In any case, the quasi-military posture of the erotic strategist, a distant ideal ever since his early reading of *Les Liaisons dangereuses*, was already stiffening into a habitual mode of behavior, and he would permanently persist in it, sometimes to his detriment and often in violation of his own inveterately idealistic instincts as a lover.

Another odd feature of Beyle's journal during these last months in Italy is its moments of sober philosophic reflection. These are, it is safe to assume, as utterly self-conscious as the sexual cynicism: one detects the theatrical note of a bright adolescent making weighty pronouncements on the Purpose of Existence. This particular pose, however, would have more constructive consequences than that of the erotic strategist. For if the sententiousness of these entries is something of an affectation, Beyle nevertheless expresses through them the fundamental seriousness with which he was already approaching his life. There was real urgency in his posing the questions of what his life was for and how he was to make use of his gifts (and though he could not yet know this, writing such flimflam as *Selmours* was clearly no answer to either question). The urgency of the questioning would soon lead him to submit himself to an improvised intellectual discipline, and once back in Paris, he would begin to collect a series of reflections, ideas for literary exploration, and thoughts picked up from his philosophic readings in a sort of commonplace book which he conceived as a guide for his intellectual development and which he gave the grandiose, bilingual title, *Filosofia Nova*.

This impulse of the determined self-improver is already prominent in this paragraph from the journal dated July 12, 1801: "Let us make haste to enjoy, for our moments are numbered, the hour spent grieving has nonetheless brought me closer to death. Let us work, for work is the father of pleasure; but let us never grieve. Let us reflect soundly before making a choice; once we have decided, let us never swerve. With stubbornness, one succeeds in everything. Let us give ourselves talents; one day, I shall regret time lost." All those hortatory first-person plurals give the affirmation a hollow forensic ring, but the ironic fact of the matter is that the young diarist was articulating in these gesturings a view of life which one day he would discover he could actually live by.

At the end of 1801, the hoped-for convalescent leave was finally granted. Beyle, just short of his nineteenth birthday, left at once for France, heading first, as both geographical logic and his physical condition dictated, to his native town. During his three-month stay, he was to find Grenoble in certain respects a more agreeable place than he had known it to be when he was growing up there. By mid-April, though, he was once more in Paris, in pursuit of what he convinced himself was a new love and preparing to muster all his resources for an assault on the world of literary fame. Italy was behind him, and he would not see it again for ten years, but it was to remain, like the woman he associated with the beauty and passion of the country, a beckoning horizon of his imagination.

IV

RETURN TO PARIS

(Aetat. 19–22)

BEYLE'S THREE-MONTH STAY in Grenoble was a pleasant interlude of indolence in what he now discovered was a rather urbane center after his army experience in the Italian hinterland. He quickly recuperated from his lingering illness. Free of all responsibility, he spent his time reading, paying social calls, attending balls, and, at last an adult in his native town, probably enjoying at least one or two transient sexual liaisons. (Either now or during a later visit to Grenoble, he gave one young woman such solid satisfaction, seven times in a row as he proudly remembered [*Brulard*, chaps. 18, 19, notes to diagrams], that the incident has been invoked by the most patriotic of Stendhal's French biographers to refute the calumny that the author of *Armance*, a novel about impotence, was himself a poor performer in the boudoir.[1] But the one great emotional, or perhaps we should say cerebral, event during this stopover in Grenoble was his encounter with Victorine Mounier.

Victorine, exactly Henri Beyle's age, and her brother Edouard, one year her elder, had gone into emigration with their parents in 1790; after the Republic was replaced by the Consulate, the family returned from

1. Henri Martineau, *Petit Dictionnaire stendhalien* (Paris, 1948), pp. 233–234.

Weimar to Grenoble late in 1801. To Beyle, bent on proving himself capable of a grand passion, the cultivated Victorine, with her fine oval face, her large gentle eyes, her dark curls, seemed a dazzling creature. The actual contact between them was superficial, and he dared not breathe a word to her of the feelings she had inspired, but he soon became quite preoccupied with her, and cultivated the friendship of Edouard, with whom he otherwise had little in common, in order to have some access to Victorine. Her departure from Grenoble for Paris in March 1802 was the principal reason for Beyle's decision to move on to Paris himself, which he proceeded to do in early April. He had no opportunity, however, to see her there, for soon after her arrival in the capital city she went on to join her father in Rennes, where he had just been appointed to a prefecture.

It was no doubt easier for Beyle to maintain the cerebral purity of his passion for Victorine at this distance. Barred by shyness as well as by social propriety from initiating a correspondence with her, he hit on the characteristically quixotic expedient of composing letters to Edouard with veiled allusions to his love for Victorine in the hope she would come to read the letters. There is no evidence that Edouard ever showed this peculiar correspondence to his sister, and indeed, the carefully planted hints may well have been lost on him. Victorine was the first of the very few women Beyle thought of as a possible wife, but she eventually married a more financially suitable mate. The one objective achieved by the stratagem of indirect love letters was to keep the emotional fires flickering and flaring for almost three years while he intermittently pursued one other woman and became the lover of another, until he finally found a more realistic object for a grand passion.

In fact, the two Parisian women immediately in question in 1802 were mother and daughter, Magdeleine and Adèle Rebuffel. The charming pubescent Adèle whom Beyle left in the spring of 1800 had now blossomed into an attractive young woman. Already on a footing of easy intimacy with his lively, playful young cousin, Beyle was by no means as timid as he had been with Victorine, though he does eventually reproach himself in his journal for not having been still bolder with her. The plausible inference is that their erotically charged relationship was never actually consummated, but the somewhat ambiguously worded journal entry for August 26 would seem to suggest the contrary: "Three times, and putting out the candle, I encounter [*rencontre*] Adèle. Going out, at 3:45, I kiss her." In any event, the bond between the cousins appears to have consisted mainly of romantic gestures—a gift of a lock of hair by Adèle, a cryptic inscription in a volume given by Beyle to Adèle, the promise of intimacy when she rests her head on his shoulder as the two watch a display of fireworks.

Meanwhile, Adèle's mother, a seasoned erotic campaigner who had no need of such paraphernalia of flirtation, decided to avail herself of the young Beyle. Although his romantic interest remained centered on the daughter, this unexpected sexual opportunity may well have had its piquancy for him, and given his delicate involvements in this household, Mme Rebuffel was clearly a liaison he could not have easily declined. He accepted the favors of the mother while trying to conceal from her—no doubt without much success—his avid interest in the daughter. This must have entailed some highly acrobatic maneuvering in the late summer and fall of 1802, and if one puts a sexual construction on the verb *rencontre* in that journal entry for August 26, he was kept very busy indeed, for here is his entry for August 27, striking the note of self-consciously brutal *machismo* we have already observed in his Italian journal: "I see Mme Rebuffel in the evening at 7. I find M. Rebuffel there, who greets me with the greatest cordiality. He leaves, I fuck Rebuffel. Adèle returns at 11 in the evening. She behaves toward me with the most natural indifference."

Despite the pressing ambiguities and excitements of this particular involvement, it was actually the company of men rather than women that was more important to Beyle during most of this second sojourn in Paris. At the time of his first stay in the capital, as we noted, he felt painfully isolated. Now he found himself part of a small circle of close friends whom he saw daily. Most of them were former schoolmates from Grenoble. The first of the series of lodgings he lived in during this period was in the same building as Félix Faure, and he continued for several years on a basis of easy confidentiality with Faure. Another daily companion of Beyle's whom he had known before at the École Centrale was Louis de Barral, and the two would remain lifelong friends. Also among Grenoble contemporaries with whom he now spent a great deal of time in Paris were Louis Crozet and Fortuné Mante. Mante played an important role in two respects, first influencing Beyle, out of fervent republican principle, to anti-Bonapartist sentiments, and then encouraging him, as we shall have occasion to see, to join in a business venture. Finally, after their months together in Milan, Beyle and Martial Daru were intimate and constant companions. One might guess that the continuous society of these young male friends would lead Beyle toward a life of dissipation—Martial's exploits as an erotic intriguer had from the first impressed his young cousin, and Barral at the time was addicted to gambling—but almost the opposite was the case. This was above all a period of serious self-improve-ment for the future writer, and one or another of his friends was always available to share in the intense discussion of literature, theater, politics, and history, even to participate in certain of the formal lessons he undertook.

Early in July 1802, Beyle officially resigned his commission in the army, so he was entirely free to concentrate on his preparation for a career of letters. He managed to maintain himself, more or less, on an allowance from his father, but as the months went by, he found the level of support increasingly inadequate and the payments unconscionably delayed, so that his journals and letters begin to bristle with recriminations against his father, whom he now regularly designates as the Bastard. Nevertheless, by means of this paternal dole, he was able, though sometimes on the edge of poverty, to devote himself to exactly what he wanted to do, and even somehow to keep himself in the dandyish fashionable attire he deemed necessary. (His letters to his sister Pauline contain urgent and repeated requests for formidable quantities of gloves, with uncompromisingly precise specification of color.) Soon after his arrival in Paris, he engaged both an Italian and an English tutor and now made appreciable progress in his ability to read both languages. Still an aspiring playwright, he sedulously attended the theater, became a passionate advocate of certain actors and actresses, filled his journal with notes about the productions he was seeing.

By the summer of 1804, this involvement with the theater led him to enroll for a series of group lessons in play reading with the prominent actor Jean La Rive (dramatic recitation was at the time a fashionable salon activity). A few months later, dissatisfied with La Rive, he switched to a course offered by a rival actor, Jean-Henri Gourgaud, known under the stage name of Dugazon. The purpose of these acting lessons, as he explained to his family, was to get rid of his Grenoble drawl and also, from his point of view, to understand stagecraft from within and to have the chance to play out the fantasy of being an actor. The play-reading sessions also clearly appealed to him for the occasion they provided of close social intercourse with professional actors and actresses and aspirants to the stage, and this, as we shall see, had important consequences for him.

The journal entry for August 24, 1804, gives a vivid sense of how Beyle spent his days during this period. At 9 A.M., he comes to pick up Martial for breakfast, after which the two go together to a ten o'clock lesson at La Rive's, where Racine is being recited. After the lesson, Martial and Henri stop for a lemonade at the Café de Foy; then Martial invites his cousin to dine with him. Beyle takes a moment to pay his respects to his relative Sophie Daru, then goes home to work on a play from two to five.

Back at Martial's, the cousins are joined by a male friend and go for an early evening stroll during which they run into Adèle Rebuffel with some girl friends. The young men and women joke together, and Beyle is pleased by the fact that he has made as good an impression as Martial. Continuing on their way, they come across a former mistress of Martial's, whom he introduces with some clowning to his cousin. Afterward, they proceed to the opera—Beyle hesitates a moment for lack of funds—where a play called *The Bards* is being presented. Throughout the evening, Beyle admires the simple spontaneity and charming manner of his cousin Martial; he at once enters into the pleasure of the whole experience and remains at an observer's distance, carefully recording data for future reflection.

The intellectual work Beyle was doing in the midst of this round of social activity and entertainment deserves closer inspection. The readings he was undertaking daily at home, at the Bibliothèque Nationale, and in public reading rooms were both literary and, in the eighteenth-century sense, philosophical. He enthusiastically discovered Tasso, began to read his beloved Shakespeare in the original, went through *Tom Jones* in translation, and found it not much to his liking (later, when he reread Fielding in English, he was to become a fervent admirer). The chief priority, however, in his private reading program was given to writers like Helvetius, Locke, Hobbes, Adam Smith, Montesquieu, La Rochefoucauld, Pascal, and, most important of all, the inventor of the rationalist system called Ideology, Destutt de Tracy, whose devoted follower he became by the end of 1804.[2]

There is something in all this of the lucid spirit of geometry that had beckoned to him through his secondary school studies in Grenoble (in a curriculum, one recalls, inspired by Tracy). There is surely some instinctive attempt to counterbalance his passionate emotionality with an intellectual apparatus adopted from thinkers who were hard-headed rationalists, utilitarians, materialists, mechanists. Most important of all, however, is the young Beyle's naive desire to get an unshakable grip on life—on his own daily experience, on his perceptions of other people, on his future enterprise as a writer—by translating its seeming shapelessness into the crystalline order of analyzed principles. It is noteworthy in this regard that he adopts a group of thinkers who by the first decade of the nine-

2. A detailed discussion in English of Stendhal's readings and what he made of them is provided by Geoffrey Strickland's *Stendhal: The Education of a Novelist* (New York, 1974). An excellent consideration of the specific importance of Tracy for Stendhal is Robert M. Adam's chapter, "Tracy: or the Advantages of Ideology," in *Stendhal: Notes on a Novelist* (New York, 1959).

teenth century were already beginning to go out of fashion. (Chateaubriand, after all, was the successful new writer in France, and in England, the *Lyrical Ballads* had just appeared.) "I must take myself entirely out of my age," he notes in the collection of maxims and jottings he alternately called *Pensées* and *Filosofia Nova*, "and imagine myself under the eyes of the great men of the century of Louis XIV. To work always for the 20th century."[3] Such a remark may again be something of an affectation in a nineteen-year-old, but it sharply expresses the future novelist's need to put a distance between himself and the intellectual fashions of his period—something many major writers have needed to do—and it is prescient, for the mature Stendhal would in fact preserve the classicizing passion for transparent lucidity of the preceding ages of French literature and by so doing write less for his contemporaries than for posterity. What seems more questionable in the young Beyle's personal system of intellectual discipline at this time is his reiterated notion, especially evident in the *Pensées*, that from his readings and careful observations he was deriving a set of assured principles out of which he would be able to create immortal literary works. His early rationalist faith is almost touching when he observes, after praising Corneille's genius, "What this great man owed almost to chance, by means of my method I shall obtain easily and surely."[4]

The long letters that Beyle was writing to his sister Pauline offer a luminous reflection of the regimen through which he sought to train himself for all the challenges of life. Pauline was the one woman he could relate to with utterly unguarded intimacy, free of all concern for the elaborate battle plans of amatory strategy, and he repeatedly tells her how much he misses her, how he would like her to come live with him in Paris, how he dreams of a woman like her for a wife. Everything he thought would benefit himself he also wanted for Pauline (his feminist notions about the education of women are already apparent), and so he gravely instructs her in letter after letter, as a twenty-year-old man of experience addressing an unformed but promising adolescent protégée, to read with scrupulous care the very books he has been reading, to pursue the study of Italian and English, and to learn from the guidebooks of rationalism he has recommended how to reduce the actions of those around her to a precise calculus of desire and the avoidance of pain. Through this quasi-mathematical knowledge of character and motive, securely grounded in the indubitable realities of sensory experience, she could discover the means to control the

3. *Pensées*, ed. Henri Martineau (Paris, 1933), vol. 1, p. 16.
4. Ibid., p. 169.

behavior of others toward herself and, even within the limitations of her social role as a woman, achieve the power and freedom she deserved as a superior soul.

The need for manipulation and control, it is clear, was a major preoccupation of Beyle's at this point in his life. This is, of course, the intellectual reflex of a very young man still unsure how to cope with the intricate arrangements of power of the private and public worlds. What balances the hardness, the cultivated cynicism of Beyle's egoistic posture is his constant impulse to subject the ego itself to unflinching scrutiny. His journal, his correspondence, his *Pensées* are all self-conscious acts, partly as performances of self-display but even more as investigations of self-knowledge. "Don't lose my letters," he writes Pauline on May 11, 1804, "They will be useful to both of us; to you, for you can understand later what you did not grasp at first; to me, for they will give me my mind's history [*l'histoire de mon esprit*]."

Some of the most bracing moments in Beyle's private writing during this period are the probing insights into his own character which he is equally capable of reaching by himself or accepting from the testimony of others. Thus, he records a comment by Mme Rebuffel (Mme Nardon in the code of pseudonymity he was already imposing on his acquaintances in his journal and letters) which suggests that on occasion she was prepared to instruct him in more than sexual adroitness: "You are awesome in a group, when you are delivering a peroration before twenty people, but in a tête-à-tête you are only a child" (letter to Pauline, April 29, 1805). A finely complementary perception from within about his constant need to make a dazzling social impression, and the price paid for it, occurs in the *Filosofia Nova*: "This cursed mania of appearing brilliant causes me to be concerned more with leaving a profound impression of myself than with perceiving what goes on in others. I am too concerned with watching myself to see the others."[5]

What is equally essential for his growth as a writer is the awareness he evinces that the knowledge of self and others has a linguistic correlate—finding precisely the right word for the thing observed and avoiding the obfuscating verbiage of mere emphasis or ornamentation.

The *Journal* and the *Pensées* are in part exercises in stylistic self-scrutiny: "When I reread these memoirs I often hiss at myself; they do not sufficiently render my sensations, the *good* of *good principles* just now is, for example, detestable. It's like a man who, speaking of a woman's com-

5. Ibid., p. 137.

plexion, would say, 'It's flesh-color' " (*Journal*, August 26, 1804). Reading Mme de Staël's novel, *Delphine*, Beyle admires her passion and her penetration into the code of society, but he deplores the effusiveness and the discursive explicitness of her style: "There is a way of moving which is by showing the *facts*, the *things*, without stating the effect."[6] It is a stylistic ideal of chastely efficient understatement that may have occurred to few writers of fiction before Hemingway, and the mature Stendhal would brilliantly realize it, but for the moment, his actual attempts at imaginative writing were no more than inept flounderings.

In 1803, he was solemnly drawing up lists of the comedies, tragedies, narrative poems, and prose works he intended to compose during the next fifteen years. These include a *Hamlet*, an *Othello*, a *Paradise Lost*, an *Art of Love*, histories of the French Revolution and of Bonaparte, but as yet no novels (though the *Pensées* contains two passing allusions to the possibility of writing a novel). Beyle quickly decided, however, to concentrate on the emulation of Molière, devoting his energies to the creation of a satirical comedy about contemporary French life.

His first sustained effort in this direction was *Les Deux hommes*, which he began working on early in 1803. The play dutifully juxtaposes with heavy didactic insistence the products of two systems of education, an honorable young man raised in the spirit of the *Philosophes* and a worldly young hypocrite nurtured in ancien régime piety; and it might be regarded as an advance over the earlier dramatic sketches simply in being based on the observation of real contemporary problems. In point of fact, *Les Deux hommes* pays only intermittent attention to its own ideological argument and is still another stale comedy of conventional intrigue, in which the last-scene appearance of a supposedly dead father rescues the young lovers whom a calculating mother has contrived to separate. Beyle, following a common neoclassical practice, cast the draft of the play in prose with the expectation that he would then be able to translate the text into the prerequisite alexandrine rhyming couplets. The result was a process of slow self-torture eventually subsiding into the concession of defeat. He carefully counted the number of lines he was able to produce daily: it was a Herculean effort for him to squeeze out ten, and these often enough proved to be flat, clumsy, and metrically imperfect. Beyle had even less of a gift for verse than for dramaturgy; indeed, as Jean Prévost has demonstrated, the very balanced rhythms of the twelve-syllable alexandrine line with its symmetrical caesura ran counter to his own natural inclination to

6. Ibid., p. 169.

create asymmetrical rhythmic patterns.[7] In this single-minded determination to make himself the new Molière, Beyle was like an athlete with the capacity to become a champion distance runner who insists on competing in nothing but the pole vault, where his efforts to soar end only in broken poles, twisted ankles, knocked-down crossbars, and mouthfuls of sawdust.

By the summer of 1804, Beyle had abandoned *Les Deux hommes* and had conceived the idea for a new satirical play on a loosely related subject. This prose comedy was to run through half a dozen or more titles and changes of personae, but he most frequently referred to it by the name of its protagonist, *Letellier*. This play would occupy Beyle on and off as his one concrete literary project for the next dozen years: he would carry draft materials with him on his sundry travels, actually working on scenes of the play when he was in Moscow with Napoleon's army in 1812, going back to it in Milan in 1816, and even as late as 1830, when the project had long been dormant, jotting down more notes on the idea of the play. One may wonder what it was about *Letellier* that absorbed his attention for so long. It is, to begin with, simply the gear in which he gets stuck in his futile efforts to become a playwright. Having worked out what seemed to him a really likely subject for a successful comedy, he will not let go of it: for more than a decade, it is virtually his sole remaining grip on his promise to himself to become a great writer.

Something should be said, however, about Beyle's attraction to the particular subject he chose for *Letellier*. The protagonist was explicitly modeled on the drama critic, Julien-Louis Geoffroy, and the other main satirical figure in the play was to be based on Chateaubriand, so that, as Beyle conceived it, both the political and the neo-Christian aspects of the reigning literary fashions would be exposed. He was hostile to Geoffroy because the critic had taken the part of Mlle George against Mlle Duchesnois in the debate raging over the merits of the two actresses, but he also imagined Geoffroy as a kind of anti-Voltaire, set on subverting all the values of the Enlightenment which the young man cherished. *Letellier*, then, is in the first instance an expression of Beyle's need to interpose distance between himself and the literary vogues of the moment, to define himself as a writer by criticizing prevalent literary values and the institutional corruption of the literary establishment.

There are, however, both political and psychological ramifications to this critical literary stance. Letellier, in the repressiveness of his censorious character—"I praise only to blame" is his motto—and in his antirepublican

7. *La Création chez Stendhal* (Paris, 1951).

sentiments, is meant to be a safe, comically malleable surrogate for Napoleon, whom the angry young Beyle was privately denouncing as a despot around the time of the play's inception. One should keep in mind that Napoleon had himself crowned emperor at the end of 1804, and the city, which five years earlier had hopefully greeted the Consulate as a stabilizing extension of the Republic, now quickly assumed the ceremonial pomp and the ostentatious monuments—they still stand today—of imperial pretensions. Beyle's feelings toward Napoleon would continue to vacillate over the years, as his two abortive lives of Napoleon attest. Long after the fall of the Empire, rereading his anti-Bonapartist notes for *Letellier*, he would comment in the margin more than once: "I beg your forgiveness, O most eminently great man. I was young and full of Alfieri." [8]

Underlying the political as well as the literary resentment of the play is the opposition Beyle makes central to his boyhood in *Henry Brulard*, between youth and age. The real Geoffroy was in his sixties; the more middle-aged Letellier "evinces scorn for the present youth of Paris" and in particular for the ideal young man in the play, Vardes, who is meant to represent Beyle and his friends. A brief note on the play written in 1816 makes even clearer how close to home its central situation was: here Beyle openly says that the young man in the play is himself, "abhorring the contact of people like the Bastard," which virtually avows that Letellier is ultimately a stand-in for Chérubin Beyle.

But if *Letellier* engaged Henri Beyle's most vital emotional interests, he had no way of transforming his idea of the play into a finished work. The initial models were to be *Tartuffe* and *Les Précieuses ridicules*, but none of Molière's sparkling wit, his ability to make comic situation and plot move is evident in these drafts. Working from the "method" he was vaunting in the *Pensées*, Beyle produced long catalogues of conceptual formulas for characters and scenes, but the few pages of actual dramatic dialogue that have survived—half the manuscript was lost in the retreat from Moscow—are sluggish, leaden things. In any case, even if one adds to the balance the lost material, there would be many pages of notes, explanations, and scenarios for every page of playscript, and it is safe to say that over this decade of Stendhal's literary apprenticeship he was writing about writing a play more than he was writing the play itself.

One way of stating Beyle's difficulty is to note that he was working out of a scant fund of experience, consciously willing himself to be a writer

8. Conte Vittorio Alfieri was the late eighteenth-century Italian playwright whose fervent devotion to the cause of freedom was one of the early inspirations of the movement of national liberation and unification in Italy.

when his deepest impulse at this stage of his life was for experience itself.
Indeed, the thirst for experience is the ultimate motive of his relentless
preoccupation with romantic entanglements, and that finally is what
makes the responses he registers to these entanglements so interesting.
"Your true passion," he observes of himself in the journal entry for June
19, 1805, "is that of knowing and experiencing. It has never been satisfied." He was just then in Grenoble again, on his way to Marseilles, where
he was following the woman who for the past several months had
seemed repeatedly to hold out the promise of the elusive knowledge and
intensity he was seeking.

When Beyle joined Dugazon's acting class in mid-December 1804, one
of his fellow students was a twenty-five-year-old novice actress named
Mélanie Guilbert, also often referred to by her stage name, Louason.
Mélanie's real nature remains an enigma for us, as it long was for Beyle.
She had a five-year-old illegitimate daughter, and she clearly must have
had more experience of the world than the young man who would soon
become her admirer. How she supported herself at this juncture is not
altogether apparent (she seems to have had some savings), but she surely
showed impressive resolution in deciding to prepare for a career on the
stage, with the responsibility for a small child, when she was already in
her mid-twenties. Was she, Beyle wondered more than once in these first
months, just a kind of elegant whore, like so many other women? Such
suspicions were reinforced by the suggestions, perhaps half-teasing, of his
male friends that she was a woman whom others had had, that at the very
moment he would do best to avoid her as an all too likely source of venereal infection. And yet Beyle was beginning to think of her more and more
as the sort of superior being he had been invoking in his correspondence
with Pauline, and at their lessons with Dugazon, he often thought he
could hear in her recitation the fine timbre of a rare and passionate
sensibility.

During the first few weeks of their acquaintance, Beyle speaks of
Mélanie chiefly as a good-spirited classmate, though he was aware that she
was also an attractive woman. (She had enormous blue eyes and what he
conceived to be classic Greek features, but the only graphic representation of her that has survived is, amusingly, his sketch of the profile of her
lips in his journal, intended to illustrate the hint of voluptuousness they
assumed in their inviting smile.) At the beginning of February 1805,
Beyle was wondering whether perhaps he might interest himself in
Mélanie as a cure for his lingering attachment to Victorine Mounier.
Within a couple of weeks, the long journal entries he was writing at the

time had been mainly turned over to a step-by-step account of his passionate pursuit of Louason. This chronicle of emotional fluctuations, frustrations, ever eager anticipations has something of the quality of Swann's
obsession with Odette in Proust—and indeed, it was in the *Journal* far
more than in *Letellier* that this future novelist was learning his subtle psychological art. We have no way of knowing whether Mélanie at first was
simply not attracted to Beyle and only gradually began to feel some
romantic interest in him because of his sheer persistent devotion, or
whether it was out of shrewd calculation that she kept him, more or less,
at arm's length; in any case, for five feverish months he remained always
just around the corner from consummation.

The predominant verb in the *Journal* for these months is "to have" in its
sexual sense, always used in the conditional: "I could have had her if . . ."
—if he had had a little more money to spend on her on a particular day,
if he had been more in possession of himself when an opportunity arose, if
he had not been so damnably chaste in his comportment (this said of an
evening when he came to pick her up and found her in the midst of dressing). Beyle devotes a kind of overfocused attention both to himself as
aspirant and to Mélanie as the uncertain respondent to his love. Holding
hands with her in an intimate conversation, he feels her palms sweating,
takes it as a sign of passion, and, seeing her eyes moist with tears, concludes that at that moment she must love him (*Journal*, March 17). His
self-consciousness about his own unprepossessing appearance becomes
more pained than ever. It is to be through a combined display of wit and
sartorial elegance, he hopes, that he will distract Mélanie from his ugliness.
"*Maximum of wit in my life*," he notes in the comic approximation of
English with which henceforth he will pepper all his private writing; and
after going on to catalogue the silk trousers, black stockings, cinnamon-
bronze jacket, and splendid frill-front shirt that he had donned to enhance
his conversational brilliance, he concludes, "My whole soul could be seen,
it made one forget the body, I had the appearance of a very handsome
man, in the style of [the actor] Talma" (*Journal*, February 25).

Beyle's pursuit of Mélanie Guilbert was not so single-minded as to prevent him for fleeting moments from entertaining other possibilities. There
was a young woman named Tullia whom he thought of trying for, but
he was held back by his usual timidity. One afternoon right after a visit
with Mélanie he stopped in to see Adèle Rebuffel and managed—perhaps
impelled by an immediately preceding frustration with Mélanie—to get a
hand on her breast (*Journal*, April 30). But these were minor exceptions.
By the early spring of 1805, the elusive actress was his one most absorbing

concern, in the face of which all other interests, including his ambitions of worldly success and a literary career in Paris, faded. In a climactic moment on the afternoon of April 8, Mélanie tearfully announced to Beyle that more than half her financial reserves had been spent and that she would soon be compelled to move to the country with her daughter. One may wonder whether there was an element of calculation in this ostensibly spontaneous avowal, but the devoted young lover never even thought of questioning her good faith. He responded by declaring that he was prepared to go live with her in whatever corner of France she chose, that he would even assume the role of her daughter's tutor in their rural retreat. Deeply moved, Mélanie wept at his goodness, or so at least he interpreted her tears. Characteristically, Beyle observes that this was still another of his missed opportunities: "With a little more assurance, or a little less love, perhaps I could have been sublime on this day and I could have had her" (*Journal*, April 8).

Sometime in the next few weeks, Mélanie received an offer to join a provincial stage company in Marseilles for what was to be a year's engagement. Financially, she could hardly decline the handsome annual salary of 6,500 francs, and this would provide her the opportunity for a full-scale debut. Beyle, consistent with his April 8 declaration, immediately affirmed his intention to join her in Marseilles. Though he gave Mélanie the impression that he was renouncing everything for her, the departure for Marseilles was actually a possibility he had been contemplating on other grounds. His friend Fortuné Mante, equipped with capital supplied by his mother, had become a partner in a colonial import and brokerage firm in Marseilles, and several months earlier had urged Beyle to join him in the enterprise. Now commercial and amatory success seemed to have chosen the same sun-graced port. Beyle left Paris with Mélanie on May 8—the two were still not technically lovers—and accompanied her southward as far as Lyons. From there, she proceeded to Marseilles to begin rehearsals, while he headed for a two-month stay in Grenoble, where he could be with Pauline again and where he would have to confront his father in order to get the capital that would enable him to become Mante's associate. Afterward, so he imagined, he could hurry on to the Mediterranean shore at last to reap the fruits of love and also plant the seeds for his future prosperity.

Part Two

The Initiate

With Stendhal we undergo, at first hand, the rites
of initiation into the nineteenth century.

Harry Levin,
The Gates of Horn

V

MARSEILLES

(Aetat. 22–23)

GRENOBLE this time proved to be an unmitigated ordeal. Impatient to pursue his shimmering dream of love and success in Marseilles, Beyle found himself marooned in the early summer doldrums of his native town for over two months. He had imagined obtaining from his father a sum of 30,000 francs to launch him in the world of business; he got nothing but an uncompromising refusal, justified by a long series of arguments and recriminations. "I feel the pleasure that I had promised myself from my trip to Marseilles being spoiled by the stupid, sad, humiliating discussions it occasions with my father and grandfather" (*Journal*, June 21, 1805). Beyle's sense of being betrayed by his family must have surely been heightened by the fact that his sometime ally, Grandfather Gagnon, had so decisively joined forces with the enemy. To him, it seemed that both his father and grandfather had simply shown themselves to be petty-minded pinchpennies, but there were reasons other than avarice for their opposition to his plans. As lawyer and doctor, they could readily support his decision to become an engineer, a military bureaucrat, or perhaps even, despite its economic precariousness, a man of letters. But to imagine him haggling over import duties, juggling the prices of cocoa, calico, spices, and rum, was quite another matter, for, in the mobile and ambiguous class hierarchies of postrevolutionary France, it implied a slipping in social status to these aristocratic-minded bourgeois. The venture itself, moreover, must have struck them as altogether too risky, and not without reason. Economic activity in Marseilles was being rapidly choked off by the British blockade, and this was hardly the moment to sink funds into the import trade. As a matter of fact, though none of the Beyles knew this at the time, the house of Charles Meunier & Co., which Fortuné Mante had joined, was in serious trouble. Finally, there was a practical barrier to Chérubin Beyle's supplying his son with any substantial amount of capital: his own resources at this time had become increasingly tied up in vineyards and sheep breeding—schemes of enrichment that, for all their solid pastoral setting, were every bit as perilous as Henri's notions of extracting a fortune from colonial cargoes.

Three days after his arrival in Marseilles in late July, Beyle summed up his stay in Grenoble with the following grim words: "*I arrived in* Grenoble *the . . . After two months and . . . days of* torpor, bleak boredom and *somewhat despair*, I finally left for Marseilles on the 3rd of Thermidor the Year XII" (*Journal*, July 28).[1] We have seen the reasons for the torpor and gloom. The "somewhat despair" (and Beyle may have used the English "somewhat" mistakenly for "sometimes"), on the other hand, was the result of his separation from Mélanie. Her letters to him in Grenoble were brief, businesslike, noncommittal, and that was a sufficient signal for the extravagant, insecure young lover to fling himself into paroxysms of self-torment. In the only extant letter from Beyle to Mélanie from this period (June 18–20), he castigates her at great length for the coldness of her written words to him, wonders whether she really loves him or whether she might care more for one of the admirers that surrounded her in Paris, and tells her of the acute anguish these doubts have caused him, crazed as he is with love for her. Caught between the stone wall of parental obduracy and the sickening pit of fear that he might be losing Mélanie, Beyle could not tolerate his stay in Grenoble too long, and on July 22, he set out for Marseilles without a *centime* of the capital he had expected to bring with him. This meant that he could offer himself to Meunier & Co. as nothing more than a clerk, but that would at least allow him to learn the business, while he clung to the hope that his father would sooner or later relent and make possible his translation from menial functionary to financier.

---

1. Unless otherwise stated, italics in quotations from Stendhal's *Journal* and letters will henceforth indicate that the phrase appears in English in the original.

The moment he escaped the confines of Grenoble, his mood changed. Hastening southward, first by coach, then by boat down the Rhône, he abandoned his role of anguished lover for that of observant tourist. The long retrospective journal entry for July 28 is really his first essay as a travel writer, an activity to which in later years he would devote thousands of pages. He records the various stages of his journey under the blistering summer sun, notes the flaking, heat-baked outcroppings of rock along the shore of the Rhône, is struck by the Italianate look of the dust-powdered, dazzling white houses of Avignon, sees in the features of a boatman and his son faces out of a painting by Raphael. All these Italian associations were perhaps inner preparations for his imminent entrance at last into a bourn of romantic fulfillment. On July 25, he arrived in Marseilles and went directly to see his friend Mante. "H, H, H, H, at 8 in the evening," he jotted down in his journal, which the Stendhal cryptographers have deciphered as "happy, happy, happy, happy."

Mélanie Guilbert's role in this access of happiness was as yet still a matter of promised satisfaction. That first evening in Marseilles, he saw her only in public circumstances, at the Grand Théâtre. The next morning he called on her in her room—Mante had exercised the friendly foresight to take a room for Beyle in the same hotel as Mélanie—but the actress, in what looks suspiciously like a calculated act of final coyness, kept her eager lover in suspense for a full four days. Finally, on the night of July 29, after a walk across the bridge with Mante for a full view of the sea, which he was seeing for the first time, Beyle joined Mélanie in her room and, some hours later, back in his own bed, recorded in his journal his elation in a cryptic English sentence: *"The evening till the mid-night, for ever."*

Such forevers, of course, are doomed to have considerably briefer duration than first conceived by the strenuous stretch of romantic imagination. In this instance, Beyle's unalloyed honeymoon bliss with Mélanie seems to have lasted from this midsummer night to no later than the early fall. During the weekdays, he was kept busy for the most part at Meunier & Co. with what could not have been very fascinating work—doing correspondence for the firm (much as he had done for the military in Pierre Daru's office), taking care of minor bookkeeping, going over to check price fluctuations in the stock exchange housed on the main floor of Marseilles's city hall, perhaps occasionally running errands for the firm at the wharves, where fresh cargoes were unloaded. The dust and heat and hurrying-about that his professional duties entailed were such that in his letters to Pauline he had to make urgent requests for new supplies of shirts and stockings to replace the ones he was soiling so rapidly. Mélanie, meanwhile, had rehearsals during the day and frequent roles to play in the evenings. This left the nights for love, though only till a certain hour, for they were careful to observe propriety by maintaining separate rooms at their hotel.

The middle-class scruples were probably Mélanie's, but the couple in fact was surrounded in Marseilles by an ambiance of raw, undisguised concupiscence. Their hotel on the rue Sainte, virtually at the doorstep of the Grand Théâtre, was on a block crowded with streetwalkers. The whores actually made it a practice of coming into the theater itself to pick up customers, and at times, the verses of Racine and Corneille declaimed from the stage were not easy to make out over the noise of the less lofty negotiations going on in the aisles and the cheap seats. Even the common European practice of mitigating marriages of convenience with stable extramarital liaisons was carried out in Marseilles with a particular lack of finesse. As Mante had explained in a May 4 letter to Beyle, most of the husbands had mistresses and most of the wives had lovers, but such arrangements were so open that it was common for husband and mistress, wife and lover, to dine all together, including the children.

The more idyllic passages of Beyle's first weeks with Mélanie occurred on Sundays, when they regularly went for outings to a variety of scenic spots in the surrounding countryside. It was during one of these outings, on August 25, that the future novelist was vouchsafed that vision of Mélanie's slender naked body bathing in the Huveaune, which brought back to him the raptures he imagined as a boy in examining the painted landscape with nude bathers in M. Le Roy's studio and which he would later recall in *Henry Brulard*. In a letter to Pauline dated August 27–September 5, he offers a delicate description of this particular Sunday, of course sparing his young sister any erotic details but reporting the whole experience as a kind of *Gesamtkunstwerk* in which the sight of a château with "melancholy" towers and a splendid avenue of plane trees reminds him of the sublime music of Cimarosa, and architecture, nature, even food (the menu of a delectable picnic) orchestrate the satisfaction of all the senses in a subtle experience of plenitude. A recurrent theme in Beyle's letters to Pauline at this time, even as he solemnly pursues his role of mentor, is his euphoric happiness with Mélanie. In the innocence of his passion, he does everything he can to bring the two women together. He repeatedly tells Pauline how much Mélanie resembles her, particularly in the fineness and the sublimity of her nature, and how impatient the actress is to meet the younger woman; he even manages to have his sister and his mistress write to each other. Pauline was so far persuaded, or so loyal to her brother, that she actually added a codicil to her will leaving a bequest to Mélanie's daughter, whom Beyle had been passing off as his own in his letters to Pauline and to Henri Gagnon. (All this time the child was being boarded at Neuilly, near Paris.) As soon as he and Mante would establish themselves as independent bankers, Beyle proposed to his sister, they could all live together in Paris, Mante marrying Pauline, Beyle and Mélanie completing the little community of superior souls.

In possessing Louason, Beyle seemed at last to have fulfilled the dream he had nurtured since childhood—enjoying the love of an actress, whose beautiful physical presence and rare sensibility were at once instruments of passion and of great dramatic verse. Life and art, of course, do not often join hands with such choreographic neatness, and by November, he was beginning to wonder whether the Mélanie who had become his bedmate really corresponded to the splendid creature he had imagined from a distance. On the stage of the Grand Théâtre, she was far from a stunning success, though this may reflect at least as much on the audiences as on her abilities. She had no inclination for the heavily emphatic style of declamation then in favor with Marseilles theatergoers and scarcely enough power of projection—she habitually complained about her "weak chest" and frailness—to get her lines across over the noise and distractions in the audience. Beyle makes some angrily contemptuous remarks about the Marseilles public in his journal, but he also begins to wonder a little whether Mélanie is as talented as he thought.

During the early fall, when he had begun rereading Destutt de Tracy with religious attention, he made an effort, in the most comic of lover's delusions, to have Mélanie read Tracy's *Logic* along with him. Mélanie was certainly not an intellectual, and there is no evidence that Beyle made any progress in getting her to share his philosophical or even his literary interests, though many years later, he would still admire the fineness of her sensibility among the women he had loved. Altogether, Mélanie seems to have had a certain practical cleverness and a good deal of dogged determination, but there is little to indicate that there was anything very extraordinary about her, perhaps not even, as we shall see in a moment, in the boudoir. She had made the decision to entrust herself to Beyle and had a certain faith in his devotion to her and a sense of gratitude for it. By the time she became his mistress, she was also devoted enough to him in her way, but that way involved the continual need for a good deal of fairly serious flirtation. By the autumn of 1805, four different Don Juans of local renown were after her in Marseilles, all of them older men, one actually in his sixties and an aristocrat. Though Mélanie probably did not betray Beyle in the technical sense, she hardly appears to have made a vigorous effort to discourage these admirers. It was over one of them that the first clear fissures in her relationship with Beyle became evident.

On November 8, the lovers were on another of their Sunday outings. After lunching on cold fowl and wine and pie under an apple tree, they went for a walk across the meadows, and Mélanie commented to Beyle that he "looked as though he were dying to do it." The silent sad remark he makes on this in his journal suggests a brooding dissatisfaction with Mélanie and how she responded to "doing it" with him: "It was true, but that was not all I desired; I would have wanted from her a little more rapture, or, more precisely, a little rapture." And this essential lack in Louason leads him to think longingly of Angela Pietragrua: "One could not be more fortunate in regard to beauty, what I had was beyond my wishes, a perfect, sublime beauty, the grace of the most beautiful Greek figures, but I would have liked a little of the rapture I imagined Angelina possessed." Perhaps Beyle was beginning to sense that what bound Mélanie to him was not passion but dependence, for, after they had walked on a bit and then paused to rest, he confronted her with the following analysis of her relation to him: "You are a vine, you have attached yourself to a little tree and you are worried about it, while what you needed was to attach yourself to a big tree in which you could have full confidence."

Mélanie immediately granted the justice of the observation, and the discussion of a bigger and better tree for her then naturally opened into Beyle's jealousy of her admirers. On this occasion, he tried to get her to admit to him the precise nature of her relationship with a certain M. Baux (in Beyle's odd code called "Leases" because of a pun on "bail"). Frustrated by the scant revelations he was able to extort from her, he proposed a bet: if she failed to identify correctly the tree under which they had eaten, she must tell him frankly whether "Leases" addressed her with the intimate *tu;* if she won the bet, he would agree to whatever she demanded. Mélanie, after countering that he had no secrets on his side to divulge, made a most revealing stipulation of the stakes he was to offer against hers: if she correctly identified the tree, he was not to sleep with her under any circumstances for the next five and a half months. Her proposing these terms suggests that indeed there was not much rapture on her side, and his agreement to the terms suggests that the violence of his jealousy had already clearly overtaken the violence of his passion. Leaping a ditch, he dashed off toward the tree she had designated, which proved innocent of the leavings of their picnic. Mélanie paid her debt as the loser: yes, she admitted, M. Baux addressed her as *tu* (*Journal* November 8).

Even before this November outing, Beyle had written to his old school-mate Plana, now in Turin awaiting a precocious appointment to a professorship of astronomy, asking Plana to procure for him a lethal and painless poison. From a December 15 letter from Plana, we learn that Beyle had contemplated using the poison to commit suicide. It has been suggested that it is more plausible to date the thoughts of suicide back to the early summer in Grenoble, when Beyle was altogether despairing of Mélanie's love, than to his Marseilles idyll, when he was only sometimes fearful that he might be sharing it with others.[2] The arithmetic clarity of this line of reasoning is surely questionable as a way of comparing different emotional intensities of distraught love, and in any case, an earlier letter from Plana to Beyle (November 5) states clearly that there would be no point in sending poison from Italy because Turin had nothing that could not be obtained as readily in Marseilles. It was in Marseilles, then, that Beyle thought of suicide, and the pangs of jealousy could have been his only motive. We must be careful, however, not to see this scheme in the lurid melodramatic light that the twenty-two-year-old Beyle himself no doubt fancied for it. He had, after all, read *The Sorrows of Young Werther* the previous year in Paris, and the Romantic gesture of suicide was just as much a *literary* notion for him as his ideas of passion, heroism, and fame. It was a notion that he would make part of his permanent repertory, later trotting it out with the appropriate indications of pistols and daggers in his journal during two other fits of despair over disappointed love. The contemplation of suicide for Beyle is less an indication of a depressive character than of an extravagant one. In the present instance, he took care to play the sorrowing Werther several safe paces from the brink of oblivion: instead of trying a local pharmacy for poison, he wrote to a friend in a foreign country; Plana, as a student of mathematics and astronomy, not medicine, would have had no special access to poisons; and one of the most sensible of Beyle's friends, he would have been one of the most likely to refuse the commission, as his reasoned argument to Beyle (in the December 15 letter) against the idea of suicide actually demonstrates.

Another motive for Beyle's toying with the idea of suicide in the fall of 1805 may have been that it was a means of fanning the embers, persuading himself that his love for Louason, in fact already fading, was a fiery, fate-

2. See Henri Martineau, *Le Coeur de Stendhal*, vol. 1, p. 198.

ful matter of life and death. Beyle's journal entries touching on his feelings about Mélanie toward the end of the year are increasingly marked by notes of irritation and disenchantment. The last really blissful moment was recorded on Christmas eve, 1805: "*The next night ago was perfectly happy; the morning, two in the arms* of Mélanie: pleasure [*volupté*] and happiness" (*Journal*, December 24). But two weeks later, Mélanie was telling him of plans to return to Paris and of the money difficulties she would have in establishing herself there, and Beyle's response was neither anger nor desperation but a dispirited sense of distaste for the whole relationship: "At 4:30, beginning of the deepest chagrin without despair, gloomy disgust, depression with no trace of vigor" (*Journal*, January 9, 1806). Mélanie on her part showed no inclination to sever the attachment to—or dependency on—her lover, but economic necessity dictated a move from Marseilles. The growing paralysis of trade in the port city resulting from the blockade had drastically cut back theater attendance, and the actors were not being paid. In January, the performers of the Grand Théâtre organized a strike. Mélanie resolved to return to Paris, hoping that after her experience as a leading lady in the provinces she would be able to find an opening in one of the major companies in the capital city. On March 1 she left Marseilles. Beyle's response to her departure aptly summarizes his feelings about her at the time, his mood as he stayed on alone in Marseilles, and the new adult perspective on the complexity of the pursuit of happiness that he was already deriving from this collapse of his grand romance: "The state of slavery in which Mélanie held me often weighed on me; the state of abandonment in which her departure leaves me bores me. So it is necessary to correct myself in order to be happy. I need to impose new habits on my desire for happiness" (*Journal*, March 25).

Meanwhile, Beyle's dalliance with commerce had gone sour on him as quickly as his liaison with Mélanie. Toward his employer, Charles Meunier, he felt little but antipathy; even his friend Mante, viewed in close working quarters, was proving to be far from the elect companion he had imagined: "Mante from day to day is becoming coarser and more stupid, say Mme Cosonnier and Mélanie; unfortunately, it is true, it seems to me he was worth more two years ago" (*Journal*, February 2). The work itself was for the most part simply troublesome, and by January, having given up on the idea that his father would actually provide him with capital, the abortive entrepreneur was already beginning to look to other horizons.

This time, the plan for worldly success that he conceived was one his family could wholeheartedly endorse. His high-placed cousin, Pierre

Daru, was now chief of the imperial Council of State. Beyle hoped that through Daru he could obtain an appointment as a commissioner [*auditeur*] in the military intendancy. He fancied that with such a secure position, and an annual income of 8,000 francs, he could have all the women he wanted as well as a good deal of freedom to pursue literary fame. Beginning in early January, he mounted a concerted seige by letters on Daru, writing separately to Pierre and to Pierre's mother, contriving to have his father and grandfather write as well, even enlisting his uncle Romain to write to Martial (who was back at work in the intendancy) and asking various Parisian friends to intercede personally, all to obtain a post for himself. Daru, however, was still smarting over the way the young man had ignored the well-laid plans for his advancement in resigning his commission in the army four years earlier, and now he refused to answer Beyle's entreaties, and the oral response reported back to Marseilles by Beyle's friends in Paris was a brusque rebuff.

Beyle nevertheless persisted, for, as the prospect of war with Prussia became imminent, a career in the imperial service seemed more and more the one sure way of establishing himself in the world. Perhaps his dealings with an impecunious mistress as well as his exposure to the harsh realities of commercial life had led him to conclude that without financial security there could be no happiness, for he was now prepared to lay aside republican principle when a career in the imperial service looked like the main avenue to material independence. Awaiting the call from Pierre Daru, Beyle hung on in Marseilles, dispatching his dull duties in the import business, keeping company for the most part with other outsiders to the city like himself, equally bored by the long card-playing parties and the flirtations in which he found himself involved, lonely and discouraged. Mélanie was writing to ask urgently why he did not join her. He responded, taking to the offense as the best defense, by accusing her of not loving him. She countered with a vehement denial in which she reaffirmed her devotion to him and told him what anguished days of weeping she had spent wondering if he still loved her. Whether her tears were real or rhetorical, her assessment of his feelings toward her was accurate enough. Perhaps an inclination for the moment to keep several hundred miles between himself and Mélanie was in part what made Beyle stay on in Marseilles, though a more pragmatic reason has been suggested by Arbelet: the desire to demonstrate to Pierre Daru, after his quick abandonment of his military career, that he was capable of persistence in a chosen professional activity.[3] A letter to Martial Daru, written when Beyle was

3. *Stendhal épicier* (Paris, 1926), pp. 233–234.

finally en route to Paris, seems to go out of its way to stress something of the sort: "Here I am in Grenoble, but it is not out of inconstancy"; it was only his grandfather's "terrible letters," threatening to do nothing for a grandson who had become a vile tradesman, that persuaded him to leave Marseilles (*Correspondance*, June 1, 1806).

Beyle's mood during his three months in Marseilles after Mélanie's departure was an acrid mixture of dejection and indifference to things in general, which leads one to suspect that an additional reason for his remaining was a kind of emotional inertia: as insipid as his existence in Marseilles had become, there was simply no point in his moving anywhere until he had some overture from Daru. His relations with women during these months provide the clearest index to his prevailing mood. Circulating in a milieu of sexually restless wives and readily accessible young working girls, Beyle succumbed to the crude sensualism of the Marseilles ambiance, fitfully pursuing different women, and when that proved too arduous, enjoying the favors of others quicker to be taken. A journal entry dated April 23 vividly illustrates this sad condition of emotional apathy and mechanical hedonism. Beyle picks up a certain Rosa, and dispensing with the barest preliminaries, they couple standing up in a doorway in the shadowy half-light of a distant streetlamp. Then he follows her to her room, where they proceed to a night of sexual gymnastics, reported by him in the coarsest language. He leaves at six in the morning, "thoroughly disgusted and ashamed." In the midst of his revulsion, he contemplates going back to Rosa to take advantage of her polymorphous availability for an experiment with anal intercourse. The best thing he can say of her, however, "is that she did not speak to me about Mlle Louason."

Beyle could hardly have wanted to linger in this self-reviling fashion among the ruins of what during the previous summer had been his great love, and by the latter part of May, he allowed himself at last to be persuaded by his family to abandon his desk in the countinghouse. He arrived in Grenoble again on May 31, after having made a pleasant week's tour on the way from Marseilles. In Grenoble, he hoped to receive some response from his letters to Pierre Daru, but nothing arrived, not even some word from Martial. The apathy of his last months in Marseilles persisted in his hometown: "Nothing gives me much pleasure. Rapture is dead for me, except for the half-hour raptures with women" (*Journal*, June 27). He needed somehow to get himself a fresh start, and so he decided to go on to Paris, where he could renew old connections, perhaps see how things stood between him and Mélanie, and break through the stubborn silence of Pierre Daru with a direct personal appeal.

Beyle left Grenoble on July 1 and nine days later arrived in the capital city. He immediately resumed his old routine, and a spirit of briskness again becomes evident in the pages of his journal. He was once more enthusiastically attending the theater and the opera, seeing Martial daily, studiously making his way through Montesquieu's *The Spirit of the Law*, escorting the Rebuffels, mother and daughter, to the Jardin des Plantes, and wondering whether Adèle might not after all be worth pursuing again (but he already saw Alexandre Petiet in the background and sensed a marriage in the making between Adèle and his former dueling adversary). On August 3, following the example of Martial, he was initiated into the Masons, a step he appears to have taken solely in the hope it would provide him useful connections for the advancement of his career. The Lodge had little intrinsic appeal for Beyle, and his careerism was by no means single-minded enough to make him persevere in the Masons against his personal inclinations. Within a couple of years, his name was dropped from the membership roles for nonpayment of dues.

As early as August 18, he renewed his sexual connection with Mélanie (in the journal entry for August 19, he remarks, quite parenthetically, "exhausted from having done it twice with Mélanie and having sweated horribly all night long"), but the relation now was something between a habit and a convenience, a worldly way of passing the hot summer nights. Arbelet aptly calls these encounters the "mediocre mornings-after" of what had been a beautiful, fleeting love.[4] Indeed, the resumption of the liaison with Mélanie brings back into Beyle's journal that note of enervation which had been predominant through the spring: "I can't take it any more, I am worn out, exhausted to the last drop, morally and physically"—a state of exhaustion attributed to a tedious dinner, a discussion of his affair with Mélanie, and having spent the night with her (*Journal*, September 2). It begins to look as though Beyle now felt he was being "drained" by Mélanie, both physically and psychologically, a not surprising consequence of his perception of her dependence on him. They continued to sleep together, at least from time to time, until Beyle's departure from Paris in mid-October, but they both must have known that it was all over between them. After this two-month postlude to their romance, they lost touch with one another. Mélanie made her debut at the Théâtre Français, but observers thought her acting weak, and she was not able to win a place for herself on the Parisian stage. Subsequently, she left for Russia with a traveling company, where she met and married a certain

4. Ibid., p. 198.

General Barcoff. Beyle later had news of her, and tried to seek her out when he was in Moscow in 1812, but she was in Petersburg at the time, pregnant. He left word that if she ever returned to Paris she would be welcome as his guest, and in fact the next year when she came to Paris they saw something of each other, now on the basis of amiable old friends. It was utterly characteristic of Beyle that he should retain a kind of emotional loyalty over the years to all the women with whom he had once shared love. In *Henry Brulard*, he would still remember Mélanie Guilbert as one of the four great passions of his life.

Beyle's plan of a direct assault on Pierre Daru meanwhile had yielded no substantive results. Daru was prepared to be reconciled to his feckless young cousin but not to make any firm commitment about obtaining a place for him. War had been declared on Prussia in July, and Paris was astir with excitement over the beginning of a new imperial adventure. Daru went off to Prussia with the conquering army. Martial, after being married on September 30, was preparing to follow his older brother. Seeing that his friend Henri was still without an appointment, Martial proposed that Beyle join him as a simple companion, with the expectation that once they were in occupied Prussia, Pierre would finally consent to arrange a post for his wayward protégé. The pair left Paris on October 17. Eleven days later they arrived in Berlin, in the footsteps of Napoleon, and of Pierre Daru. Two days after their arrival, Beyle at last was given the first handhold on the rungs of imperial bureaucracy that he had sought for almost a year: Daru appointed him provisional deputy to the Commissariat of Wars at Brunswick.

The sobering aftermath of Beyle's Marseilles adventure had been a time he seemed to use chiefly for a regrouping of inner forces before another leap outward into worldly experience. In Marseilles, his readings—Tracy and the astringent comedy of Diderot's *Jacques le fataliste*—had been relatively intermittent; back in Paris, he pursued his self-education once more with his earlier assiduity, deriving a quiet sense of gratification from the grasp of human nature he felt he was acquiring through his readings in the eighteenth-century philosophers and historians. On the day he left for Prussia, he summed up in his journal the three months he had just spent in Paris: "I have not had very lively pleasures, but often contentment. The liveliest pleasures I have had were given me by the consciousness of my progress in the knowledge of the world," and this, he goes on to say, was mainly from his reading. The Beyle who sets out after the Napoleonic armies to begin another career does seem, in the tone and tenor of his private writing, to have a more measured, less fantastic approach to experience than the Beyle who had headed southward a year and a half earlier on the trail of love and wealth. War in Prussia and Austria, in contrast to the relative insulation of his Italian expedition, would begin to confront him with disturbing realities, but he was better prepared now to see them precisely, without flinching, just as he was readier now to face the dull routine of duty in an army of occupation with the inner resources of a sensitive adult.

VI

PRUSSIA AND PARIS

(Aetat. 23–28)

HENRI BEYLE'S SITUATION in Prussia was in certain respects the obverse of what it had been in Italy. Professionally, his administrative post at Brunswick, where he arrived on November 13, 1806, was a position of responsibility. He supervised revenues from imperial lands, corresponding scrupulously with bailiffs, intendants, prefects, inspectors, and the like, and within a few months, his competence won him official recognition: in July 1807, his title of provisional deputy was converted to regular deputy, and then in January 1808, at the instance of Pierre Daru, he was named Intendant of the Domains of his Majesty the Emperor in the Department of Ocker. He would soon note in a letter to Pauline (May 26, 1808) that he had become an important figure in the eyes of those around him, a personage addressed in official correspondence as *Monseigneur* or *Monsieur l'intendant*. Beyle's duties, moreover, left him ample time to pursue the leisure activities of a gentleman: he took lessons in equitation, hunted with some frequency (though in later years this would sometimes seem to him a barbaric pastime), practiced shooting, and explored the environs in a series of long excursions. During his first sixteen months in Brunswick, by his own calculation (*Journal*, March

11, 1808), he made twenty-six separate trips, not counting a month's furlough to Paris at the beginning of 1807. One town in the region to which he did not make any special expedition, but whose name he would remember, was Stendal, about fifty-five miles to the east of Brunswick and roughly halfway to Berlin.

But if Beyle could at last enjoy some sense of coming up in the world through his work in the imperial bureaucracy, Germany, in contrast to Italy, offered very little to excite his imagination. Quickly, and perhaps too facilely, he assimilated what he could observe of Prussia to the north-south polarities of national character which he had valued as a principle of explanation from Grenoble onward. The Germans, he complained repeatedly in journal and letters, were heavy, dull, cold, unimpulsive, flatly practical, in consequence, he conjectured, of their chill climate and of the black bread, butter, and beer they consumed in such large quantities. To his prejudiced ear, the German language sounded like the "croaking of crows," and he never made much effort to acquire a mastery of it. After a year or so, he had picked up enough German to follow, more or less, a Mozart opera, but his official business was conducted in French, and he could converse perfectly well in French with the few friends he made from the Prussian nobility and upper middle class. Instead of concentrating on German while he was in Brunswick, he actually engaged another English tutor and was soon reading Shakespeare, Samuel Johnson, Thomas Gray, and (this time enthusiastically) *Tom Jones*. Beyle provides the perfect emblem of his sojourn in Prussia in the journal entry for March 11, 1808: "I write all my official letters at the foot of the portrait of Raphael, which changes its features according to the hours of the day. This fine figure, who drew happiness from his heart, prevents my soul from becoming entirely desiccated." Thus, amid the aridity of bureaucratic work in what seemed to him a Prussian cultural wasteland, Beyle clings to a talisman of Italian art with its delicate visual adumbrations of beauty, passion, happiness.

At the same time, inevitably, he had tried to escape the threat of desiccation by attempting to discover passion plain and simple in a relationship with a woman. The candidate he chose was not a very likely one. Wilhelmine (Mina or Minette) von Griesheim was the daughter of a Prussian general, a proper enough companion for Beyle on outings in the company of several friends, but too virtuous or too prudent to become his mistress and hardly a matrimonial prospect for a French bureaucrat with no financial resources beyond his limited salary. Her portrait shows a face with firm Germanic features: broad mouth, prominent nose, wide-set eyes, high forehead framed by a tightly plaited palisade of symmetrical curls, in sum, a far cry from the "Grecian" and Italian beauties Beyle had recently fancied. His preoccupation with Mina was especially strong through the spring and early summer of 1807, but when he learned that she had become engaged to a Dutchman, he quickly abandoned the chase, both practically and emotionally. On November 9, he tersely noted in his journal, "I am cured of my love for Minette," then recorded the sensible regimen of his cure: "Every three or four days, out of physical necessity, I go to bed with Charlotte Knabelhuber, a woman kept by M. de Kutenvilde, a rich Dutchman. I have been pleased with myself in this regard." The neatest of arrangements: convenient pleasure without attachments or expense, and cuckolding a Dutchman into the bargain. About a year later, Beyle was involved for a time in an affectionate relationship of uncertain character with Livia Bialowiska, the newly widowed Italian consort of a Polish officer, whose attractions were no doubt considerably enhanced for him by his unflagging nostalgia for Italy. His liaisons with women, however, during his stay in Prussia, 1806–08, and then in Austria in 1809, were decidedly of the Knabelhuber variety, mere exercises in physical hygiene.

Having launched on a career in the imperial service, Beyle's most consuming passion during this period was ambition, not love. For the first time since he had left the paternal home, he experienced through his administrative work a degree of independence in the adult world, but he was keenly aware how precarious his position was unless he could advance in the hierarchy and obtain the means to secure his future prosperity. Advancement, to be sure, remained always a means to an end for Beyle. He imagined that unless he married, he would retire from the service by the age of thirty-one and then lead a life of cultivated leisure in Italy— something he eventually did anyway, though without the comfortable income he had expected.

Two extended stays in Paris while awaiting new assignments—first from December 1808 to the end of March 1809 and then, after participating in the Austrian campaign (to which we shall return), from the beginning of 1810 to late summer 1811—whetted his appetite for worldly success by placing him in the center where it was resplendently enjoyed and near the corridors of influence where, in this imperial age, it might be suddenly obtained. During his second and longer stay in Paris, he took steps, after having lived in the capital in near penury a few years earlier, to support himself in the style to which he wanted to be accustomed.

With a small but dependable income of his own and some prospects for substantially increasing it, he gave full rein to his impulse to play the dandy. His wardrobe now boasted eighteen different waistcoats, no less than forty-three dress shirts (laundering service could not have been very prompt), and of course innumerable pairs of gloves, of the sort he had earlier been soliciting from Pauline, in precisely the appropriate shades. On April 30, 1810, he purchased a cabriolet *"très à la mode"* for 2,100 francs, about the equivalent of his annual income (for a twentieth-century counterpart to this spiffy two-wheeled carriage with folding top, one might think of a particularly elegant sports car like a silver-tinted small Mercedes). He was keeping two servants and two horses, dining in the best places, retaining choice seats at the theater. Toward the end of October, he rented a spacious and fashionably appointed apartment with a new friend, Louis de Bellisle, a stylish young man of society then the lover of Countess Marguerite Beugnot, to whom Beyle was duly introduced (his friendship with the Countess was to prove lasting and would later have interesting ramifications). Though Beyle was certainly living beyond his means, he was not at all the sort of compulsive spender and accumulator of possessions that Balzac or, in a somewhat different style, Sir Walter Scott was. He felt, rather self-consciously, that he owed it to himself to cut a brilliant figure in society, and at least the dandyism was given special urgency by his continuing apprehensiveness about his unattractive physical appearance—in his late twenties, he was already visibly expanding from stocky to stout. There was also an element of calculation in all this conspicuous consumption, for with the meteoric upward mobility that was possible in the imperial service, he wanted to demonstrate, even as he pursued specific schemes of promotion, that he was a man already known to be moving in the best circles.

Beyle, however, did not have much real zest for the whole enterprise of worldliness: as he would make memorably clear later in the heroes of his novels, the self-imposed duties of ambition can be the most onerous a man has to perform. He was trying again to work on that Penelope's loom (as Martineau has called it), his play *Letellier*—for a while in July he actually put in eight-hour days on it—but there were simply too many distractions: "The visits, the servants, the laundresses [all those shirts!], and many other things just about as important disturb me five or six times during a morning, inflame my irascible temperament, and I get nothing done" (*Journal*, entry headed August-September 1810). Toward the end of the year, he sums up his social activities on this sour note: "Yesterday from six to eleven, I paid five visits, four of which were for the sake of ambition. What a bore!" (*Journal*, December 29).

However much a bore, careeristic advancement was an effort to which

Beyle had fully committed himself, and because of it, he was becoming involved in a growing tangle of disbursements. At the beginning of August 1810, he received a new appointment, as commissioner for the Council of State—the post he had set his eye on four years earlier in Marseilles—at an annual salary of 2,000 francs. Later that month, he was granted the additional title of Inspector of Crown Furnishings and Buildings, carrying a salary of 6,000 francs. As Inspector, he was actually given a good many weeks of work on a project close to his real interests, the establishment of a catalogue for the artworks contained in the Musée Napoléon. In any case, his total annual income of 8,000 francs was at least 6,000 short of his actual expenses as a Parisian man-about-town, and so he was forced to borrow, occasionally stopping the gap with a money order from Pauline (who in 1808 had married François Périer-Lagrange, scion of a prosperous Grenoble family). By the latter part of 1810, Beyle had hit upon the idea of attaining a baronetcy for himself as the prerequisite to securing an upper-echelon administrative appointment (his fiery republicanism was now quite extinguished). In order to do this, he first had to obtain from his father a *majorat*, the legal transmission of the title of the estate to the firstborn son according to the Continental system of primogeniture. He besieged Chérubin Beyle by letter, but with no success. This new rebuff confirmed his notion of his father as the Bastard implacably hostile toward him; what he did not know was that Chérubin Beyle's disastrous agricultural speculations had already entrammeled the family holdings in mortgages, so that the father was in no position to confer the sort of *majorat* the son needed. Although Henri Beyle would persist in the hopes of ennoblement and advancement for another three years, he had in fact already reached the summit of his bureaucratic and financial ascent; his debts alone would climb higher.

There is a curious disjuncture in Beyle during this period from 1806 to 1811 between will and temperament, chosen commitment and feeling. He is perhaps inflamed by ambition but not deeply impelled by it. As always, he longs for the condition of being in love, but beyond his casual affairs, the best approximation of it he can achieve is an oddly self-coerced facsimile of passion fixed on the most improbable object, as we shall presently see. This split between natural inclination and actual experience drives him more into himself, makes him for the first time not just rationally self-analytic but genuinely introspective, alternately musing and brooding over how his life feels and how it felt before. This new note is especially evident in the long, confidential letters he writes Pauline from his post in Brunswick. Memory and, strangely enough for a twenty-five-year-old, nostalgia become leading motifs. Thus, in the very letter of May 26, 1808, in which he boasts of being addressed as *Monseigneur*, just four years after the sojourn in Paris when he had but "a single pair of boots with holes in them, without a fire in the dead of winter, and often without a candle," he thinks longingly of that period of youthful poverty:

If one could put life where one wanted, like a pawn on a chessboard, I should still be going to study recitation with Dugazon, to see Mélanie with whom I was in love, in a shabby frock coat, a fact that made me desolate. When she didn't want to receive me, I would go to read at the library, and finally, in the evening, I would walk in the Tuileries, where from time to time, I envied those who were happy. But what delicious moments in that unhappy life! I was in a desert where from time to time I found a spring; [now] I am at a table covered with dishes, but I don't have the least appetite.

An earlier letter to Pauline (March 26, 1808) formulates this disposition to nostalgia in more delicate terms, for here one can already begin to see the lineaments of a distinctive Stendhalian notion—that elegiac pursuit of happiness, where in a curious way memory itself becomes the medium of happiness, the means through which intimations (scarcely ever realizations) of bliss in the past, recalled in the proper configuration of associations, acquire a sustaining luminosity, like an achieved work of art.

I take note of a rather sad thing; in losing a passion, one loses little by little the memory of the pleasures it has given. I've told you about when I was at Frascati, at a lovely fireworks display, how at the moment of the explosion Adèle leaned for an instant on my shoulder; I have no words to say to you how happy I was. For two years, whenever I was overwhelmed with grief, this image restored my courage and made me forget all unhappiness. I had long since forgotten it; I wanted to think about it again today. Despite myself I see Adèle as she is; but in my present state there is not the slightest happiness in this memory. Mme Pietra Grua, that's another story: her memory is bound to that of the Italian language; as soon as, in a woman's role, something pleases me in a literary work, I automatically put it in her mouth.

The distinction between his memory of Adèle in those first two years and his conscious, futile attempt to recall the plenitude of the experience in 1808 corresponds, at least in part, to Proust's distinction between involuntary and voluntary memory. For Stendhal, the sudden infusion of involuntary memory is almost always linked with the image of a desired woman, beginning, at least chronologically and perhaps etiologically, with that remarkable erotic image of his mother embracing him recorded in

Henry Brulard. The recollection of the desired woman is in turn associated with the harmonious sense of completion in art—even Adèle's leaning on his shoulder is happily synchronized with the sudden splendid pattern in the night sky of a *feu d'artifice*—and sometimes with specific
works of literature, painting, music. Angela Pietragrua is a better focus
for involuntary memory than Adèle, not only because she is distant and
ultimately mythic for him, but also because she belongs to the realm of
Cimarosa and Raphael and so can be imagined walking among the graceful
lines of every Italian play or poem that Beyle reads.

Late in 1808, in another letter to Pauline (October 29), this student of
the pursuit of happiness pushes his reflections on these matters one
extreme step further. Again he recalls the experience with Adèle at the
fireworks display, calling it "the happiest moment of my life" and connecting it with his euphoria at the performance of *Il Matrimonio Segreto* in
Novara in 1800. Speaking to his newly married sister with a new sexual
frankness about his relations with women, he suggests that the pleasures of
love pale before the pleasures of art: "It seems to me that none of the
women whom I've had has given me a moment so sweet and so uncostly
as that I owe to the musical phrase I just heard. The pleasure has come
without my expecting it in any way; it has filled my whole soul." And to
complete this thoroughly Proustian meditation, Beyle, as he ponders how
precarious passion is, how tedious it can become, wonders whether art
may not have primacy over what we call reality, at least in regard to the
intensity and purity of experience: "All this makes me think, dear Pauline,
that the arts, which first please us by painting the delights of the passions
and, so to speak, by *reflection*, as the moon shines, can end up giving us
stronger delights than the passions [H. B.'s emphasis]."

What one may infer from these various meditations is that inner preparations were going on in the young careerist Beyle for the emergence of
the mature Stendhal. He was at moments becoming aware now of a deep
impulse toward withdrawal from the world of action, enterprise, engagement into which he had flung himself with such energy. He would act on
that impulse, at least to a degree, when the turn of poilitical events dictated; he would realize it fully in the denouements of his two greatest
novels. At this juncture in his life, he offers one vivid ideogram for this
hidden aspect of his nature. The enigmatic journal entry for September 9,
1810, is headed by the title: "My Tower." There follows a plan for the
tower, with a drawing of the structure in the margin. It is to be eighteen
feet in diameter, sixty feet high, with a circular balcony surrounding the
author's study on high, to which one ascends by one hundred twenty

steps. This elevated refuge, with the lovely symmetry of its measurements divisible by twelve or six, of course remains a paper tower, a fantasy of retreat sketched out with quasi-mathematical precision at the very moment Beyle is dashing about in his new cabriolet and preparing to rent a fine apartment. Behind the fantasy lie the Alps that loom above Grenoble, the mountain retreat at Les Échelles, the bell tower at Rolles that rang out for him in 1800. Beyle never withdrew to such a tower in his personal life, but one day he would reinvent it as a paradoxical gift of grace for Julien Sorel in his lofty condemned man's cell and for Fabrice del Dongo in the intoxicating isolation of the *Tour Farnèse*, a tower built upon a tower, looking out over Parma all the way to the Alps.

While beginning to dream of towers, Beyle had by this time witnessed at bloody close quarters what went on in the armed melees below, and though there is no evidence that he brooded much over the carnage he had seen, it surely must have had some bearing on his fantasies of a perfect sanctuary, on his skeptical view of the shifting human realm outside memory and art. The earliest record of his observing the violence of war firsthand is in a letter to Pauline dated September 19, 1808. It is the report of an attempted Prussian insurrection that had just taken place in Brunswick. The bantering tone Beyle adopts is, to say the least, curious. He is, of course, writing to a younger sister and no doubt trying to be witty and amusing about events that might otherwise be viewed as horrible, and the odd playfulness may also be his own defense against the horror of what he has seen. In any case, his description opens with manifestly misplaced irony, a Swiftian mordancy with no satirical object to justify it:

What is more, the day before yesterday, that is, the 10th [*sic*], a battle! A fusillade I was in, in which an old woman, both hands crossed over her belly, had the advantage of having them pierced like Our Saviour, and the belly besides, and to go off instantly to experience the effect of His mercy. Not counting several saber cuts which no one boasts of. Magnificent moonlight; broad street full of people. *Fer-flou-Ke-ta-Françauze*, which is to say, d——— French rascals, raining from all sides on my uniform hat; a rifle shot, twenty people stretched out around me; the others had flung themselves against the walls, I alone standing. A pretty girl of eighteen, her head almost under my boots . . .

On this occasion, fortunately, Beyle is able to give his story a touching happy ending after the three suspension points he inserts in the letter: the girl is alive and unharmed, only trembling with fear; he gently picks her up and carries her out of the line of fire, whereupon she leaps to her feet, makes him a little curtsey, and flees.

Seven months later, in the Austrian campaign, he was to see much worse things. On leave in Paris after the termination of his Brunswick assignment, Beyle received orders on March 28, 1809, to join the French forces in Strasbourg. Throughout April and early May, he was on the move with the advancing army; on May 13, he entered the conquered Vienna, where he would be stationed till the end of the year, except for a brief mission of unknown nature to Hungary and a few weeks, beginning in December, at Linz. As an administrative officer, he was never in the front lines, and he never actually witnessed any decisive battles (though once more a wishful memory would later lead him to imagine he had been at Wagram), but he came close enough on the heels of fierce fighting to see the devastation that had been wrought on both sides. On the one hand, he is inclined to view the war as an exciting adventure, an escape from boredom, a grand spectacle—he uses that word repeatedly—at which he constitutes himself a tourist of terror. But he is also aware of the human meaning of the terror, as he hears a dying officer pleading for water in a nasal voice, sees piles of corpses by the roadside, notes that to take a particular point the French attacking forces lost one out of two, even three out of four, men. The imperial enterprise, the great occasion for Beyle's own career, clearly had its horrendous side. The worst moment for him came at the town of Ebelsberg, where the French had just captured at an awful cost the bridge over the Traun River. Only in the retreat from Moscow would he see scenes this terrible:

Arriving on the bridge, we found corpses of men and horses; there were still thirty or so on the bridge; we were forced to throw a great quantity into the river, which is extraordinarily wide; in the middle, four hundred paces below the bridge, was a horse, erect and motionless; a singular effect. The entire town of Ebelsberg had just finished burning, the street through which we passed was filled with corpses, mostly French, and almost all burnt. Some of them were so badly burnt and blackened that one could barely recognize the human form of the skeletons. In several places, the corpses were piled up; I examined their faces. On the bridge, a brave German, dead, his eyes open; German courage, fidelity, and goodness were painted on his face, which expressed only a little melancholy.

Little by little the street grew narrower, and finally, under the door and in front, our carriage was forced to roll over these corpses disfigured by the flames. Some houses were still burning. A soldier coming out of a house seemed irritated. I admit that this whole scene made me sick to my stomach. [*Journal,* May 5, 1809]

Almost thirty years later, he would draw on a finely distilled residue of these memories in creating the great Waterloo scenes for *La Chartreuse de Parme*, but at this moment, in newly conquered Austria, he was focusing his emotional energies in quite another direction. On October 21, 1809, Alexandrine Daru arrived in Vienna to spend a month with her husband, Pierre. The two had been married in 1802, about the time Beyle returned to Paris after his service in Italy. By the date of her visit to Austria, Mme Daru, who was exactly Beyle's age, had already given birth to four surviving children and was eight months pregnant with her fifth. She and Beyle had been on cordial terms since 1806, though his recollection that he first "paid her court" then is probably an anachronistic exaggeration. In the fall of 1807, when Mme Daru was visiting her husband in Brunswick, Beyle was struck by the special kindness she showed him and began to muse over the possibility of a different sort of relationship with her. It was during her month in Vienna, however, that Beyle first thought he could detect hints of romantic encouragement in Mme Daru's comportment toward him and so laid plans to court her in earnest. At her departure, as he gave her a cousinly kiss through her veil, he was silently berating himself for his lack of boldness during these weeks and faintly wondering, though he knew it was implausible, whether the tears in her eyes might be for him. After his own return to Paris in late January 1810, this preoccupation with his patron's wife began slowly to build momentum, finally attaining the characteristic Stendhalian state of feverish obsession during the spring of the following year. In retrospect, Beyle would include this with his few great passions, but it was the oddest, the most disembodied of them all.

Alexandrine Daru was, by the testimony of various contemporaries, a decent, sensible person, strong in religious principle, loyal to her husband (sufficiently so, one might note, to undertake a journey to see him in the last weeks of pregnancy), and devoted to her children. She was well enough disposed toward Beyle to be willing to act as his advocate to her husband on more than one occasion, but there is not the slightest indication that her feelings toward the young bureaucrat ever went beyond friendly concern. Although it is a ritual for the Stendhal cultists to invoke the beauty of all his loves, the formal portrait of her by David—which, if anything, would have been devised to flatter—shows little in the way of physical charms. Thin-lipped, broad-mouthed, thick-browed, a fold of fat beneath her large moonshaped chin, she exudes matronly heaviness rather than the *embonpoint*, or voluptuous plumpness, then much in favor. Why was Beyle so drawn to her? Her connection with Pierre Daru seems the most obvious explanation, and a curious document of Beyle's involvement with her, which he composed at its height, confirms this suspicion while suggesting certain important nuances peculiar to his imaginative way with relationships.

In April 1811, Beyle, in collaboration with his friend Louis Crozet, wrote a "Consultation for Banti," Banti being his pseudonym of the moment and the subject of the consultation being his prospects and his strategic options for becoming the lover of Alexandrine Daru. The high density of pseudonymity in this whole affair is itself worth observing. It was becoming Beyle's general practice to assign a pseudonym to any woman with whom he was involved (and, indeed, to his male friends as well), but there is a positive proliferation of invented names in the case of Mme Daru. In the "Consultation," she is referred to as the Duchess of Bérulle; elsewhere, she is variously called Lady Palfy, Countess Z., Countess Marie, Elvira, Alexandrine Petit. All this suggests Beyle's fanciful notions of the need for an elaborate secret code in the deep, dangerous game he imagined he was playing; it may also reflect the degree to which Mme Daru was for him an object of fantastication rather than of desire. The "Consultation" takes the form of a lover's catechism in which Beyle is referred to for the most part in the third person. The salient aspects of Mme Daru's character and principles are coolly assessed, the stages of her relationship with Beyle reviewed, and a course of action proposed —with the usual military metaphors—calculated to make her his mistress. Revealingly, the "Consultation" is supplemented by a kind of appendix, which is a coldly unsympathetic character study of Pierre Daru.

It is tempting, and perhaps not entirely off the mark, to conjecture that Beyle unconsciously resented Daru as a father figure and that the perennially pregnant figure of Alexandrine attracted him precisely because of its maternal associations. But if there was an underlying Oedipal drama here, the important thing is to see the specific literary terms that Beyle imposed on it. In the "Consultation," he invokes the model of Valmont, the arch-seducer of Laclos's novel, *Les Liaisons dangereuses*. His portrait of Mme Daru, moreover, though it does not mention the character from Laclos, makes her sound quite like the Présidente Tourvel in the novel—the woman of perfect virtue and piety who has not yet known true puberty, which is, Beyle tells us, to experience in sexual intercourse a combined rapture of body and soul, not just physical pleasure. He will besiege her as Valmont besieges the Présidente Tourvel because of the seeming impregnability of her virtue and because he fancies he can introduce her to a whole new realm of experience. One sees how autobiographical statement camouflaged with pseudonyms begins to tilt in the direction of autobiographical fiction, as the contours of the writer's experience are made to conform to the conventions of the novel. Such imaginings, of course, had a great deal to do with Beyle's youthful reading and very little to do with his actual relationship with Alexandrine Daru. Stubbornly, he had set up the challenge of winning Mme Daru as the test of his decidedly quix-otic conception of his manhood, which probably explains the edge of fanaticism in his devotion to so dubious a prospect of conquest. He con-cludes the body of the "Consultation for Banti" by observing, "If he did not have Mme de Bérulle, he would reproach himself for it all his life." And indeed, in his notes on the manuscript made when he reread it in 1819, he upbraids himself more than once for his failure in 1811 to "Attack! Attack! Attack!"

In hesitating to attack, Beyle could enjoy his preoccupation with Mme Daru as an inexhaustible source of emotional perturbation through the dullness of relatively idle times. The terms he chooses in a letter to Pauline (July 14, 1809), when his involvement was just getting under way, indi-cate the kind of excitements he could provide himself in such a relation-ship by an unchecked exercise of the imagination: "Insurmountable obsta-cles and the greatest danger for each of us have prevented us from speaking except through expressive looks. . . . As for all the details of our conduct, you must imagine a courtier in love with a queen: you can see the nature of their dangers and their pleasures." Thus, alternately conceiv-ing himself as a cunning Valmont and as the star-crossed hero of a courtly romance, Beyle, as his journal shows, could work over every trivial exchange between himself and Mme Daru—a casual conversation during an afternoon visit, a remark or a glance at a dinner party—and find in it subtle and ambiguous signals of his advancing in her opinion, of a growing intimacy, of his coy mistress at last silently avowing nascent love. Tensely expectant, erotically charged self-consciousness was becoming at times virtually a way of life for the future novelist, and Alexandrine Daru, as he contrived to imagine her, provided the perfect occasion for it. A recent French biographer, Victor Del Litto, has nicely caught the tenor of this disposition: "What Stendhal in these circumstances calls love is a sort of fixation of his cerebrality and his sensibility. The object is named in turn Louason, Alexandrine, Métilde, Countess Sandre; the procedures and the process do not vary at all. The worst of things—for disenchantment would have irremediably followed—would have been to have heard the whisper: 'I will expect you at midnight. . . .'" [1]

Meanwhile, Beyle had found another means for attending to simpler

---

1. *La Vie de Stendhal* (Paris, 1965), p. 134.

carnal needs. In June 1810, he met a young singer for the opera buffa company of the Théâtre Italien named Angéline Béreyter and before long began maneuvering to establish a liaison with her. On January 29, 1811, she became his mistress and thereafter slept at his fine new apartment on the rue Neuve-du-Luxembourg almost every night. The connection was to last three years and was the closest Beyle ever came to actually living with a woman. Their relationship appears to have been one of good-spirited sensual companionship, and it even had certain artistic amenities— Angéline would sing arias to her lover over their intimate late suppers at home. Beyle was affectionate to her, bought her gifts, and took her on outings, but there was no intense emotional involvement on his part. In his journal, he referred to her with gentle condescension as "little Angéline" or "the little Jewess." Once they had become lovers, he quickly developed a sense of his bond with her as perhaps too much of a good thing. The journal entry for March 17, 1811, aptly summarizes this feeling: "It strikes me that my physical happiness with Angéline has robbed me of much of my imagination." Then he adds, in his distant approximation of English, a numerical notation about their sexual transactions which indicates just how happy he was kept and what was the formidable degree of Angéline's responsiveness in bed: "*I make that one or two every day, she five, six and sometimes* nine times." But imagination—which is to say, romantic quest —had far more appeal for him than any such regimen of unimpeded physical rapture. Even as Beyle was getting accustomed to this comfortable eroticism with Angéline, he was becoming more and more obsessed with Alexandrine and pursuing his campaign for her to a crisis. At last, in the late spring of 1811, he forced things to a confrontation with his lady of many pseudonyms. The result, though in itself hardly unexpected, led directly to an important turning, and returning, in his life.

VII

MILAN

(Aetat. 28–29)

IN the "Consultation for Banti," Beyle, with the aid of Crozet, had reconnoitered the terrain for his grand attack. Then, at the end of April, he gave himself a furlough before the final movement of his campaign by going off on a brief excursion to Rouen and Le Havre with Crozet and Félix Faure. The odor of tar in the port at Le Havre brought back to him his time with Mélanie in Marseilles, and that memory triggered a momentary recognition of the duplicity he was practicing on his own emotions in his siege of Alexandrine Daru: "Is it then quite impossible that I should ever again be in love? Still so young, must I give up on my own heart?" (*Journal*, April 30, 1811). Nevertheless, he was committed to this effort of conquest, and a few weeks after his return to Paris, he made his avowal to "Lady Palfy," afterward habitually referring to that fateful encounter on the night of May 31 as the Battle.

But to use these terms at all is to succumb to the falsifying rhetoric Beyle himself adopted in his determination to endow his emotional life with epic grandeur, even when there was no epic occasion. (It is instructive that he should allow his feelings to be so strongly colored by conventional metaphors; later, as a novelist, he would take pains to maintain a coolly unmetaphorical presentation of his material.) The fact of the matter is that nothing much of consequence happened on the night of May 31, although Beyle exerted all his imaginative faculties to think otherwise. He was staying at the Daru château at Bècheville, on the banks of the Seine about fifteen miles west of Paris. Pierre, of course, was not present, detained by his official duties. After dinner, responding to an invitation from Mme Daru, Beyle stepped out through the French windows and joined her for a leisurely twilight stroll on the garden path: later that night, he would trace in his journal a diagram of their route, carefully lettering points on the path where particular exchanges between them had taken place. Mme Daru asked him, perhaps with a hint of maternal concern, whether anything had materialized of his tentative matrimonial designs on a young woman named Jenny (nothing had, and the relationship was so tenuous that we cannot be entirely sure now whether the prospective bride was a certain Jenny Leschenault or someone else camouflaged in the *Journal* by the pseudonym "Jenny"). To be questioned by his beloved about marriage plans was more than Beyle could bear; he responded with a sudden confession: "You feel nothing but friendship for me, while I love you passionately," and with that, he grasped her hand tightly and then actually tried, unsuccessfully, to kiss her. Mme Daru's reaction was all that it should have been. She hastened to say that her feelings toward him had only been, could only be, cousinly affection, that he had no right to expect any other relationship between them, and then she deftly guided the conversation back to his marriage prospects and the role they might play in his professional advancement (*Journal*, May 31, 1811).

The refusal sounds unequivocal enough, but so ardent an addict of the imagination as Beyle was not prepared to accept it as such. During their conversation on the garden path, Mme Daru's face had been hidden from him by the shade of the large-brimmed straw hat she was wearing. A few minutes later, when they rejoined the rest of the company, he got a better look at her and thought he could detect an unusual pallor in her face, a redness in the eyes that might be a sign of recent weeping and "that certain surge of emotion which comes from happiness" (*je ne sais quoi de l'attendrissement du bonheur*). It is in principle possible that Beyle's perception of Mme Daru's response to him was a correct one—that as a virtuous wife she of course was compelled, at least at first, to reject his advances but that she was in fact overjoyed, moved to tears by this confession of passion from a man whom she had secretly come to love. The overwhelming likelihood, however, is that Alexandrine Daru was chiefly embarrassed (though perhaps also just a little flattered) by this unsought avowal from her husband's cousin and that she had no intention except to preserve their relationship as a cordial friendship—an inference borne out by all her subsequent behavior toward him. The discrepancy between Beyle's reading of the encounter and what in all probability were the facts teeters on the edge of comedy, but in recording these events in 1811, Beyle shows no awareness that he is making himself the farcical dupe of an elaborate self-deception. He was, however, on some level, perhaps not yet a conscious one, learning the intricate emotional rhythms of the experience of self-deception, one of the experiences most frequently scrutinized by mature judgment in the novel, which is generically concerned with the operations of extravagant imaginations on persons, events, and relations that are in themselves banal, trivial, indifferent.

For the moment, Beyle's persistence in imagining a pale, trembling Alexandrine, her eyes moist with the tears of happiness, enabled him to continue his campaign into the summer months, of course keeping his direct appeals to her few and faint so as not to risk a rupture with her, and at the same time berating himself for his timidity, which he feared was causing him to lose his prey. In fact, he must have realized, with all his efforts to suppress the realization, that he had irrevocably lost the battle of May 31 or, rather, that it had been no battle at all. His enthusiasm for the pursuit of Mme Daru slackens, he perhaps begins to sense that the whole involvement has been the chasing of a will-o'-the-wisp and deprived of a compelling amorous cause, he becomes restive after a year and a half in Paris. Napoleon's empire was now at its apogee, and Beyle hoped for an interesting post in one of the conquered territories. In March, his friend Bellisle had left for Spain on an assignment to Carthage. Martial Daru (with whom Beyle was no longer on such good terms) had been installed as intendant in Rome. Beyle had earlier thought of a mission to Spain, and beginning in February, he made repeated attempts to obtain an appointment in Rome. When by mid-summer the Italian assignment was still not forthcoming, he decided to apply to Pierre Daru for a leave in order to make a trip to Italy on his own. On August 17, the request was granted; a week later, he paid a visit to Versailles, where he saw the Emperor and Empress in all the grandeur of their court; on August 28, he went to Bècheville to say farewell to Alexandrine Daru. The next morning he departed, accompanied to the coach by Félix Faure and a tearful Angéline Bércyter; after nine days of unbroken travel, he was once again in the place that had been the lodestone of his longings for a decade, the city of La Scala and Angela Pietragrua.

There is a recurrent quality of jaded emotion in Beyle just before his departure for Italy. The great enterprise with Alexandrine had vanished like smoke. He was tired of his devoted Angéline, even began to have some difficulty being sexually excited by her, and was thinking of other women when he made love to her (*Journal*, August 10). He was troubled by the idea that as a sensualist he might require eternal novelty and that as a romantic lover he was trapped in the solitary confinement of endless role playing, unable to experience anything immediately and spontaneously. Against this background, Milan, from the moment of his arrival, flooded him with a sense of renewal, making him feel that he had indeed entered into a realm of intense and authentic passions, where men and women knew how to give themselves to art, to experience, and to each other. Thus, he rhapsodically marks his entry into Milan at the beginning of his journal notation for September 8: "My heart is full. Yesterday and today I experienced sensations full of delight. I am on the verge of tears." Back again in this cherished city of his fantasies, he sees himself vividly as he was then, a naive eighteen-year-old pining for Angela Pietragrua and not daring to breathe a word of it to her: "I see the causes of each effect; I feel tender compassion for myself."

Now, however, as an experienced man of the world, he wasted no time in approaching Angela, making his first afternoon call on her the day after his arrival. At thirty-four, her beauty had not diminished. If she showed a little less of "that grace of voluptuousness," Beyle noted, she was altogether more imposing now, and wittier besides: "Back in my time, she was majestic only through the force of beauty; today she is majestic through the force of her character as well" (*Journal*, September 8). At first, she entirely failed to recognize him. For some reason, this pleased him—perhaps because it gave him the sense of power of confronting her after ten years as an unknown, a new and more capable man. When he coaxed her memory and identified himself as Beyle, the friend of Joinville (her lover then), it suddenly came back to her: of course, he was the Chinaman, a nickname that had had some currency among his schoolmates and his early army companions because of the slight suggestion of slant in his eyes. Recalling the time they had spent together in 1801, Beyle joked about the ridiculous, voiceless love he had felt for her in those days. "Why didn't you tell me about it then?" she asked, twice, in response, and one can easily hear her velvety tone of invitation, perhaps joined with a note of playful amusement. From this first meeting, then, a bond of intimate understanding was established between them, though not without a certain awkwardness still to be overcome. As Beyle quite properly observes, concluding his account of the September 8 tête-à-tête with Angela, "After ten years, it is a new acquaintance to be made."

How formidable an acquaintance it was to be Beyle could hardly have guessed. For the next two weeks, until she "surrendered"—in Angela's case the double wink of quotation marks is obligatory—she led him over a wild obstacle course, and once having yielded, she time after time found ingenious ways to renew the chase. The comic last lap, Angela's ultimate contrivance, would not be run for another four years. Beyle had loved professional actresses, but for Angela, acting without benefit of stage or script seems to have been a way of life, the means of transforming the flatness of daily existence into the zest and flair of adventure. No one has caught this aspect of her more brilliantly than Robert Martin Adams: "Alternately tender and savage, timid and fearless, coy and experienced, she could look as majestic as a sybil and fight like a cornered vixen; yet when she melted into amorous pliability, no one could be more seductive. She was in fact a thoroughly practiced coquette, past mistress of the art of encouraging a lover and putting him off, a versatile, volatile libertine of a woman." [1] Adams ranks Angela with Matilde Dembowski and the retreat from Moscow one of the three decisive influences on Stendhal's imaginative life, and he plausibly argues for a direct filiation between her and her namesake Gina in *La Chartreuse de Parme*—that supreme actress and endearing manipulator of men and effects.

The only feature one might quarrel with in Adams's radiant account of Angela and Beyle's liaison is the notion that Beyle fully entered into the game, even to the point where it is hard to distinguish between the leader and the led. To be sure, Beyle was allured by the indomitable will, the quicksilver temperament, the endless resourcefulness of his mistress, but there are a good many indications in his journal that he was far more often an unwitting victim than an equal partner in the game. Indeed, there are moments when he is just a little afraid of Angela, though it is manifestly the kind of fear that enhances attraction. "I don't know how she was led to tell me," he comments after they had become lovers, "in the natural manner that distinguishes her, and without vanity, that some of her friends have told her she was frightening. It is true." And to confirm the idea, he observes her face as they sit together over coffee in the quiet recesses of an unfrequented café: "Her eyes were brilliant; her half-lit face had a supple harmony, and yet was terrible with a supernatural beauty. One might have thought her a superior being who had taken on beauty because that disguise suited it better than another, and who with its penetrating eyes read the very depths of your soul" (*Journal*, November 2).

1. *Stendhal: Notes on a Novelist* (New York, 1959), p. 86.

The Initiate

What were Angela's intentions toward Beyle? She clearly must have found it piquant that the bashful "Chinaman" of 1801 had in his peculiar way remained loyal to her all these years, and no doubt she thought it would be amusing to grant him, in due time, the sexual privileges he wanted. After all, why should she exclude him where she had welcomed so many others? There is not much evidence that Angela was ever what one could call in love with Henri Beyle. If she were to admit him as a lover, she would take careful steps to ensure that he did not become an impediment and that he would not interfere with the free exercise of her libertinism. And with those penetrating eyes of hers, she may well have seen in him from the start a contradiction of character that tempted her as a female Machiavelli of amatory intrigue—a man of intellectual brilliance and rare sensibility who in the insecurity and self-consciousness of his postures as a lover could be as malleable and gullible as the rawest country rube.

The day after his first interview with Angela, Beyle purchased a stylish walking stick, with the idea that it would make him look four years younger—at the age of twenty-eight, courting a woman six years his senior!—and prevent him from putting his hands behind his back *à la papa* when he went to see her. Two days later, as he left her house, he observed her engrossed in conversation with Lodovico Widmann, the Venetian officer who was at the moment her reigning lover, and he stalked off to his hotel room filled with jealous rage, at the same time guessing or hoping that his appearance on the scene had nettled the good Captain Widmann. The next day, Angela began to address him with the intimate *tu* and kissed him, but when he tried actively to embrace her on his part, she coyly warded him off with a terse maxim: *to receive but never to take.* When they discussed the possibility of his leaving Milan, she exhorted him in a carefully modulated tremolo: "Go, go; I feel you must go for the sake of my tranquility; tomorrow, perhaps, I will no longer have the courage to say it to you" (*Journal*, September 13). All this was just what Beyle had always dreamed of hearing from the lips of a mistress, and he was quite taken in by it, or at least allowed himself to be taken in. The day afterward, Angela combined with her histrionics an expertly managed sexual tease which she would keep up for another week. Her eyes wet with tears, "she abandoned herself" in his arms, but even as she welcomed his caresses and embraced him tenderly, she resisted his efforts to kiss her on the thigh, gently chiding him: "Who would stop us from going farther? Is that the way for us to part? We are losing our heads more and more." Beyle's comment on this moment is at once an assessment more accurate than he may have realized and something like the punchline of a joke: "I sensed the presence of a superior reason" (*Journal*, September 14).

A week later, Angela decided to capitulate, meticulously arranging the time, place, and manner. In his journal (entry misdated September 20), Beyle announces the event as an official war bulletin: "The 21st of September, at half past eleven, I carry off that victory so long desired." He shows little awareness of the extent to which he has been led around by the adversary in this supposed victory. At nine forty-five that morning, at Angela's behest, he had gone to the little church at the corner opposite her house. (Did he remember this ironic choice of a church as a signaling point for an assignation when he invented the crucial meetings between Fabrice and Clélia in *Chartreuse*?) He was so overwrought that he did not hear the bells peal ten o'clock. Five minutes later, there was still no sign from Angela. He walked off, returning at ten twenty-five, and finally was vouchsafed the agreed-on signal. He rushed up to her house and, after a full hour of no doubt finely controlled preliminaries, was granted his conquest. A little wistfully, he notes in his journal that his happiness was not quite complete, for the first time was merely a victory, while real intimacy was acquired in the next three times. Such a consummation, however, his mistress was not of a mind to permit. Having allowed herself, as she must have impressed on her lover, to take the fatal step from which she had so recoiled, she enjoined him to leave Milan at once. Frustrating as this command must have been, Beyle surely took a certain delight in enjoying the love of a woman so passionately imperious: his Milanese Angela would not cloy him with easy pleasure like his Parisian Angéline. He hastily packed his things, engaged a place on a coach, and by one thirty that night, he was on his way to Mantua. From there, he would continue on a rapid grand tour of Italy to Bologna, Florence, Siena, Rome, and Naples. It would be over a month before he saw Angela again.

He did a good deal more than mark time on the trip. He was rapidly becoming a professional tourist, and his journal for this whole stay in Italy is an odd mixture of a chronicle of a love affair and a formal travel book. It is divided into chapters like a book, and Beyle had some notion of publishing it, despite its incongruous personal elements, as a *Voyage in Italy*. Now driven southward on his lady's orders, he was keenly attentive to the changing landscape; the behavior of his travel companions; the character and customs of the various Italian regions; and, above all, to the music, painting, sculpture, and architecture that on all sides confirmed his vision of Italy as the homeland of the arts. On his arrival in Milan, he had proposed in his journal (September 8) that the two years of sighs, love, and melancholy spent in Italy when he was on the verge of manhood had forever tuned his sensibility, so that he could respond to the finest details of a landscape with page after page of painterly description. Whether or not that connection is a real one, there is a perceptible sympathetic vibration between his state of lover's exaltation—the product of love Italian style, not the blasé Parisian variety—and his excited responsiveness to the masterworks of Italian art.

In the midst of his peregrinations as a tourist of sensibility, Beyle also spent some time with two old acquaintances. In Rome, he saw Martial Daru, on whom he would have had to call in any case as the intendant of the city, and Martial took him to meet the great sculptor Canova at work in his atelier. (He neglected to pay his respects to the French chief of police in Rome, as military protocol also required, because he knew the incumbent to be a particularly disagreeable fellow; the omission would make trouble for him when he returned to Paris.) From Rome, he traveled to Ancona, where he had a reunion with Livia Bialowiska, the friend he had known at Brunswick, and whom he found plunged in a state of dire boredom. In what had become his usual reflex in an ambiguous situation with a woman, he ventured an exploratory grip on an erogenous zone; far from objecting, she encouraged him with kisses. It was really Angela he wanted, though—Livia seemed a poor substitute in regard to both mind and body—and Beyle abandoned the effort before anything of consequence happened (*Journal*, October 19).

On October 22, Beyle arrived back in Milan, again, or still, in a condition of romantic exhilaration. Angela, however, was not there, having gone with her husband and son on an excursion to Varese, to the northwest in the lake country. He hastened after her, on October 24 reaching the village a few miles from Varese where the Pietragruas were staying. Her husband greeted Beyle cordially, as doubtless he had greeted a long procession of Angela's lovers for the past seventeen years. She on her part had assigned her complacent spouse a rather different role in the scenario she was now improvising for the sake of her French admirer. She had been horribly compromised, she frantically explained to him, one of their rendezvous had become known, a maid had betrayed her. Signor Pietragrua was represented as a raging lion of jealousy; in a furtive note that Angela slipped Beyle two days later, she proposed a midnight meeting but warned of the need to exercise extreme caution, for the husband's jealousy had been violently roused. Her initial invocation of danger had been coupled with a stern rebuke: while Beyle was away, she had opened a letter

from Faure to him—according to the instructions he himself had left!—
and thus learned that he had come to see her in Italy with the basest
designs of seduction. These criminal intentions of his, however, were
quickly enough forgiven for her to arrange the midnight assignation, but
horror of horrors, she then discovered, or invented, two nuns lodged in
the room through which he would have to pass to reach her bedroom; and
so, accompanied by her sixteen-year-old son, she managed to convey to
him another clandestine note warning him of the danger. Never mind, she
would be back in Milan by Monday, and they would have ample privacy
then. Angela's sense of timing in this elaborate farce is perfect. At the
point when the two nuns were introduced, even Beyle, after a day's
reflection, began to question their reality (without realizing, however,
that he had been caught in a whole net of fictions), but forty-eight hours
later he was back in Milan and once more happy in bed with his sublime
Angela.

Or to speak more precisely, as happy as his uncertain situation vis-à-vis
this formidable woman would allow. Outmaneuvered by her in the
romantic hide-and-seek of *billets doux* and midnight meetings, he was
uneasy about whether he would prove her equal between sheets: *"This
morning I made that a time, this night I should go to a very respectable
number. But at first the anxiety of waiting and then what she said to me
agitated my mind too much for my body to be brilliant"* (*Journal*, October
29). During the next few days, he noted, with a tentative sense of satisfaction, that Angela "had pleasure," which may well have been the case,
though with so consummate an actress one could never be sure where
the performance stopped. Meanwhile, she regaled him with protestations
of passion punctuated by warnings about the perils of her husband's
jealousy. She offered to leave Italy and go with her lover to France, a
course of action she certainly did not contemplate seriously and which
may even have been, as one biographer has suggested, a ruse to scare him
off.[2] On the other hand, she announced that she must make another excursion, and perhaps actually absented herself from Milan for a few days,
and she tried to convince Beyle to go off on his own to Venice in order
to "avert suspicion." This time he resisted.

In any case, his stay in Italy was almost over. He had received notice
toward the end of October in a letter from Faure that he had been
granted a month's extension of his leave, but this still meant that he had to
report back for duty in Paris by late November, and he wanted to allow

2. Martineau, *Le Coeur de Stendhal*, vol. 1, p. 286.

himself three or four days to visit with Pauline and her husband at their estate near Grenoble on the way, so he had to set out from Milan on November 13. All in all, he had enjoyed at most two weeks of physical intimacy with Angela, but she had sent him through enough gyrations to keep his head spinning for another four years, and she had impressed upon him an image of splendid and extravagant womanhood which he would draw on for a lifetime.

These tempestuous weeks in Milan also had moments of literary occupation. While waiting for Angela in the furnished room he had rented for their assignations, he read Ossian and, more significantly, Lanzi's *History of Painting in Italy*, a work that caught up the resonances of his own just-completed tour of the galleries of Florence, Rome, Bologna, and elsewhere. On October 29, the idea occurred to him of translating Lanzi. He composed a brief prospectus in the form of a letter to be sent to publishers, which reflects the hazy distinctions he made at this early point in his career between translation, plagiarism, and original work. The note in his journal had spoken of a translation project; the prospectus proposes an original study, conceding only that "the history of M. Lanzi has been quite useful to me" (*Journal*, entry dated October 30 or 31). By December, back in Paris, Beyle was actually happy at work twelve hours or more daily dictating a translation of Lanzi (this new procedure of composition by dictation would later play an important role in his career as a novelist), and in six months, he managed to finish half the large history. The first page of the manuscript bore the inscription, "To milady Angela G." The transformation of this preliminary material into his own *History of Painting* would not be completed until 1817, but the beginnings of the book in 1811 are worth noting, for they mark the moment when, without entirely relinquishing his youthful fantasy of becoming what he called "the Bard," he begins to think in more practical terms of embarking on a career of professional writing. He still deluded himself in imagining he might realize enough of a fortune from his projected history to retire to a life of ease in Italy, but that is of course a delusion that has been shared by many writers from his time to ours, and is, indeed, one of the things that makes them professionals.

Beyle arrived back in Paris on November 27 and reported to his office the next morning. "Battle lost," he noted cryptically of the occasion. He had hoped, it appears, to receive a decoration in recognition of his four and a half years of faithful bureaucratic service, and this he may have conceived as a preparatory step for promotion. Instead, his superiors greeted him with icy disapproval because of his violation of protocol in failing to visit the chief of police in Rome, and Pierre Daru, who had been elevated to the position of secretary of state some months earlier, was particularly incensed at this new instance of irresponsibility in his protégé. The ladder of ambition was slipping from Beyle's grasp, but he refused to abandon hope of moving up in the imperial hierarchy. In early February, he requested an appointment as a commissary of war, and at the same time in his letters to his family in Grenoble, he was still pursuing his scheme of obtaining a baronetcy. After several months of waiting, his suit for an appointment in the commissariat was rejected on the grounds that his work status till then had been officially defined as civilian, not military. He was left with little recourse and with not much to do in Paris except for his self-imposed labors as a translator.

He had anticipated on his return a cozy welcome from Angéline Béreyter, but to his exasperation, she was out of town, not to return till December 18. They continued thereafter to sleep together, but as we have already seen, there was not much in the relationship to engage him. He tried half-heartedly to stir the embers of his passion for Alexandrine Daru, but after Angela, he was scarcely capable of it. He grudgingly admitted that his love for her "was dying," and he inscribed the epitaph to it in a letter to Pauline written July 14, 1812, at last seeing Mme Daru in the cold light of day: "*For six weeks* there has been an emptiness *in my heart. A passion who lived in it, since two years* suddenly died around the 13th of last month, *by the sight of the mediocrity of the object.*" This sense of emptiness, aimless drifting, depression was alleviated only in the hours when Beyle was dictating his translation. But in general, coming back from the romantic excitement of Milan to a Paris of faded loves and frustrated ambition was for him a daunting plunge into a fallen world. The vividness and the dramatic detail with which he elaborates this feeling in a letter to Pauline on December 5, 1811, just ten days after his return, are worth observing:

Imagine a man at a charming ball, where all the women are gracefully dressed; the flame of pleasure shines in their eyes; one detects the glances they cast on their lovers. This beautiful setting is decorated with a taste rich in voluptuousness and grandeur; a thousand candles give off a celestial brightness; a suave fragrance has the effect of making one ecstatic. The sensitive soul who is present in this place of delights, the happy man, is forced to leave the ballroom; he encounters a thick fog, a rainy night, and mud; he stumbles three or four times and finally falls into a hole full of dung.

That in a few words is the story of my return from Italy.

Rather than stumble on without a goal in this dismal miasma that life in Paris had become for him, Beyle was prepared to undertake a completely new venture. Napoleon had invaded Russia in June 1812, and the general feeling in France was that this would prove to be one of his grandest exploits and, after the bloody Austrian campaign, a relatively easy one. Each week a commissioner of the Council of State was sent out from Paris as a courier to the eastern front with official dispatches and documents to be signed. Beyle asked for an assignment as courier, and the request was promptly granted. On July 14, he was given a mission to carry a set of portfolios to Vilna. He left on the 23rd, first making a visit in full uniform to the Empress at Saint-Cloud, who accorded him a brief interview. His impulse to join the Grand Army in Russia was a compound of the quiet desperation engendered by boredom and frustration and a flippant eagerness for adventure. The latter mood was clearly reflected in a journal entry more than a year earlier (March 27, 1811), when the prospect of a Russian war first appeared on the horizon: *"They speak much of war with Russia.* It would be charming, after coming back from Italy, to join a really active army." But rereading this comment on February 25, 1813, after having undergone the terrible months of the military disaster in Russia, Beyle added a terse, acidly understated note on his own recent illusion: "That is what happened. Charming is not exactly the right word."

VIII

MOSCOW TO MILAN

(Aetat. 29–31)

ON AUGUST 14, 1812, Beyle reached Napoleon's headquarters at Boy-arinkova and delivered his dispatches. At that point, he was assigned to the staff of Pierre Daru, and in this capacity, he would remain in close prox-imity to the imperial command till early December, when the Grand Army would break up in the chaos of the retreat. On August 18, he arrived in Smolensk and saw the town in flames. As in Austria three years earlier, he was eager to witness the "spectacle" of war, but the actual course of military events and the company in which he found himself very quickly made this aesthetic stance impossible. In his journal, he com-plains of a constant state of enervation beginning from his week in Smo-lensk, a condition perhaps caused by demoralization as well as by long work hours and the stubborn case of diarrhea he had contracted.

At an encampment between Smolensk and Moscow, he had a brief unexpected pleasure—a meeting with his erstwhile rival in Milan, Lodo-vico Widmann. The two happily exchanged reminiscences of Angela Pie-tragrua, then parted in comradely good feeling. Soon, Widmann would be one of the countless victims of the invasion.

Beyle arrived in the newly conquered Moscow on September 14, where he appears to have enjoyed a few weeks of relative respite from the ardors of the campaign, though he now suffered from a bout of fever. He had brought along with him the notebooks containing his translation of Lanzi and *Letellier*—most of this would be lost in the retreat—and he actually spent some time in Moscow working on the two projects. On October 15, Moscow was put to the torch by Russian incendiaries, and the calamitous folly of Napoleon's venture was now inescapably clear. The Grand Army was left virtually without shelter and with scanty provisions in the face of the Russian winter, its supply lines unmanageably long and exposed to attack. Napoleon ran the risk of being cut off in Moscow and losing all of Europe. The order for an immediate retreat was given. As the city was engulfed in flames, a vast cloud of copper-colored smoke towering above it, Beyle, after having appropriated a volume of Voltaire from the house where he was quartered, headed westward with Pierre Daru's staff. Looking back at the burning city, he made a last, unsuccessful attempt to see things from an aesthetic distance; after this, there would be nothing but a desperate scrabbling for survival: "We left the city, which was lit by the loveliest conflagration in the world, forming an immense pyramid that was like the prayers of the faithful, the base on earth and the apex in the heavens. The moon appeared, I believe, above the conflagration. It was a grand spectacle, but one would have had to have been alone to see it or surrounded by discerning people. That is the sad circumstance which spoiled the Russian campaign for me, having done it with people who would have made the Coliseum or the Sea of Naples seem small" (*Journal*, entry misdated September 14 to 15). If this sounds like the chilling elitism of an aesthete, one should juxtapose it with the following comment on the devastation of Moscow which appears in a letter addressed to Countess Beugnot dated October 18: "Just one thing saddens me: . . . the spectacle of this charming city, one of the loveliest temples of pleasure, transformed into black, stinking ruins, in the midst of which wander a few unfortunate dogs and a few women looking for some food." There still may be an element of elitist sensibility in the stress here on a charming temple of pleasure, but one must keep in mind that in the perspective of Beyle's philosophic hedonism centers of civilized life existed precisely for the elaborate ordering of pleasure, and in any case, this second comment on the destruction of Moscow clearly reflects a sharp sense of the human cost involved.

Beyle fled with the imperial forces across a countryside that had been laid waste in the march of conquest and that now offered neither food nor shelter. The fine autumn weather of the first days of the retreat was soon broken off by a sudden freeze and the first snowfalls. The 700,000 men Napoleon had marched into Russia—only 300,000 were Frenchmen—were being fearfully decimated by desertion, frostbite, starvation, and enemy bullets. Only 55,000 of the French troops would see France again. Guerrilla bands and Cossack cavalry conducted daily raids on the ragged line of retreating French soldiers. On October 24, Beyle's unit, as it was preparing its evening bivouac, found itself surrounded by what he estimated to be 4,000 or 5,000 Russian infantry. He and the officers with whom he was traveling drew the obvious inference that this was the end. With impressively steady resoluteness, they decided to spend the night on their feet, then at dawn to attempt to break through the Russian lines in a tightly drawn square assault formation. It was better, they reasoned, to die fighting than to be tortured to death by the peasants if they surrendered. They distributed gold coins to their orderlies, drank the last of their wine, prepared packets of personal effects to discard in the attack. When day broke, they were enveloped in impenetrable fog, and as they made their way cautiously through it, guns ready, they discovered that the Russians had moved on (letter to Alexandrine Daru, November 7, 1812). Toward the end of the long retreat, in Prussian territory, Beyle had another close call, fleeing across the ice of the Frisch Haff from a Cossack squadron, when the ice broke beneath the runners of his sled (*Essai d'autobiographie*, 1822).

Beyle's coolheaded resourcefulness and his powers of endurance through the whole retreat are noteworthy and, on the basis of his past experience, perhaps a little surprising. Till now, he had been pretty well insulated from the hardships and dangers of war in his military service, a tourist among the smoking embers of Napoleon's battlefields rather than a combatant on them. And his personal life, of course, had been largely devoted to the pursuit of pleasure and prestige and to a richly various cultivation of fantasy. But faced with the most urgent threats to his survival, surrounded by the dying and the despairing, himself weakened by illness, he demonstrates extraordinary toughness and practical capability. He is concerned, moreover, not only with saving himself but with performing his duty in the most exemplary fashion. In later years, he would take pride in the fact that as quartermaster he had managed to find the sole provisions to sustain the Grand Army on one of the last legs of its retreat. Even Pierre Daru was for once impressed by the performance of his protégé. This most trying of Beyle's experiences of initiation during the Napoleonic years was in one sense, then, a victory, for he had eminently proved himself in what was quite literally an ordeal.

One must not infer, though, that Beyle returned from Russia with a new inner strength. Almost the contrary is true: something had been crushed in him during the Russian campaign. It would take him many months to revive, and he would never again view the world of public events with the same quality of innocent hopefulness. The year 1813 is a crucial period of transition in Beyle's life, and it is important to try to see what was going on inside him at this long moment of low ebb. In mid-December of 1812, he reached Koenigsberg. After two weeks there, he proceeded through Prussia to France, arriving back in Paris on January 31. During the rest of the winter and the early spring, while the allied forces advanced toward France, he attempted to pick up more or less where he had left off—which, as we have seen, was nowhere in particular—but plunged into a deep depression by his Russian experience, he had little energy and no enthusiasm for whatever he contemplated doing.

Angéline Béreyter again shared his bed in the apartment on the rue Neuve-de-Luxembourg, but as he put it with the linguistic brutality he now adopted toward his own feelings in his journal, his "thirst for [her] was slaked" in three days (*Journal*, February 4). By the time of his departure from Paris in the latter part of April, their liaison, on his part always an emotionally shallow one, was virtually over, though the final break would not come until 1814. Mélanie Guilbert, now Mme Barcoff, was back in Paris from Russia, and he saw something of her on a friendly basis. Incredibly, he made some feeble gestures at exhuming his buried devotion to Alexandrine Daru, imagining that he detected clear signs of love in her now that she saw him again after he had passed through the crucible of battle. No man was ever more persistently faithful than Beyle to his own mental conceptions of what and who his passions had been, but these imaginings about Mme Daru were the mere misplaced reflexes of an exhausted spirit, and they did not continue long.

On the strength of the courage and competence he had demonstrated during the campaign, Beyle again hoped for a decoration and again pursued the possibility of an advantageous appointment in the commissariat, and once more he took up the matter of the elusive baronetcy in his letters to Grenoble. He made no more headway toward any of these goals than he had in 1811–12, and indeed, his maneuvers of ambition now seem more the expression of inertia than the result of real eagerness for worldly success. His enthusiasm for *The History of Painting* had faded, and still another time, he began to accumulate draft materials for *Letellier*, but the play as always resisted his efforts, and he remained as distant from being the Bard as the baron.

Beyle had returned from the front with little more than the clothes on his back, an abundance of new gray hairs, and, as he wrily remarked, the advantage of being for once thin. He felt fatigued, and as he confessed in a letter to Pauline (February 4, 1813), he was constantly cold and hungry —as though the physical hardships of the retreat were still gripping him inwardly. Coldness, in fact, is the constant theme of his journal, letters, and marginalia at this time, the Russian winter having imposed on him a kind of metonymic emblem of his emotional life: "I am right now in a state of perfect coldness; I have lost all my passions. . . . I feel dead at this moment; an old man of sixty could not be colder" (*Journal*, February 4, 1813). A month later, he wonders, hovering between plaintiveness and desperation: "Is this state of moral death the necessary effect of a six-month struggle with disgust, malaise, and danger? . . . What are the quickest means to shake this premature old age?" (*Journal*, March 15).

It is curious that Beyle is so reticent about what he actually underwent on the great retreat—curious in any case for him, who was accustomed to render such richly detailed accounts of his experience in his correspondence and diaries. Even if there were journal notebooks lost in the retreat (there is no way of knowing), he remained strangely reticent about the whole debacle once he was back in Paris. From his view of Moscow as a pyramid of flames till his return to France, the only discriminated incidents he reports are the night of encirclement by Russian infantry and—retrospectively, ten years later—the escape over the ice near Koenigsberg. Of his three summary terms for the Russian campaign—disgust, malaise, and danger—the first is the psychologically crucial one for him, and it would seem that there was something so utterly distasteful (or, if one prefers, traumatic) about what he had undergone that he could not bring himself to write about it. The closest he comes to specifying the source of his revulsion is his journal entry for May 21, 1813, written against the background of the cannon fire at Bautzen. He had approached the battle, he observes, where some 300,000 men were engaged, ensconced in a comfortable calèche, in a perfect position to witness the spectacle of war, but with no heart for it. "Unfortunately, I was thinking of what Beaumarchais says so well: 'In every kind of good, to possess is nothing; it is to enjoy that is everything.'" Then, revealingly, he responds to this elegantly turned eighteenth-century aphorism, which seems to define his own condition so accurately, with a movement of verbal violence: "I no longer get a hard-on over that sort of observation. I am sick of it, may the expression be forgiven me; it's like a man who has drunk too much punch and has been forced to throw it up; he is disgusted with it for life. The interiors of the souls I saw in the retreat from Moscow have forever disgusted me with the observations I can make on the gross creatures, the murderous oafs [*manches de sabre*] that compose an army."

It was, most fundamentally, a sense of man's nature that was destroyed for Beyle in the wreckage of Napoleon's Russian adventure. He had drawn his views of human behavior and human potential from two different kinds of literary sources. On the one hand, he had cherished a heroic ideal of the gifted elite ever since his youthful readings of *El Cid*, Tasso, *La Nouvelle Héloïse*. On the other hand, from the *Philosophes* and their immediate heirs, he had cultivated the notion of a rational quasi-mathematical analysis of man as a bundle of impulsions toward pleasure and away from pain obeying uniform laws of motivation. Both approaches were profoundly shaken on the retreat from Moscow. The elitism was not abandoned—indeed, he was driven to cling to it more tenaciously as an anchor in the abyss of degradation—but any heroic ideal he had of human potentiality would now have to undergo a radical ironic qualification. One can assume that the manifestations of selfless heroism he saw in the retreat were not very frequent, and one might guess that he also discovered in himself, especially in the last weeks of 1812, when he finally headed on out before the straggling army in order to save himself, a naked animal fear of imminent death beneath the admirable discipline of his soldierly efforts. As for the eighteenth-century calculus of moral and social behavior with which he had sought to train himself as an observer, it was not that it had been refuted but that it had come to seem grotesquely inappropriate in manner and mood. Whatever Beyle actually saw of cowardice, crudity, savage egoism in the masses of men fleeing across the frozen Russian countryside conveyed to him an abysmal vision of human nature (parallel in a way to what many sensitive writers experienced in World War I) for which the polished precision and the cool confidence of the language of the *Philosophes* were somehow beside the point. Beyle's involvement in rationalist moral psychology, as we noted earlier, was motivated by his desire to obtain control over human relations, but the extremes of brutalization he saw on the retreat must have made him feel that the very ideal of rational control was chimerical and that it was pointless merely to stand at a distance and formulate universal folly in an epigram. It is symptomatic that he should hurl aside Beaumarchais's nicely put perception with an obscenity: Russia, as he notes precisely, through what it had revealed to him of "the interiors of souls," had disgusted him with his own carefully acquired intellectual strategy for analyzing such interiors.

After the Russian experience, Beyle would tend to place himself as much as he could within the civilized, protected perimeter of that symbolic clean well-lighted place he had described in his letter to Pauline on his return from Italy to France—the ballroom of a high culture that knew how to translate desire into a perfectly choreographed pattern of repeated fulfillment. This is the point where Stendhal's doctrine of the Happy Few begins to take definitive shape, for after Russia he begins to fear that the mass of humanity is too horrendously unredeemable to work with or hope for. On July 15, 1815, when the news reached him in Milan of Napoleon's second and final defeat and of the restoration of the Bourbons, he would vilify his countrymen for their baseness, and these angry thoughts, symptomatically, would lead him back by an obvious path of association to a reflection on the Russian campaign: "The filthy aspect in which one discovers humanity under difficult circumstances, in a word, what I saw in Russia, makes me disgusted with [even] slightly dangerous voyages" (*Journal*).

Beyle focuses his disillusionment with humanity at large and his need for a refuge in a recurrent set of images: the French and their politics and wars are a marshy lowland, a sea of mud, excrement (one recalls that the man who leaves the ballroom stumbles into a hole full of dung); Italy offers the highlands of love and art where clarity, order, harmony are possible. This opposition of key images, which was to become one of Stendhal's characteristic imaginative orderings of the world, is already vividly present at the beginning of the Russian campaign, in a letter to Félix Faure from Smolensk dated August 24, 1812. Beyle complains that "everything is gross, filthy, stinking, both physically and morally." No prize of ambition, he goes on to say, could possibly compensate him "for the mud in which I am buried. I imagine the heights that my soul (composing works, listening to Cimarosa, and loving Angela,[1] in a beautiful climate) that my soul inhabits, like delightful hills; far from these hills, on the plain, are fetid marshes in which I am plunged, and nothing in the world but the sight of a map brings back to me my hills." The debacle of the French empire in 1813–14 was to force Beyle twice back into active duty, but as he began to recover slowly from the inner numbness with which he had returned from Russia, he was more and more committed, as the one escape

1. Henri Martineau believes that the Angela in question is Béreyter because Beyle had entrusted her to Faure and because she is mentioned, with that form of the name, at the end of this letter. But the juxtaposition of Angela with Cimarosa and the fine climate of Italy, as well as the affirmation of the ideal nature of his love for her, makes it almost certain that he is thinking of Angela Pietragrua. See Martineau's note in his edition of the *Correspondance* (Paris, 1962), vol. 1, p. 1361.

route from the "premature old age" that had seized him, to find some way back to Angela, Cimarosa, the hills of Lombardy, and to all the values they represented for him.

In mid-April 1813, Beyle, still smarting over his failure to receive the recognition of a promotion for his recent distinguished service, was ordered, much against his will, to join the army on the Prussian front. His mood in the combat zone was not very different from what it had been in Paris, a mixture of boredom and disgust, and he was even beginning to wonder whether Napoleon was mad. We have already seen a sample of his frame of mind as he rolled up to witness the battle of Bautzen in his calèche on May 21; a later passage in the journal entry for that same date raises a technical rather than a temperamental objection to viewing the spectacle of war. "We perfectly perceive Bautzen from the top of the slope opposite which it is situated. We see quite well, from noon to three o'clock, everything that can be seen of a battle, which is to say, nothing." That acerbic observation, as has often been noted, contains the kernel of his conception of the Waterloo scenes in *Chartreuse*, where poor Fabrice stumbling through the chaotic mayhem of the field wants to know whether he has really been in a battle. One could add that Beyle in 1813 might not have come to so astringent a perception had it not been for the radical disillusionment he underwent in the Russian campaign: he was now prepared to look on war with the eyes of the writer who would produce the first adequate fiction about the madness of modern warfare, in which the individual is seen as a speck of flotsam tossed on tides of senseless, shapeless havoc.

An armistice was declared on June 4. Two days later, Beyle was appointed intendant at Sagan in Silesia. He assumed his duties on the 10th, and for a couple of weeks, his situation looked much like the one he had had at Brunswick six years earlier, though with more administrative authority now. He established social contacts with the town notables, paraded about in his dandyish finery, planned tours of places of interest in the region, began to read Tacitus, and of course found himself utterly bored. But in the first days of July, he began to run a high temperature that was to have few remissions for the next two months. After the debilitation of the great retreat, from which he had not fully recovered, he must have had very little resistance to whatever infection he was exposed to. The terminology of the day that he uses—"nervous fever," "gastric fever"—does not enlighten us much on the nature of the disease, but its gravity is made clear in a July 16 letter to Pauline, which begins with these words: "I believed I was going to have the honor of being buried in

Sagan," and goes on to offer the following cool analysis of his own feelings: "I've been amazed at the small effect of the proximity of death; it derives, I think, from the belief that the last pain is no worse than the one before the last." Beyle suspected, perhaps with some warrant, that he was not receiving adequate medical care in Sagan. On July 27, he set out for Paris, pausing on the 28th at Dresden, where, despite his weakness, he went to see a performance of his first operatic love, *Il Matrimonio Segreto* (he was burning with fever by the time he came out of the theater). He made a two-week stopover in Dresden, then proceeded to Paris, arriving August 20. He at once put himself in the care of a highly recommended doctor, whose regimen seemed to him to afford some immediate relief and who concurred in the advisability of a convalescence in a mild climate. Having obtained an extended sick leave, Beyle left Paris at the beginning of September. It hardly needs to be said that his destination was Milan, where he hoped to find balm for his bruised spirit as well as for his ailing body. He was not disappointed on either account.

Beyle reached Milan on September 7, still so weakened by his illness that at moments of excitement he became shaky: as he sipped his first coffee back in this capital of his happiness, he lost control of the cup and spilled it all over his fine new gray cashmere trousers. Two years earlier, his stay in Italy had been a delirium of romantic excitement. Now, wrung out by his war experience and enervated by his illness, he could hardly feel the same exuberance, but in compensation, his journal shows a quality of quiet self-possession and purposefulness that he did not have in 1811. The moment he first caught sight of the cathedral of Milan on the horizon, it occurred to him that "my travels in Italy make me more original, more *myself*.[2] I am learning to seek happiness more intelligently" (*Journal*, September 7). The perception is beautifully accurate and explains as well as could be explained in brief compass why Beyle was from this point on to spend more than half his life in Italy. The comment also suggests how Italy almost at once was helping him to emerge from the emotional torpor in which he had been sunk ever since Russia: already he was thinking again of the pursuit of happiness, imagining possibilities of realizing his own distinctiveness and thus of standing apart from the frightful heap of humanity. To be sure, the process of recuperation was neither instantaneous nor without its reversals. On his first visit to the art galleries of Milan, he complains that he viewed the splendid paintings with a deadened responsiveness, but less than two weeks later, he would add in a note that

2. Italicized in French in the original.

he had gone back to the galleries and had seen the pictures with his "soul of former days" (*Journal*, September 9).

Angela Pietragrua was of course the most potent elixir for Beyle's emotional malaise. One gets the impression that she was more measured, less extravagantly provocative, in her stratagems than she had been in 1811. Perhaps she was touched by this weakened, visibly aged Henri who had returned from the wars still stubbornly faithful to her. One can assume that she admitted him again to the privileges of lover within a few days after his arrival, but he seems less concerned now with physical passion than with the inner satisfactions of affectionate intimacy. The word *bonheur*, happiness, recurs in his journal for these weeks, accompanied by a pronounced reticence about describing it in detail, for fear of spoiling it. A comment in the entry for September 15 nicely summarizes his mood: "I don't feel the intoxication of 1811. But it seems to me that I am in the second stage *of love* in which there is more intimacy, confidence, and naturalness." Beyle fancied he could observe in Angela indications of real love that he had not seen two years earlier, but in this mistress of amatory maneuvers, a lover's confidence was always a little misplaced.

Very quickly, Angela initiated a new round of hide-and-seek. The specter of Signor Pietragrua's jealousy was once again roused. Promised notes never reached her expectant lover. She found it necessary to go off on more of her excursions to the lake country and elsewhere, before long making difficulties, for the sake of dreaded propriety, about Beyle's joining her. He had spent some idyllic days with Angela in Monza, on September 9–10, and then a week later at Como, but after returning to Milan, he was left dangling several days before he received word that he could come back to see her at Monza. In between trysts, he was making notes for a commentary on Molière, and thinking again of writing a history of Italian painting (both projects were surely signs of psychological recuperation), but there were times when he found himself too distracted by Angela to concentrate on anything: "I am in the painful position of a man who waits" (*Journal*, September 25). For the most part, however, he seems to be able now to enjoy her evasiveness with something like equanimity as a source of piquancy in their relationship, like the elaborate semaphore of closed and half-opened windows she was once again inventing to signal the changing hours of their assignations. Through this extended second encounter in Milan, Beyle most commonly refers to Angela with the sobriquet "Countess Simonetta" (apparently after the Villa Simonetta, which they had visited together early in their relationship in 1811). His adherence to that designation may reflect the degree to which he was consciously pleased to let her play a literary role in an amorous intrigue, this

**Presumed portrait of
Stendhal's father,
Chérubin Beyle.**
*Courtesy of
Victor Del Litto, Grenoble.*

**The Abbé Raillane,
Stendhal's tutor.**
*Courtesy of
Victor Del Litto, Grenoble.*

Entrance of the French army into Milan in 1796, by Vernet.
Courtesy of Victor Del Litto, Grenoble.

**Alexandrine Daru,
portrait by David.**
*Courtesy of
Victor Del Litto, Grenoble.*

**Presumed portrait of
Angela Pietragrua.**
*Courtesy of
Victor Del Litto, Grenoble.*

A box at La Scala in the 1840s.
Courtesy of Victor Del Litto, Grenoble.

Luini's *Hérodiade*, in whose Salomé Stendhal saw Matilde.
Uffizi Gallery, Florence.

**Presumed portrait of
Matilde Dembowski.**
*Courtesy of
Victor Del Litto, Grenoble.*

**Bust of
Countess Clémentine Curial.**
*Courtesy of
Victor Del Litto, Grenoble.*

Alberthe de Rubempré.
Courtesy of
Victor Del Litto, Grenoble.

Giulia Rinieri.
Courtesy of
Victor Del Litto, Grenoble.

**Contemporary engraving of the capture of the
Palais Royal during the July Revolution of 1830.**
Courtesy of Victor Del Litto, Grenoble.

LE ROUGE
ET LE NOIR

CHRONIQUE DU XIXᵉ SIÈCLE,

PAR M. DE STENDHAL.

TOME PREMIER.

PARIS.

A. LEVAVASSEUR, LIBRAIRE, PALAIS-ROYAL.

1831.

Stendhal at fifty, portrait by Jean-Louis Ducis.
Courtesy of Victor Del Litto, Grenoble.

**Sketch by Alfred de Musset of Stendhal dancing
on the trip down the Rhone, December, 1833.**
Courtesy of Victor Del Litto, Grenoble.

Manuscript page of *Lucien Leuwen* with Stendhal's revisions and planning notes.
Stendhal Collection, Bibliothèque de Grenoble.

Stendhal's map for the washerwomen scene in *Lamiel*.
Courtesy of Victor Del Litto, Grenoble.

libertine wife of a petty Milanese functionary elevated into the figure of a proud and imperious lady, always mysterious and difficult of access even as she surrendered herself to him.

When in late September it became apparent that she would remain out of town and unavailable for two weeks, Beyle calmly set off for a tour of Venice, which he appears to have enjoyed with no serious perturbation over his separation from Angela. By the second week of October, they were both back in Milan, going to the ballet together (an art Beyle was just discovering) and sharing daily intimacies. In a month, Beyle's leave would be over, but these last weeks together, from what one can infer from the sparse revelations of his journal and marginalia, had the mellow quality of an autumnal idyll. On November 10, four days before his departure, he notes in his journal: "Spent *with* Gina from 8½ to 10. I was weak, having a bit of fever. Charming hours, sweet tenderness, the most charming perhaps of this trip." One might even speculate that Angela herself had found, at least for the moment, that Beyle was after all not only an incorrigible dupe who invited her deceptions but a fascinating man, and a touchingly devoted one, for whom she could on occasion feel a spontaneous impulse to be tender Gina instead of the formidable Countess Simonetta.

In any case, Beyle returned to France, though still not fully recovered from his physical illness, with his frozen emotions at last thawed, with a renewed sense of the richness of the arts in Italy, and with a revived ambition to take up a career as a writer. Meanwhile, political events were about to thrust him into a last turn of imperial service. Beyle reached Paris again at the end of November and immediately prepared to resume his old routine of cultivated life in the capital, making notes for a treatise on comedy, taking a subscription for the theater, beginning a round of dinner parties. He was exempted from the general conscription, but on December 26, he discovered that he had been appointed as administrative assistant to Count René de Saint-Vallier, who was being sent to organize the regional defense of Grenoble and environs as the allied forces moved toward the invasion of France. An assignment in Grenoble, of all places (that "dung heap," that "headquarters of pettiness"—*Journal*, March 2, 1814), was hardly an alluring one, but the state of national emergency left no time for second thoughts or for official appeals. He called on his new superior, who proved to be more agreeable than he had imagined; then he hastily packed, and on December 31, accompanied by his sister Pauline and her husband, then visiting Paris, he was off for Grenoble.

Beyle undertook his administrative duties with considerable zeal, but with little thanks from the citizens of his old hometown. Some anticlerical measures that he was enjoined to enact met serious resistance, and many Grenoble residents looked on him as an upstart who had abandoned the paternal hearth for a Parisian life of dubious character and who now had returned with the presumption of ordering them around. His official directives were signed with the particle of nobility, de Beyle, to which he was not strictly entitled, as the townspeople knew perfectly well, and some of them took pains to cross out the offending letters or to add a jeering commentary on the proclamations that were posted on public walls. At a point in Beyle's life when he had little sympathy for the French in general, his hometown was confirming the worst suspicions he had harbored about it since childhood. The precarious state of his health must have made his vehemence against Grenoble even sharper. It soon became apparent that he had not really shaken his illness during his Italian vacation. Under the pressure of hard work, he fatigued rapidly and by early February suffered a relapse and was for a time bedridden. He requested leave to return to Paris for reasons of health, and Saint-Vallier, though sorry to lose his services, recognized the justice of the request. In mid-March he departed for the capital, in fact exactly at the moment when Napoleon's last defenses were collapsing. He arrived in Paris during the final days of March and so was just in time to witness on March 31 the Battle of Montmartre, won by Russian troops, and the triumphal parade of allied forces down the Champs Élysées. On April 7, along with thousands of imperial functionaries, he prudently signed an act of adherence to the decrees of the senate restoring the Bourbon monarchy. The Empire was finished, and with it, Beyle's dream of worldly ascent on the crest of the imperial tide. During the Hundred Days of Napoleon's return in 1815, Beyle would be in Italy, again entangled with Angela. The idea of Napoleon, however, would continue to haunt him as it would haunt so many original imaginations in the nineteenth century: having observed the great man firsthand, together with the ambiguous consequences of the Emperor's actions, he eventually would engage the Napoleonic phenomenon in his fiction with a peculiar and forceful conjunction of acute judgment and impassioned sympathy.

For the moment, he did what he could to provide for his own future. The civil service had been his only visible profession, and now as the whole elaborate Napoleonic administrative scaffolding was thrown down, he could no longer hope for a brilliant place but only for a comfortable sinecure—ideally, as he imagined, some modest consulate in Italy that would give him 4,000 or perhaps 6,000 francs per annum and the leisure to cultivate the arts and to write. With the Restoration, his protector, Pierre Daru, of course could no longer be of any use to him, so he sought the aid of Countess Beugnot, whom he had come to know through his friend Bellisle and with whom he had remained on the most cordial terms. The countess's husband was at first minister of the interior in the new regime, a position which encouraged Beyle's hopes of a consulate. When Count Beugnot was transferred in mid-May to the directorship of the ministry of police, Beyle despaired and contemplated simply leaving for Italy at once without resources. Or to speak more precisely, without resources and with a mountain of debts—by now 37,000 francs, 2,100 owed to his tailor alone. To make some decent financial provision for himself, then, was a matter of considerable urgency.

The ex-commissioner hung on in Paris for another two months, his once great expectations dwindling daily. At the beginning of July, Count Beugnot petitioned Talleyrand on Beyle's behalf for an Italian consulate, but nothing came of it. Some scholars have conjectured that if Beyle had only had the patience to continue waiting, Beugnot would have obtained something suitable for him within a few months. Patience with the French, however, was at this juncture a commodity almost as scarce for Beyle as cash, and though he realized that the sensible thing for him was to secure an income through the foreign service, by now, after eight years of frustrated ambitions in the administrative hierarchy, he had little stomach for persisting as a supplicant at the doors of the new government. In his journal for July 4, he notes: "I am jaded with Paris, not at all in anger. I've become thoroughly disgusted with the calling of commissioner and with the insolent stupidity of the powerful. Rome, Rome is my native land; I am burning to depart." On July 18, he submitted a request to the ministry of war that he be awarded the regular pay due him (900 francs per annum) as an inactive deputy of the commissariat of war, and two days later, he left for Italy, stopping on the way near Grenoble to visit again with Pauline and her husband.

But before his departure, in those last two months as a petitioner for office, Beyle had undertaken and actually had completed a curious literary project. It is odd that he should have written such a book, or any book, at this moment of uncertain transition in his life. His sudden involvement in this particular subject and the ambiguities of authorship in the way he at last made his literary debut reveal a good deal both of his state of mind in 1814 and of the course on which he was now set.

In early May, Beyle hit upon the idea of putting together a book on the lives of Haydn, Mozart, and the rococo librettist, Pietro Metastasio. The immediate inspiration was a recently published book he had probably brought back with him from Italy, a life of Haydn by Giuseppe Carpani presented in epistolary form. "Inspiration," however, lends a theological dignity to the operation which it scarcely deserves, for what Beyle did was to plagiarize Carpani wholesale, even robbing him, as the Italian musicologist later protested, of his age, his personal peculiarities, and the fever he happened to have when he was writing the book. This literary looting was as careless as it was unscrupulous: names were garbled; arbitrary excisions made; facts of time, place, and circumstances confused; Italian terms mistranslated. Nor did the borrowings stop with Carpani. The life of Mozart was a more or less verbatim transcription—no translation was necessary because the original was in French—of a biographical article by C. Winckler, and the section on Metastasio drew heavily on an Italian article by Giuseppe Baretti and on the ideas of the Swiss historian J.-C.-L. Sismondi. When in 1816, a year after the publication of the book, Carpani, its principal victim, inveighed against the larceny in print, the culprit did not hesitate to attack Carpani vehemently in return, literally adding insult to injury. It is hard to think of another writer of genius who launched his career in so dubious a vessel, and in such a morally questionable fashion.

Why did Beyle do it? There is nothing to suggest that in general he was deficient in a sense of professional honor or plain honesty; yet in the unfortunate episode of *Haydn, Mozart, et Métastase*, he exhibited an egregious lack of both. Perhaps the curious facts of this book's composition may make more sense if they are considered in the context of the long period of desperation he had undergone in 1813 and the radical disorientation he was experiencing now with the fall of the Empire. After all those years on the treadmill of *Letellier*, and after the abandonment of *The History of Painting in Italy*—which he apparently was unable to resume until he could have around him an actual Italian environment as a stimulus—he desperately needed to get himself going as a writer in order finally to have a vocation, and he had reached the conclusion that there was no other vocation for him. He was prepared to propel himself into literary action even if it meant beginning with large-scale borrowings from the writings of others, to which he would merely add some personal modifications and interpolations. It was not exactly honest, but it was a way of escaping the state of impotent inactivity in which he found himself in the spring of 1814 and which, in some sense, had been his professional fate through most of the Napoleonic era. Using the system of translation by dictation that he had adopted while working on Lanzi's *History*, he sailed through the translation/adaptation/composition of the book in less than two months, having found in the project, whatever its unworthy aspects, a beautifully efficacious remedy for a fourteen-year-long writer's block.

This habitual user of pseudonyms—even in his most intimate correspondence—of course presented his *Vies de Haydn, Mozart et Métastase*
under the camouflage of a pen name, and the madcap invention he chose
in itself suggests that he conceived the whole undertaking as something
of a lark; and this playful attitude may in part explain why he felt he
could be irresponsible about his uses of sources. The supposed author of
the *Vies* was one Louis-Alexandre-César Bombet—the first two names
alluding to two detested monarchs in these first days of the Restoration,
Louis XVIII and Czar Alexander, the third name referring to Napoleon
himself, while "Bombet" evokes in French associations of swollen con-
vexity (like its English cousin, "bombast") and perhaps also the notion
of going on a spree. The dedication of the book was equally, if less
farcically, pseudonymous, to "Mme Doligny," Beyle's private designation for Countess Beugnot. He was pursuing with the countess (though
not very vigorously) his usual course of flirtation, but as he happily dictated the final section of the book in late June, he was also, after a lapse of
eight years, again sleeping with Mélanie Guilbert. This is a time of recapitulation and preparation for Beyle: in an affectionate revisiting of passion spent, he once more becomes Mélanie's lover for a couple of weeks,
while he is busy staking out a literary future. And in the same breath in
which he mentions his new liaison with Mélanie (*Journal*, July 4), he also
records being struck by the fine face and candid eyes of Countess Clémentine Curial, the twenty-six-year-old daughter of Countess Beugnot. Those
eyes would rest on him again with passionate attentiveness a decade later.

Meanwhile, his thoughts were directed toward Italy and its arts, and
toward a reunion there with Angela Pietragrua. The book he had
decided to write was for him, among other things, an inward turning to
Italy, even though two of its three biographical subjects were German
composers. Haydn of course came to him refracted through an Italian
lens, and in Carpani's stress on music as a sensuous rather than an intellectual experience, on the interconnection of the arts, and on the changing
nature of music from country to country according to national climate
and language, he found the confirmation of ideas he had long cherished,
which may be why he was so unwilling afterward to concede that he had
drawn directly from Carpani's formulations.[3] The Mozart whom Beyle
venerated was the composer of operas, the supreme Italian art form—a

3. Richard N. Coe, in the admirable scholarly introduction to his rather free translation of the *Vies*, has proposed that Carpani be seen as a decisive influence on
Stendhal's conception of music and the other arts, but the seminal ideas that Coe
lists had long been entertained by Stendhal. See *Haydn, Mozart, and Metastasio*, ed.
and tr. Richard N. Coe (New York, 1972), pp. xxii–xxiv.

figure of astonishing genius, he recognized, though in his "Germanic melancholy" less appealing finally than the divine Cimarosa. And on Metastasio, Beyle heaped the most extravagant praise because he saw in the Italian poet (who was responsible, among much else, for the libretto of *Il Matrimonio Segreto*) a writer endowed with the supreme gift of perfectly marrying words with song and dramatic occasion to effect a kind of apotheosis of language as the enactment of bliss. Here was inchoate desire translated into the lucid harmony of art: "His heroes retain almost nothing of drab reality. He has created figures that possess an element of verve and genius which the most fortunate of men have encountered only in the luckiest moments of their lives: Saint-Preux entering Julie's bedroom" ("Metastasio," Letter I). Thus, the sumptuousness of music combined with drama; the grace of poetry; and the moments of rapture a "sublime" woman such as Angela might vouchsafe a man, coalesce in a single image, the highest pitch of Rousseau's imagination realized in Italian art, on Italian soil.

The world of private associations, then, in which Beyle immersed himself in composing the *Vies* was richly alluring for him, but there was little practical good to be gotten from the publication of the book. He brought it out at his own expense, at a cost of 1,150 francs (at a moment when he was loaded with debts!). The printing was 1,000 copies, and since his share of the list price was to be five francs a copy, he would have scarcely made any inroads on his amassed debts even if the printing had sold out. As a matter of fact, not much more than a hundred copies were actually sold. It was a humiliating debut, and Stendhal was to have more disappointments like it, though at least this commercial failure could be attributed to one L.-A.-C. Bombet, an absurdly named fellow whose real identity was not generally known. But he seems to have been not overly concerned with either money or success at this point, despite a lingering feeling that he *ought* to be concerned. When at the beginning of July he moved out of his stylish apartment on the rue Neuve-de-Luxembourg into a little furnished room, selling his household goods and his cabriolet, he felt perfectly content, perhaps a bit relieved at lightening himself of all that baggage. He was heading, unencumbered, for the land of happiness, and the book he was finishing was itself an extended intimation of that happiness.

Beyle arrived back in Milan on August 10; as early as the 13th, he made one of his cryptic marginal notes, "two times," indicating that he was quite satisfactorily bedded down with Angela once more. Almost as soon as he arrived, he began work again on *The History of Painting in Italy*, a measure of the momentum as a writer that he had developed through his just-completed work as an "adapter." Toward the end of the month, he wrote a brief essay, "A Letter Concerning the Present State of Music in Italy," which he appended as a conclusion to *Haydn, Mozart et Métastase*. One passage near the end nicely summarizes what was now to be his thinking about public and private realms in a Europe ruled by the spirit of the Congress of Vienna:

I find it very convenient to live in a country endowed with a liberal constitution; but, unless one has an extremely touchy sort of pride, and a sensibility ill-suited for the concerns of happiness, I do not see what pleasure one can find in constantly attending to matters of constitutions and politics. With the present state of the enjoyments and habits of a man of the world, the happiness we can derive from the manner in which power is distributed in a given country does not amount to much: it can harm us, but it cannot give us pleasure.

This is a kind of zero-degree liberalism, founded on the most far-reaching skepticism about what can be achieved for the individual under even the best of circumstances by political institutions. Beyle would remain avidly interested in politics as an analytic observer, but the philosophy of disengagement he articulates here was what he lived by, for after the trauma of the Russian experience he would never again imagine that politics could be an appropriate sphere for the pursuit of happiness. It was this sense of disengagement that dictated both his writing a book on music (chiefly opera) and his immediate move to Italy at the very moment when Europe was entering the shadow of Metternich and Talleyrand. "I fell with Napoleon in April, 1814," he was later to announce dramatically at the beginning of *Henry Brulard*, but in consciously withdrawing from the ranks where from first manhood he had hoped to advance in the world, he was actually making possible the emergence of a long-thwarted self. Residing in Italy, he would possess not only the inner freedom to pursue the pleasures of life in culture as he had not before but also the perspective to begin articulating in rapier-quick prose the distinctive vision of man and society he had slowly been shaping. In other words, he could now become both an accomplished dilettante and an original writer. In the debacle of the Empire, for all the pangs of disappointment and anger it cost him, Henri Beyle had his first sure intuition of how he might make himself Stendhal.

Part Three

The Free Lance

The two caryatids of the old style of literary studies are called, one may recollect, the man and his work. The exemplary value of the Stendhal phenomenon comes from the way he shakes these two notions by altering their symmetry, by confusing their difference, by deflecting their relations.

Gérard Genette,
Figures II

IX

MILAN

(Aetat. 31–38)

FROM AUGUST 1814 to the late spring of 1821, Beyle was to be a resident of Milan, the city that had been the geographical focus of his dreams of art and love since the verge of manhood. By 1820, already brooding over his own mortality, he would conceive the first of the meticulously designed plans for his own tombstone in which he asked to be identified as "Errico Beyle, Milanese" (*Souvenirs d'égotisme*, chap. 6). But if he now thought of himself as essentially Milanese, the combination of unlimited leisure and unlimited cultural curiosity also made him a constant tourist during this period. In a long series of expeditions, he explored the landscape, architecture, museums, restaurants, and social textures of Verona, Padua, Venice, Florence, Rome, Naples, Genoa, and other points of interest in the Italian peninsula. Family and business concerns necessitated four trips back to Grenoble, during three of which he touched base in Paris as well, once, in 1817, also managing at last to spend a fortnight in London. But Milan remained the center of his world, and despite the spectacular fluctuations of his emotional life, to which we shall presently attend, the city did not disappoint his expectations.

How did this cultivated bachelor with no visible employment spend his time in Milan during these years after the fall of Napoleon? One must begin describing his daily routine from the evening because it was around La Scala that his schedule was ordered. "In sum," he wrote his Parisian friend Adolphe de Mareste (March 21, 1818), "Italy pleases me. Each day I spend from 7 P.M. till midnight listening to music and watching two ballets. The climate does the rest." Instructively, a moment later in the same letter, he adds a general reflection on the stance of self-protective egoism he has adopted, and he stresses the equanimity of his life in Milan by transmuting the horrors of the Moscow campaign into an image of the nonchalance of the Milanese cafés: "The only thing worth the trouble in this life *is oneself* [H.B.'s emphasis]. The good side of having such a character is taking a retreat from Moscow like a glass of lemonade."

We had occasion to note earlier the central Milanese social institution of nightly appearances at the opera house. In order to understand what this involved, one must keep in mind that a box at La Scala was more like a small parlor than the little overhanging pockets jammed with fixed seats of modern theaters. A party of eight or ten could comfortably deploy themselves where they chose, around a pedestal table convenient for reading and card playing, in movable chairs by the railing, or on the cushions of the divan set against one wall of the box. This meant that a party at La Scala was very much a social group whose activities were limited neither in nature nor duration by the performance on the stage below. Often, as Stendhal reports in *Rome, Naples et Florence en 1817*, he and his companions at the opera would remain in their box playing faro to one in the morning in a darkened house emptied of spectators, until the janitor would finally ask them to leave. Then the group would go out to dine, separating only after the break of day. Stendhal confesses that he had no really intimate friends among these parties frequented at the opera, and throughout his sojourn in Milan, his closest personal connections were his correspondents in Paris. Nevertheless, he hardly seems to have been lonely, and Milan's easy routine of cultured hedonism often made him feel a spontaneous sense of pervasive well-being—*ces soirées de naïveté et de bonheur*—he had rarely known during the years of the Empire.

If these evenings till dawn were in fact very frequent, that would have often left only the afternoons, following a few hours of sleep, for reading and writing. Beyle continued to pursue his vocation as a writer by fits and starts, though during this seven-year period he began at last to build some momentum in writing for publication, and by the end of his stay in Milan, he would finish a book in which he fully discovered his original voice. In any case, such professional writer's work as he performed did nothing at all to improve his financial state, and it is something of a puzzle how he managed to support himself in his life as a dilettante. His lodgings in Milan were modest, and he did not permit himself the extravagances in which he had indulged a few years earlier as a Parisian man-about-town. Nevertheless, when he traveled, he liked to travel in style, eating at good restaurants, stopping at the better hotels; as always, he felt compelled to make a considerable outlay on his wardrobe; he also made substantial expenditures on the purchase of books; and the interest alone on his Parisian debts amounted to 2,000 francs per annum. Early in this period, moreover, he was either invited or deemed it prudent to provide a monthly stipend of 200 francs to Angela Pietragrua—an arrangement which makes one wonder equally at the nature of their relationship (as a married woman, she would not fall into the category of *femme entre-tenue*) and at where he got the money.

Beyle's one known source of dependable income at this time was an annuity of 1,600 francs he received as interest on the legacy left him by his grandfather, who had died in 1813. He also had a pension of 900 francs per annum coming to him in his capacity as ex-commissioner, but this was paid only intermittently, as his repeated letters of entreaty to various official personages indicate. Between 1817 and 1819, after his father—in Beyle's letters to Pauline still grimly designated the Bastard for his supposed miserliness—had ceded to him a house in Grenoble in order to help him legally establish his *majorat*, the son was able to realize enough money from the sale of the place to pay off his Parisian creditors. A recent scholar,[1] by carefully sifting autobiographical documents, has noted that Beyle had a peculiarly fluctuating amount of capital invested with his friend Félix Faure in Paris between 1810 and 1822. Her very plausible inference is that Beyle, during his years in the Napoleonic administration, following the general practice of people in such positions, often received quiet "bonuses" or kickbacks from the contractors with whom he dealt on behalf of the army. Any savings accumulated in this fashion would have had to remain clandestine, which would explain the elusiveness of the sum in the hands of Félix Faure. This surreptitious fund would have been the money that kept Beyle afloat during his Italian life of leisure. No more than afloat, to be sure, for he was often compelled to send Pauline urgent requests for money, and more than once he contemplated selling some of his books to obtain needed cash. But if he felt the occasional nip of economic necessity, he was never preoccupied by it, and he was left free

1. Lily R. Felberg, *Stendhal et la question d'argent au cours de sa vie* (Aran, 1975), pp. 42–43.

enough to pursue his literary interests, even when that meant bringing out a book at his own expense, and his amatory interests, even when the lady in question appeared to require philanthropic attentions.

The lady immediately in question, of course, when he arrived in Milan in the summer of 1814, was Angela Pietragrua. Just three days after Beyle's return, on August 13, he made one of the cryptic marginal notations he fancied for such occasions, "Milan, *2 times*," indicating that Angela had promptly readmitted him as her lover. That role had never been one he could enjoy with much security, and now it was more precarious than ever before. The sense of quiet contentment he had felt in their relationship on his previous visit a year earlier had vanished. Perhaps Angela thought it a little awkward to have a French lover, a veteran of the Napoleonic service, in an Italy again dominated by Austria. In any case, it was one thing to entertain a devoted Beyle who from time to time appeared for visits of two or three months, and quite another to have this persistent admirer taking up residence in her home city, and she surely must have seen the inconveniences of the new situation. Before long, the old tired ghost of the jealous husband was conjured up. The French lover was sent off to the provinces for supposed reasons of prudence, was refused assignations, and was allowed others at out-of-the-way locations only under the greatest complications of secrecy and disguise. By October 1814, Angela was heaping recriminations on Beyle for his alleged neglect of her, threatening to break off relations permanently, and yet, whether out of genuine ambivalence or the sheer delight of manipulation, granting him another meeting in which she showed herself as seductive as ever.

The early months of 1815 were a last interlude of gratification for Beyle before the final deterioration of the relationship. (It was, as we have already noted, chiefly his liaison with Angela that kept him in Italy during the Hundred Days of Napoleon's return, which occurred at this time.) In July, he allowed himself to be talked into giving Angela 3,000 francs for a trip to Venice in which he was to join her, and he immediately had misgivings over having agreed to provide the money. In August, they reached a point of estrangement. There was a last, tenuous reconciliation in October, quickly broken, and by late December, the love Beyle had treasured for fifteen years was dead, beyond even the resurrectional powers of his doggedly determined imagination. On December 1, Angela had written him to sever their connection, condemning his execrable behavior toward her. By December 28, she was writing him again to defend herself against an accusation he had made and to "remind" him that it was he, after all, who had abandoned her. The accusation, Beyle informs us in a note made on her letter, stemmed from his having heard her threaten to denounce him to the Austrian police, presumably as a French spy.[2] This was the sour note that ended the affair.

But there exists another, more theatrical denouement to this mixture of farce and melodrama that Beyle had played out with Angela for so many years. Prosper Mérimée, in a memoir of his friend Beyle written after the latter's death, reports the following story, which one may assume Beyle told him perhaps a decade after the actual events. Angela's chambermaid, either because of a quarrel with her mistress or because she was won over by Beyle, revealed to him that his cherished Gina was almost daily betraying him with a different lover. He agreed to accept ocular proof, and hidden in the closet of Angela's bedroom, peering through a crevice, he was able to observe his mistress disporting herself with another man barely three feet away from him. His first reaction was hysterical hilarity: he could barely restrain himself from bursting into laughter, and an hour later at a café, he was still convulsed at the image of the "puppets I had just seen dancing before my eyes." By the next day, an enervating depression set in which persisted for months. Sometime later, his rejected mistress came in tears to beg his forgiveness, clinging to his jacket and dragging after him on her knees.[3]

This last touching vignette can be safely dismissed as a thoroughly implausible self-gratifying fabrication of Beyle's, no doubt encouraged by the situation of telling about an old love affair to a worldly male friend, where he would have wanted to present himself as triumphantly disdainful at the end. Whether the rest of the story is a fantasy, a heightened version of the facts, or an honest account of them is impossible to ascertain. The quality of stage farce of the anecdote is certainly in keeping with the tenor of Beyle's long affair with Angela, and if the revelation in the closet really happened as reported to Mérimée, Angela was easily capable of putting the maid up to arranging the whole voyeuristic occasion as a stratagem for getting rid of the importunate Beyle. In any case, his oscillating reaction, hysterical amusement followed by utter dejection, has the ring of emotional truth. If Beyle was not reporting the literal facts of the end of his affair with Angela, he was at least faithfully transposing them into a novelistic key. The novels he was to write would revel in such vividly theatrical contrivances of situation and would often brilliantly demonstrate how anguish and absurdity could be the obverse sides of the

2. *Correspondance* (Paris, 1962), vol. 1, p. 1241.
3. Pierre Jourda, *Stendhal raconté par ceux qui l'ont vu* (Paris, 1927), pp. 196–198, 214–216.

same set of feelings, could be different aspects of the same relationship. It was not the least of the lessons he learned through the long course of intrigue and emotional acrobatics in which he was led by this "sublime strumpet," Angela.

Meanwhile, Beyle was also pursuing the technical side of his apprenticeship as a novelist—though still unaware that the novel was to be his genre —in the art history, travel notes, and personal reflections he wrote during his Milanese period. By the fall of 1814, he was immersed in what was to be his second book, *L'Histoire de la peinture en Italie*. He continued work on it for the next two and a half years, though till his final break with Angela he was often too troubled over his difficulties with her to concentrate on writing. His sundry Italian travels, of course, were in part "research trips" that enabled him to see paintings on which he needed to comment. In any case, the amount of original observation in the book is quite modest. Beyle was for a second time getting himself up to the point of writing by climbing on the shoulders of others. As with his book on Haydn and Mozart, he was dealing with a subject to which he was attracted by sensibility but of which he had no real technical grasp. Mérimée was later to note with great justice that Stendhal's notion of painting was essentially literary and dramatic. The project had begun, we recall, as a translation of the Italian art historian Lanzi, and more than two-thirds of its bulk now proved to be a kind of compilation of materials from Lanzi, Reynolds, Vasari, and a score of other sources. All this looks a bit less like plagiarism than the Haydn-Mozart book because the accepted practice of the times did not require authors of compilations to provide reference notes, and Beyle, quite conscious that he was utilizing sources, observes several times in the margin that he does not want to fatigue his reader with references.

L'Histoire de la peinture en Italie—actually only a history of the Florentine school—was completed early in 1817. Beyle in any case had to return to France at this point to help his sister Pauline, whose husband had just died. (In November, he took her back to Milan with him for an extended visit, but now that Pauline—a plump matron rather than a promising protégée—was beginning to be a burdensome responsibility, his old sense of passionate intimacy with her faded.) He took advantage of his stay in France to deliver the manuscript to a Paris publisher. *L'Histoire de la peinture en Italie* appeared in July, at the author's expense, most of the small printing, like that of *Haydn, Mozart et Métastase*, destined to gather dust on the bookseller's shelves. The work was signed only "M.B.A.A." (*Monsieur Beyle, ancien auditeur*). Beyle had first thought of dedicating it to Angela, then to the memory of Alexandrine Daru, who had died in childbirth in 1815, but the first volume of the *Histoire* bore instead a dedication to "the greatest of living sovereigns," by which he apparently meant to designate Czar Alexander I. This astonishing political turnabout was another of Beyle's hopelessly quixotic efforts at careeristic scheming. He imagined that the flattered czar might somehow be persuaded to offer him a position as a professor of aesthetics in Moscow, though it is doubtful whether either the dedication or the work ever came to the attention of the Russian emperor—and in any case Beyle claimed to have a horror of cold climates after his experience on the eastern front. The title page of the second volume, on the other hand, carried a distinctively Stendhalian device, which he would use again, the English words, *To the happy few*, a perfect summation of the retreat into art, Italy, and the carefully guarded pleasures of private life to which he was impelled after the trauma of 1812. The phrase itself came to him from the second chapter of *The Vicar of Wakefield*, a novel whose early sections he had committed to memory as part of his program for learning English.

The chief importance of *L'Histoire de la peinture en Italie* in Stendhal's development is that it involves his own grappling with a major concept of European Romanticism: the relativity of aesthetic value, its determination by national character, which in turn is imagined to be determined by climate and geography. These notions are explored in detail in a long central essay, only obliquely connected to the subject of the book, which compares the *beau idéal* of the ancient world with that of the modern. Climate, national character, and a quasi-physiological explanation of cultural activity are invoked with a mechanistic simplicity that verges on self-parody. Thus, Southern Man, because of his warm climate, is said to seek physical repose: "Southern man, in his musculatory inaction, finds himself constantly drawn to meditation. A pinprick for him is more cruel than the slash of a saber for someone else. Artistic expression therefore must be born in the South" (chap. 100). The intellectual naiveté of that final "therefore" (*donc*) reveals Beyle as still the innocent disciple of the Ideologues and the eighteenth-century mechanists, requiring a mathematically precise system for defining the realm of the emotions and their expression in art. Before long, he would discover freer, less "scientific" ways to approach the precision of explanation he sought.

Milan immediately after the Restoration was a lively center for the discussion of the new ideas of the Romantic movement, both through its very prominent local literary exponents and through the openness of this cosmopolitan city to foreign influences. Soon after taking up residence in

Milan, Beyle discovered the *Edinburgh Review,* which gave powerful articulation to many of the ideas on the arts that he himself had been pondering. He became a devoted follower of the journal, repeatedly recommending it in his letters to his Parisian friends and dedicating the first small profit he realized from his writing, toward the end of the decade, to the purchase of a complete set. Reading Jeffrey on Byron in the *Edinburgh Review* was a revelation to him of the true nature of Romanticism.

Then, in October 1816, in the box at La Scala of a Milanese friend, Ludovico de Breme, Beyle met Byron himself, whom he admired as the greatest living poet. "I dined with a handsome and charming young man, showing the face of an 18-year-old though he is 28, an angelic profile, the gentlest manner. He is the original of Lovelace or rather a thousand times better than that chatterbox Lovelace" (letter to Crozet, October 20, 1816). For the next three weeks, Byron and Beyle saw each other almost nightly. Beyle fascinated Byron with anecdotes about Napoleon and the retreat from Moscow: one wonders whether he regaled the English poet with images like the one he soon after mentioned incidentally in *Rome, Naples et Florence,* of a hospital he saw at Vilna in which the holes in the wall were stopped up with frozen human bodies. Byron, according to the testimony of his friend Hobhouse, had a very good opinion of Beyle's judgment, while Beyle on his part found Byron a passionate and brilliant conversationalist, scintillating with original ideas, and, alternately, the captive of his own cool self-consciousness as an English lord (letter to Louise Swanton-Belloc, September 24, 1824). Though Stendhal acclaimed Byron's genius, in his own writing he would prove much less under the sway of the Byron legend than most European literary figures of his generation. The closest approach to a Byronic hero in Stendhal's novels is Octave, the tormented aristocratic male protagonist of his first novel, *Armance,* and neither Octave's suffering nor his noble sensibility is made to seem very convincing.

Throughout 1816 and 1817, which was the interregnum between the two most obsessive romantic involvements in Beyle's life, he was bustling with ideas for new literary projects. While pushing *L'Histoire de la peinture en Italie* to a conclusion, he wrote some short pieces on the nature of Romanticism, in the vain hope that he would be able to publish them in Italian translation and so join in the public debate in Milan over the controversial literary movement. He sketched out the first pages of an essay on comedy and laughter, conceived the idea of a life of Napoleon (which he was to work on briefly in 1818), and even began to fiddle again on that old, worn string of his, the play *Letellier.* But he was in fact moving away irrevocably from writing for the stage and from his Sisyphean effort to compose verse: by 1820, he would comment to Mareste, apropos of reading Byron, on his "growing disgust with verse," which he found tiresome because it was "less exact than prose" (letter, October 20). Meanwhile, as he was finishing his *L'Histoire de la peinture en Italie*, he realized that he had in hand what amounted to the better part of still another book. As early as 1811, he had toyed with the notion of converting the journal he kept of his Italian travels into a publishable *Tour d'Italie*. Now, with the sundry notes and journal entries he had amassed during the six intervening years, he needed only to write some connecting passages and to assemble his materials to have a finished book. He was turning over plans for the new book in the early months of 1817. When he arrived in Paris in May to tend to the publication of *L'Histoire de la peinture en Italie*, he also undertook negotiations for *Rome, Naples et Florence en 1817*. Terms were agreed on in June, the manuscript was delivered a month later, and the book was brought out in September, in a most modest printing of 504 copies. The publication went virtually unnoticed in the press, but this time the printing was almost entirely sold out, and within a year, an English translation appeared (an English version of *Haydn, Mozart et Métastase* had come out in the summer of 1817, which may have been the occasion for Beyle's brief trip to London).

   Rome, Naples et Florence is the first of Henri Beyle's books to bear the pseudonym by which he would become known to posterity. The title page identifies the author as "*M. de Stendhal, officier de cavalerie.*" The writer was probably remembering the Prussian town of Stendal near which he had been stationed a decade earlier. The *h*—to the eternal consternation of copy editors, undergraduates writing class essays on The Novel, and other wrestlers with orthography—was probably inserted after the *d* simply to make the name look more exotically German. Of all the conjectures that have been proposed about the choice of the name, the most plausible is that the author thought it might serve him as a political cover. Tart expressions of Beyle's liberalism, his contempt for the Hapsburg regime, his lingering loyalty to Napoleon are generously scattered through the travel book, and he seems to have hoped that presenting the author as both a German and a cavalry officer would persuade the authorities that the book was "safe." As usual, his infatuation with strategies of camouflage went hand in hand with a naiveté about what constituted an effective cover. The subversive passages were duly noted in the files of Metternich's secret police and their author identified; in the course of time, this record would cause him trouble.

Rome, Naples et Florence is the first of Stendhal's books that can confidently be called his own. To be sure, even here, for brief passages he did not hesitate to lay under contribution whatever from his reading seemed relevant to the task at hand, including the *Edinburgh Review*, Mme de Staël, and Goethe's *Travels in Italy*. This time, however, not only was the substance of the book his original conception, but the tenor of the writing —its acerbic wit, its narrative verve, and labile intelligence—was much more distinctively Stendhalian. *Rome, Naples et Florence* is a literary potpourri, part journal; part guidebook; part popular history; part chronicle of opera performances seen and art galleries visited; part compendium of anecdotes (a rather large part, that) with lengthy transcriptions of conversations heard; and part personal rumination on a variety of cultural, historical, and political subjects. Stendhal's two most recurrent preoccupations here are his opposition to the Austrian domination of Italy and his fascination with the manifold revelations and implications of national character. The latter concern, as we have seen, was also at the center of *L'Histoire de la peinture en Italie*, but national character in the later book is pursued more empirically, less schematically. Italy, as the imagined sphere of spontaneity, bold originality, passion, and energy, figures as an anti-France, the vices of the French rendered visible through the virtues of the Italians. (Two decades later, the same set of national comparisons would give *La Chartreuse de Parme* its peculiar double resonance as an "Italian" novel constantly sounding against the antithetical background of the French and their national traits.) The other exemplary culture for Beyle, England, is also frequently invoked, so sometimes a kind of triangulated vision is brought to bear on the Italian subject by focusing it through the optics of two different antitypes, France and England. Many of these supposed national characteristics were already clichés of Romanticism in 1817, but Stendhal is able to endow them with a certain freshness by the ingenuity of his juxtapositions, the shrewdness of his binocular perceptions as a Frenchman to the core and a Milanese by spiritual naturalization.

The voice that addresses us, moreover, through all this miscellaneous matter has a quality of ripe reflectiveness one would not have anticipated in so casual and amusing a travel companion. One can understand why the author of *Rome, Naples et Florence* was stung when his beloved *Edinburgh Review* criticized the book for its flippancy. In point of fact, even the seemingly capricious turns in the writing reflect a new, personally meditated seriousness about the business of living that Beyle in his Italian expatriation had managed to achieve. After discoursing, for example, on his antiaristocratic feelings, the narrator brings himself up short by citing the opinion of an acquaintance that he had a distinctly aristocratic side. On reflection, he has to admit the truth of the opinion, and if, he contends, there is something of the aristocrat in him, then there is nothing for it but to yield wholeheartedly to that aspect of himself. It was no doubt in such inconsistencies that the dour *Edinburgh Review* found the heinous flippancy for which it chided Stendhal, but the inconsistencies are in fact affirmed by the writer with a full sense of the existential consequences of his own contradictory stance. Thus, the narrator concludes this account of himself as an aristocratic antiaristocrat with the following observation: "What is the *self* [*le moi*]? I haven't the slightest idea. I awoke one day on this earth; I found myself bound to a body, a character, a fate. Shall I amuse myself vainly seeking to change them while forgetting in the process to live?" [4]

Indeed, one of Beyle's most winning traits was his readiness, in spite of his efforts to be elaborately calculating about his life, to give himself recklessly to the impulsions of experience. *Visse, scrisse, amò* was the device he conceived for his epitaph in 1820: to live meant of course to write but also to love, and within a few months of his return to Milan late in 1817, after the publication of his two books, he found himself more extravagantly and, in the most literal sense, desperately in love than ever before.

Matilde Viscontini Dembowski—usually referred to by Stendhal with the French form of her name, Métilde—was twenty-eight when Beyle met her, probably through mutual liberal friends, early in 1818. She had been married in 1807 to a Polish officer who was a naturalized Italian, and had two sons by him. Contemporary testimonies suggest that Jan Dembowski was a rapacious, brutal, and jealous man. By 1814, her husband's mistreatment forced Métilde to flee the marriage; for two years, she took refuge in Switzerland, keeping her younger son with her; she returned to Milan only when Dembowski had agreed to let her live separately without interference. There is no clear evidence that Métilde was ever inclined to take a lover after the harsh trials of her conjugal experience. Rumor implicated her in a liaison with Ugo Foscolo, the Italian liberal poet, with whom she had been friendly since the early years of her marriage, but in fact there was nothing more than friendship between them, as documents uncovered after their lifetimes have made clear. If she did have one affair, as Stendhal later believed, it would have been with Count Giuseppe Pecchio, another liberal friend dedicated to

4. *Rome, Naples, et Florence en 1817* (ed. Abravenel and Del Litto, Lausanne, 1961), p. 271.

Italian independence. Métilde's real passion in fact seems to have been directed toward political ends. She was a woman of great energy and resolution—qualities which clearly heightened her appeal for Beyle—committed to the dangerous cause of national liberation.

The years 1817 to 1821, the very period in which Beyle encountered Métilde, were the high point of activity for the revolutionary movement known as the Carbonari ("Coal-burners," the eighteenth-century guild in which they were supposed to have had their origins). The Carbonari had an underground network all up and down the peninsula, and Milan was one of its focal points. In 1820–21, preparations for an imminent insurrection throughout Italy were being made (there was actually a temporarily successful uprising in Naples in 1820), but Metternich through his Italian collaborators, in an elaborate game of double agents, intercepted letters, and betrayed confidences, was able to obtain intelligence of the revolutionary plans and to abort them.

The Carbonari were just the sort of political group to appeal both to Beyle's principles and to his sensibility. They had begun as an anti-French group (with the aid of republican French officers) in the last decade of Napoleonic rule, but they became a power to be reckoned with in their opposition to the Austrian domination after 1814. A clandestine society organized in cells of twenty, the Carbonari borrowed a certain amount of ritual from the Freemasons, and they were addicted to ceremonies like blindfolded initiations in which the initiate had to take a solemn vow that he would suffer death by horrible mutilation if he ever revealed any of the secrets of the movement. This taste for melodrama was accompanied by a certain Voltairean spirit of anticlericalism. The membership of the secret society was largely recruited from the aristocracy and the intelligentsia, making it very much a revolutionary movement from above, without much representation of the vulgar masses. What was even more attuned to Beyle's way of conceiving things was the fact that, especially in Milan, the political opposition was linked to the literary opposition as a matter of life and death. The neoclassicists in literature allied themselves with the Restoration powers; the exponents of Romanticism, like the poets Foscolo, Monti, Manzoni, all of whom were personally known to Beyle and who moved in the same circles as Matilde Dembowski, were connected with the Carbonari. Beyle's closest male friend in Milan, the lawyer Giuseppe Vismara, who may have introduced him to Métilde, was a prominent Carbonaro. It seems unlikely that the Frenchman was actually privy to secrets of the organization, but he must have had a vivid sense of the whole clandestine ambiance, and Métilde's involvement with the revolutionaries surely enhanced her charms for him.

Late in 1820, a few months before Beyle was to return to France, there was a general police crackdown on the Carbonari in Milan. Several conspirators were arrested, damaging letters were discovered, and other members of the movement were compelled to flee. Some of the Carbonari leaders were tried and sentenced in the summer of 1821, shortly after Beyle's departure, and meanwhile investigations continued. In 1822, Matilde Dembowski herself was placed under house arrest for a brief period and interrogated about money she allegedly gave Giuseppe Vismara. Predictably, she comported herself with strength and dignity through this attempted coercion by the authorities, and they obtained nothing from her. Her friends Vismara and Count Pecchio, both of whom had left the country, were condemned to death in absentia, and even the Frenchman Henri Beyle was declared a dangerous character for his dubious association with these subversives.

Métilde as a political activist may have been imposing in her courage and moral grandeur, but Beyle also saw her as the perfect embodiment of Lombard beauty, an evaluation not readily confirmed by two presumed portraits. In the tight-lipped expression, moreover, of both versions, there is an intimation of self-containment, perhaps of something withheld. What is instructive is the fact that Beyle chose to identify her visually with the principal female figure in Luini's painting, "Herodiade." The lovely Lombard Salomé in the painting shares Métilde's oval face, high forehead, prominent nose, and long graceful neck, but her features are far more exquisite, her highlighted face an image of radiant inwardness suffused with the suggestion of soft sensuality—as she demurely holds the bowl that contains the severed head of John the Baptist. The painting thus offers a more potent icon than Beyle may have consciously realized of Métilde, and of his relationship with her. It is also, of course, an exact prefiguration of his brilliant fictional creation, Mathilde de la Mole, who at the end of *Le Rouge et le Noir* marches off bearing the severed head of her lover.

By March 1818, Beyle was in love with Métilde. Toward the end of the month, he notes, as he will do again in the months to come, "battle and defeat," adopting the military terminology he had favored during his long, futile pursuit of Alexandrine Daru. But his involvement with Métilde had none of the cerebrality, none of the self-conscious effort to be in love that had characterized his campaign for Alexandrine. Beyle this time was quite overwhelmed by love, obsessed by it, at times virtually incapable of thinking of anything else. Métilde did not give him the slightest encouragement, was indeed wary of his libertine reputation, which one of her women-friends had maliciously reported to her; and after one critical moment in his pursuit of her, she even rationed his visits to her to one every fifteen days. With Alexandrine, Beyle had continually sustained himself on illusory hope; with Métilde, there was scarcely room for such illusions, and the best he can manage in his private notations is an occasional flickering glimpse of a possibility that she might after all care for him. But this was in the final analysis a desperate love accepted in the full knowledge of its desperate nature. On October 4, 1818, Beyle observes with great lucidity in a letter to Métilde: "I love you much more at a distance than in your presence. At a distance I see you kind and indulgent toward me. Your presence destroys these sweet illusions." Such clarity in no way mitigated his anguish at being separated from her. A month later (November 16), after having affirmed that he would love her as long as he lived, no matter how she treated him, he stated quite baldly, "I think I would give the rest of my life to be able to speak to you about the most trivial things for a quarter of an hour." As elsewhere in his letters to Métilde, what might in other contexts look like sheer hyperbole comes across as the immediate expression of the extremity of his emotions. "There are moments," he writes her still later (June 7, 1819), "during the long lonely evenings when, if it were necessary to murder in order to see you, I would become a murderer." If this is comically unrealistic as an assessment of what he was capable of actually doing, it seems faithful enough as a statement of the violence of his feelings. Beyle was caught in the tempestuousness of that Italian passion he had so long cherished as an idea, equally incapable of extricating himself or of bringing the love to fruition.

We may wonder why Matilde Dembowski, who obviously had no intention of admitting him to intimacy and who was in some ways discomfitted by his attentions, chose to keep this admirer dangling ambiguously for three years. Beyle in his mid-thirties, portly, rubicund, suffering from periodic circulatory ailments, already beginning to go gray in the hair showing below his toupee (in 1820 he would urgently request from Mareste a formula for hair dye), was less prepossessing physically than ever, though as an often brilliant conversationalist, a man of shrewd, experienced judgment, he must have been entertaining enough to have at one's salons. Métilde had none of Angela's theatrical coyness, but it seems likely that she, too, found the sheer extravagance of Beyle's devotion to her so temptingly piquant that she might not have wanted to be altogether rid of him. Such devotion, whatever its inconveniences, surely had a flattering aspect, and it might also have easily provoked, even in a woman of so noble a character, the desire to toy with the incorrigible devotee. One detects something of the latter motive in a particularly disquieting anecdote about Métilde reported by Stendhal in *Souvenirs d'égotisme* (chap. 3). His unattainable mistress once told him about the lover of a friend of hers who each evening, after visiting the true object of his desires, would go out to a whore. Only after leaving Milan did the real intention of the story dawn on Beyle: "I realized that this moral phrase did not in the least belong to the story of Mme Bignami but was a piece of moral advice intended for my use." As a matter of fact, during these three years of unrequited love, Beyle had become an intimate friend of the Milanese opera singer, Nina Vigano, whom he was free to visit several nights a week from eleven to the early hours of the morning, including those carefully regulated evenings when he was allowed to see Métilde. Nina's virtue, from what is known of her other activities, was far from impregnable, but Beyle, unlike the lover of Mme Bignami in the story, remained faithful to his mistress, at least as far as Nina was concerned. (He did, however, occasionally console himself physically for his frustrations with Métilde: at the end of 1819, he was complaining that he had caught the clap.)

Beyle had a gift for inadvertently turning tragic suffering into farce, a transformation that, under knowing authorial control, would characterize some of the most memorable scenes of his novels; and trailing after Métilde, he ended up stumbling into one of his most painfully comical episodes. In mid May 1819, she had left Milan for an extended trip, in the course of which she planned to spend some time with her two sons, who were at boarding school in Volterra. A fortnight after her departure, the forlorn Beyle, unable to restrain himself any longer, set off after her. He arrived in Volterra on June 3, armed against detection by having donned a new jacket and a pair of green glasses—the visual equivalent, as it were, of "*M. de Stendhal, officier de cavalerie*" on the title page, and no more efficacious. That evening at 8:15, just as he had removed the green spectacles so as not to appear too peculiar to his innkeeper, Métilde happened by and recognized him. Apparently, she was rather cordial in conversation, and that was enough to make him euphoric. He sent her two very proper letters in which there was nothing that could compromise her. She answered with a severe note objecting to the unseemly way he had chased after her. On June 5, while he was leaning over the parapet looking out at the sea, which, as he wrote her, "had brought me near to you and in which I would have done best to have put an end to my destiny," she came by again and was most distressed to find him still in pursuit. (In his letter, Beyle claims, not too convincingly, to have been entirely ignorant of the fact that she took a daily walk along the parapet.) Still another time they met, according to Beyle, by chance. Then on the 9th, Métilde sent him the following icy sentence: "Monsieur, I want neither to receive any letter from you nor to write you anymore. I remain with most respectful regards, etc." His own letter to her on June 11, in which the entire week at Volterra is recapitulated, is a tortuous effort of self-justification. In some 1,200 diplomatically chosen words, in which Beyle is careful to address Métilde respectfully only as Madame, he denies any intention of compromising her, explains that his seeming importunacy was the result of a chain of unforeseen accidents, protests the sincerity of his delicate regard as well as his love for her, and concludes with one contention about himself that seems completely convincing: "It is all too evident that a prosaic being would not have appeared at Volterra."

After this ill-fated appearance at Volterra, access to Métilde became still more difficult—she now instituted the fifteen-day waiting periods—but this most unprosaic of lovers, setting aside his green spectacles, manfully persisted in his attentions. He arrived back in Milan in late July after touring Florence and Bologna, but having received the news of his father's death, he had to depart for Grenoble on August 5. Beyle, consistent with his sense of estrangement from his father, expresses no particular feeling of bereavement. He had hoped to inherit a substantial estate, perhaps as much as 100,000 francs, but to his dismay, he discovered that the patrimony was weighed down with debts as a result of his father's agricultural speculations. The sum he actually inherited may have been less than 5,000 francs. His disappointment confirmed the resentment he had felt toward Chérubin Beyle since childhood. After attending to legal affairs in Grenoble, Beyle spent a month in Paris and was back in Milan on October 22. Apparently, he imagined that after an absence of five months Métilde's pique would have vanished and that she would at last be ready to accord his devotion the response it deserved. Instead, of course, he was received coolly once again, as he might well have expected. "This is a love," he noted in the margin of one of his books on November 25, "that lives only through imagination."

But still he could not disentangle himself. Through 1820 and the early months of 1821, he continued to pine over Métilde, in growing despair. Meanwhile, his political position in Austrian-dominated Milan was beginning to become uncomfortable. In July 1820, he was shocked to discover that a rumor was circulating among his Italian friends that he was a French agent. The following spring, during the counterrevolutionary sweep in Milan, he was suspected, perhaps more seriously, of Carbonarism, and his friend Crozet urged in a letter that it would be prudent for him to return to France. Though terribly reluctant to leave the city to which he had become so attached, Beyle concurred. By now, he was quite hopeless about Métilde, and he was also near the end of his uncertain financial resources. He imagined there might still be some inheritance to be wangled out of the intricacies of the law in Grenoble, and he vaguely thought he might obtain some remunerative post in Paris (letter to Mareste, April 1, 1821, and the letter to the same correspondent dated the next day in which he pointedly cites the English proverb: *The hunger brings the wolf out of the forest*). Beyle paid a final visit to Matilde Dembowski a week before his departure from Milan on June 13; he would never see her again. Four years later, at the age of thirty-five, she was dead. When he heard the news, he marked the date, May 1, 1825, on his copy of the book she had inspired and beneath the date four English words: *death of the author*.

Beyle had begun his residence in Milan after the fall of the Empire with the conscious resolution to enjoy life as a disengaged spirit. "Nothing that is done here," he noted in his journal on July 25, 1815, in connection with the Austrian rule, "can touch me; I am a passenger on the ship." The first two books of his Milanese period, as the observations (and borrowings) of a tourist and a dilettante of the arts, were very much the works of a passenger. But as we have seen, Beyle was imperceptibly drawn into the Milanese struggle to legitimize Romanticism in the arts and then into the cognate cause of Italian national liberation. Finally, he was engulfed by love for a woman associated through friendship with the proponents of the former movement and through actions as well as friendship with the advocates of the latter. By the end of 1819, in the final year and a half of his desperation over Métilde, he began to write for the first time in his life out of the most immediate and painful emotional involvement in his subject. His initial attempt to cope in writing with his difficulties was *Le Roman de Métilde*, a novel, undertaken in early November. His first piece of prose fiction, it was conceived as a thinly disguised account of his love for Matilde Dembowski, but perhaps because he lacked the imaginative distance from his material to elaborate it into a novelistic world, he was unable to carry out his plan, breaking off the narrative after a few pages. Then, on December 29, he hit upon a completely new idea and proudly marked in the margin of one of his books the English words, *Day of genius*. As it turned out, for once he was not exaggerating. *De l'Amour*, "a book written in pencil in Milan during my lucid intervals" (*Souvenirs d'égotisme*, chap. 5), is Stendhal's first thoroughly original book. By fixing in astringent prose the whole interior revolution that

Métilde had effected in him, he improvised a method for combining the cool analytic detachment of his eighteenth-century masters with his Romantic penchant for the extravagant extremes of emotional experience.

De l'Amour has no more "structure" than its immediate predecessor, *Rome, Naples et Florence*. It is not even a sustained essay on love, as its title might suggest, for it takes the form of a staccato series of notations, in chapters ranging from a few pages to a few lines, which define a variety of psychological, cultural, social, historical aspects of love and which intermittently illustrate the definitions with personal anecdotes (Métilde appearing here as Léonore, Beyle as Salviati, among other pseudonyms). One might say that Stendhal was preparing for his great novels by articulating here an analytic understanding of love which he would then flesh out in his fictional personages, but what is more important for his future as a novelist, what makes *De l'Amour* such an engaging book in its own right, is that he is able to express intensely personal feeling, sometimes transparently and sometimes obliquely, in a vehicle of seemingly clinical objectivity. The concise statement of stylistic purpose that constitutes all of Chapter 9 is a program steadily realized in *De l'Amour*; Stendhal's commitment to this program here and later definitively sets him apart from the more typical French Romantic writers: "I make every possible effort to be *dry* [H.B.'s emphasis]. I seek to impose silence on my heart, which imagines it has much to say. I am constantly afraid of having written only a sigh when I imagine that I have noted a truth."

The dry notation of truths, an ideal Stendhal owes to the *Philosophes*, to Destutt de Tracy, and to his early infatuation with mathematics, involves both a rigorous and an efficient form of expression and a fresh, vigorous way of perceiving things. To begin with, he tries to lay out his subject with a geometric orderliness and clarity, stipulating four categories of love; first five, then seven, stages in the process of falling in love; and a series of complementary or antithetical responses in men and women respectively as they experience the various stages and kinds of love. Obviously, and fortunately, this "mathematical" mode of discourse cannot be sustained very long, nor does Stendhal really bind himself rigidly to the neat categories he has established. He moves quickly into associative digression, anecdote, speculation, adhering to the stylistic ideal of dryness chiefly in his attachment to an eighteenth-century epigrammatic manner. The epigram may derive from cultural observation—"In England fashion is a duty, in Paris a pleasure" (chap. 45)—or, more interestingly, from introspection: "One can acquire everything in solitude, except character" ("Fragments divers," no. 1). In both cases, Stendhal repeatedly evinces an ability to disengage himself from received opinions, which produces a special shrewdness of judgment or satiric sharpness. Thus, he can approach a fashionable social scene with the "innocence" of a Gulliver viewing the court practices of the Lilliputians. (This is the same satiric strategy of creating an estrangement from the familiar—the Russian Formalists' *ostranenive*—with which he would render warfare in *Chartreuse* and with which Tolstoy, explicitly following his precedent, would render war, opera, and other subjects in *War and Peace*.) "Court ceremonies, with women's exposed breasts, which they display as the officers display their uniforms, this abundance of charms making no greater sensation, involuntarily call to mind the scenes of Aretino" [5] ("Fragments divers," no. 79). Indeed, the cultural relativism of Stendhal's two previous books becomes in *De l'Amour* a spirit of aggressively scientific detachment from most conventional attitudes. "It is from comparative anatomy," he observes in a footnote to chapter 26, "that we ought to ask for the most important revelations about ourselves." The notion of modesty, that is, and the rites of flirtation and seduction are to be studied as aspects of animal behavior, though complicated by the processes of civilization. He wants to know how the phenomenon being studied is modified not only by climate and national character, questions he had raised in his two previous books, but also by divergent political systems, economies, and, above all, social institutions.

This cognitive freedom from the bias of accepted thought and practice is perhaps most strikingly evident in his chapters on the education of women, in which he gives acute expression to the feminist views he had held since his early tutelage of Pauline. In *Rome, Naples et Florence*, he had voiced the provocative notion that women might obtain equality by learning to duel—since a pistol, after all, could be managed as well by a woman as by a man. Here he adopts a utilitarian perspective (he had long been an admirer of Bentham) to argue that depriving women of a proper education quite simply deprives society of half its potential for intellectual achievement just as it deprives men of real companions who could share with them more than conjugal pleasure and domestic chores. Some of his argument is drawn from Tracy and the *Edinburgh Review*, but it is made with a lively concision and an impetus of wit that are distinctively Stendhal's. These rhetorical virtues may be directed satirically at those who oppose the writer's argument: "This whole line of reasoning [against the education of women] comes down to this: one adopts it in order to be

5. Pietro Aretino, the elegant pornographer of sixteenth-century Italy.

able to say of one's slave—he is too stupid to be wicked" (chap. 55). Or these resources of expression may serve as instruments to focus empathy for the plight of women in society as it is presently constituted: "The debris of the charms of youth [in an aging woman] is no more than an object of ridicule, and it would be a happy fate for our women today to die at the age of fifty" (chap. 56). The feminist position that Stendhal articulates in these chapters of *De l'Amour* would have important consequences in his imaginative achievement as a novelist. In contrast to many of the other major novelists of his century, like Balzac, Dickens, and Dostoevski, he was able to conceive his female personages quite free from the stereotypes of the age (the patient sufferer, the gentle paragon of redemptive virtue, etc.), and so he could endow the most memorable of them with the same qualities of energy, willfulness, self-dramatizing extravagance, physical daring, and intelligence that he accorded his most interesting male characters.

In regard to the psychology of love, Stendhal's central perception in *De l'Amour* is the concept for which he invented the term "crystallization." Many Stendhal scholars have treated this concept with the sort of reverence generally accorded to holy writ; some twentieth-century observers may find it altogether peculiar, but it does come to play an important role in Stendhal's work and life, and it succeeds in illuminating one major aspect of the experience of love, though from a rather odd angle. The process of crystallization is imagined as follows: once the lover's attention is fixed on a single object, he imbues it with an endless variety of perfections, of luminous intimations of happiness; the image of the loved one, immersed in the alchemic medium of the lover's imagination, is magically transformed, like the bare branch left in a salt mine which, Stendhal tells us, becomes covered with brilliant crystals. (This central image, one might note, is not without its ambiguities in how it represents the love object.) Out of the pain of his love for Matilde Dembowski, whom he had "crystallized" into the radiant beauty of a Luini Salomé, and out of his protracted self-deceptions with Angela Pietragrua and Alexandrine Daru, Beyle came to the discovery of this notion, which we would now call idealization, without the clinically deflating implications often attached to that term in its modern psychological usage. For if he recognized that crystallization might well mean the flamboyant operation of the imagination on a relatively indifferent object, a bare ruined branch, he was also deeply persuaded that the excitement, the essential interest, in a sense the ultimate gratification of love were entirely owing to crystallization. Stendhal's conception of love here is in the final analysis solipsistic; later, as we shall see, after the end of his obsession with Métilde, he would have the opportunity to experience love as an interchange between two real people.

According to *De l'Amour*, then, any conditions that would promote crystallization are to be sought out by the lover. Stendhal even proposes that it is something of a disadvantage to love a very beautiful woman because not enough room is left for the operation of crystallization. Writing in the grip of his unrequited passion for Métilde, he argues that the real appeal of love is in the promise of bliss with which it kindles the imagination, not in the consummation that leaves nothing more to expect. In making this argument, Stendhal produces one of the richest accounts we have of the powerful operation of fantasy in love. And repeatedly he develops his argument with the sudden surprise of idiosyncratic perception that was to become one of his hallmarks as a writer: "The greatest happiness love can give," he observes in a characteristic, and famous, statement, "is the first squeeze of the hand of a woman one loves" (chap. 32). The extremeness of such assertions reflects in part the provocative strategy of Stendhal's rhetoric, in part the need to provide a justification for the long months of frustration he had been experiencing because of Métilde. In any event, the uncompromising stress on *imagination* as the essential element of love was one that would prove particularly congenial to the future novelist.

The defense of crystallization is brilliantly summarized in the vivid comparison between Don Juan and Werther to which the final chapter is devoted. Beyle himself, as we have seen, had aspired misguidedly since childhood to the ideal of Don Juan, first in its eighteenth-century literary embodiment of Laclos's Valmont. Now, able to bring to bear on the anguish he was undergoing over Métilde the lucid reflectiveness of a mature man, he concluded that one paid too high a price for being Don Juan. If the archetypal seducer exercised the "useful virtues" of "daring, resourcefulness, liveliness, *sang-froid*, amusing wit," Werther "open[ed] the soul to all the arts, to all the soft and romantic impressions." Historically, Don Juan and Werther represent the eighteenth- and nineteenth-century aspects, respectively, of Stendhal's imagination. One might say that *stylistically*, as a matter of literary strategy, he remains faithful to Don Juan but that *experientially*, as a matter of sensibility, he becomes firmly committed to Werther, beginning with his attachment to Métilde. The plots, in fact, of his two greatest novels are a kind of derailing of Don Juanism and the discovery of a Wertherian denouement: the protagonist in each case is made to abandon a boldly manipulative attitude toward the world at large in favor of a Romantic withdrawal from the world. In the shrewd contrast of these two figures at the end of *De l'Amour*, Stendhal repudiates the amatory code he had tried to follow since the days he admired the erotic *savoir-faire* of his uncle Romain Gagnon and his cousin Martial Daru:

What makes me believe the Werthers happier is that Don Juan reduces love to being an ordinary affair. Instead of having, like Werther, realities fashioned according to his desires, he has desires imperfectly satisfied by cold reality, as in ambition, avarice, and the other passions. Instead of losing himself in the enchanting reveries of crystallization, he thinks like a general about the success of his maneuvers, and in a word kills love instead of enjoying it more than others, as is vulgarly supposed.

By July 1820, the manuscript of *De l'Amour* was completed and mailed off to Paris. At first, Beyle had envisaged a little brochure of thirty or so pages, but with no need for padding this time, it had swelled to a work of over four hundred pages. To his dismay, the sole copy he had made of the manuscript miscarried in the mails, finally reaching its destination only toward the end of 1821. By then, Beyle himself had been back in Paris for six months. When the book appeared the following year, it was to be almost entirely neglected by French readers (though not by Balzac, who expressed his admiration and borrowed pieces for his *Physiologie du mariage*). Beyle was no closer, then, to success as a professional writer, but in channeling the frustrated energies of his personal anguish into writing this book, he had produced a quirky achievement of the highest originality, and he had prepared the ground, both stylistically and conceptually, for the major work that lay ahead.

X

PARIS

(Aetat. 38–44)

"I LEFT MILAN for Paris on the 13th of June 1821," Stendhal notes at the beginning of *Souvenirs d'égotisme*, "with a sum, I believe, of 3,500 francs, thinking it a unique happiness to blow my brains out once the sum was exhausted." At least according to his own retrospective account—he no longer kept a journal and his memoir of these years, *Souvenirs d'égotisme*, was not written until 1832—suicide was constantly on his mind during the first months of his return to France. He found himself sketching pistols in the margin of a romantic tragedy he was trying to write, finally resisting the urge to finish himself off only because of his "political curiosity." After eight days in Paris, equally depressed by what he saw as the ugliness of the city and its lack of real political life, he conceived an even more bizarre resolution, which he would record in code at the end of the first chapter of *Souvenirs d'égotisme*: "To profit from my suffering by t L 18." This has been decoded by the Stendhal cryptographers as a simple abbreviation: *tuer Louis XVIII*, kill Louis XVIII. Like the more extravagant affirmations in his letters to Métilde, these thoughts of suicide, or of suicide through regicide, seem serious, in that Beyle was able to persuade himself that he might actually be capable of carrying them out, but at the same time, they are essentially histrionic. Viewing the élan he was very soon to exhibit in Parisian social and literary life, one suspects that he was never really so "close to the pistol" as he liked to believe he was in 1821 or again, after another romantic disappointment, in 1826. But it must have been consoling for him to imagine the hand that held the pen could pull the trigger, especially consoling to fantasize putting an end to his own life by assassinating the gouty old king, "fat Louis XVIII, with his ox-eyes," whom he repeatedly saw being hauled slowly through the streets in a carriage drawn by six fat horses (*Souvenirs d'égotisme*, chap. 5) and who was, for this liberal with Bonapartist sentiments, the supreme embodiment of Bourbon mediocrity and political reaction.

Beyle's closest associate throughout his sojourn in Paris in the 1820s was Baron Adolphe de Mareste, who had also been his most faithful correspondent during his years in Milan and the informal literary agent for *De l'Amour*. Mareste, just Beyle's age and still a bachelor in the early 1820s, was an urban sophisticate and dilettante of no particular talent or intellectual ambition. He earned his living as a high-ranking functionary in the passport office. Stendhal credits Mareste in *Souvenirs d'égotisme* with a shrewdness and a mature judgment far beyond his years, though he is also criticized for his stinginess and his aristocratic snobbery. (The friendship cooled in 1829, for reasons we shall note later, and the intimacy was never resumed.) Immediately after returning to Paris in 1821, Beyle began to see Mareste twice daily. Rising at ten, he would meet Mareste and also usually his Gagnon cousin, Romain Colomb, around ten-thirty at the Café de Rouen for a breakfast of coffee and brioches. Then he would accompany Mareste to the latter's office, strolling through the Tuileries and along the quays, frequently stopping to look at the exhibits of engravings for sale. The moment of separation from Mareste, Stendhal recalls, was always a trying one because he was afraid to be alone with his dark brooding over Métilde, unable to tolerate the walls of his solitary room.

He spent his days, then, in restless, aimless movement, going to museums, sometimes buying a book that he would read in the Tuileries Gardens. At five, he would be rejoined by Mareste for dinner at the Hôtel de Bruxelles, where both lived. Then there was an evening promenade on the fashionable Boulevard de Gand, followed by a party of faro around ten-thirty at Giuditta Pasta's, the Milanese soprano, which would go on till two or three in the morning. This regimen has a certain external similarity to the leisurely routine of Beyle's life in Milan, but with none of the sense of spontaneous pleasure he enjoyed in Italy till his encounter with Métilde. Seeing the chic prostitutes sauntering along the boulevard and the elegant lovers vying with each other, he would be reminded of his plight; sometimes the Milanese friends of Mme Pasta would mention Métilde, and he would play away his money at the card table in a deep reverie; even reading Shakespeare he would find his attention broken by wrenching thoughts of the woman he had loved and never attained.

The most vivid illustration of Beyle's state of mind at this time is an incident he reports with extraordinary candor, and admirable "dryness," in chapter 3 of *Souvenirs d'égotisme*. "Love gave me in 1821," he begins, writing about his own intimate experience with the same verve and distance with which by 1832 he was rendering the experience of his fictional protagonists, "a most comical virtue—chastity." One evening in August, in an effort to cheer up the dejected Beyle, Mareste and two other friends arranged an elegant *partie de filles*, a party with whores. The four men had their choice of prostitutes, but the principal attraction was a slender, black-eyed eighteen-year-old named Alexandrine who had just recently entered the profession. Mareste went off with her first; a "frightful interval" passed before he returned to the salon, cast a comradely "your turn, Beyle" to his friend, and directed Beyle to the room where Alexandrine lay awaiting him in appropriate dishabille. He found her adorable and himself quite incapable of the act. After an attempted "compensation" (*dédommagement*) of a manual nature, to which Alexandrine proved disinclined, Beyle explained his predicament in as dignified a manner as he could and withdrew from the room. He was followed by the next in line of the four men, to whom Alexandrine, astonished by her first experience of impotence, promptly told what had happened. Gales of laughter sounded from the bedroom. The friend led Alexandrine back to the salon and revealed the secret of Beyle's fiasco to the others.

One must allow that they had all been drinking and that the occasion was one of libidinous amusement, but the harsh reaction of the supposed friends was twenty minutes of uncontrollable laughter at Beyle's expense. In his retrospective account, he claims to have been untouched by this humiliating scene, and that may indeed have been the case, for by 1821 his deeply meditated experience of love and its sharp disappointments had brought him to an inner vantage point beyond the adolescent self-consciousness about sexual prowess which many males never outgrow. "These gentlemen wanted to convince me that I would die of shame and that this moment was the most miserable of my life. I was surprised and nothing more. Somehow the idea of Métilde had seized me as I entered that room which Alexandrine was so prettily adorning" (*Souvenirs d'égotisme*, chap. 3). Because of the publicity of the incident, rumors of Beyle's alleged condition of impotence continued to circulate in Parisian society for the next few years, but there is no indication that he himself was much troubled by this false reputation, and before too long, at least one Parisian woman would be offering private testimony quite to the contrary of the rumors.

By the fall of 1821, Beyle himself contrived a much more efficacious remedy for his depression than the erotic measures his well-meaning friends had proposed. On October 18, he set out for London, not on a hasty stopover as in 1817, but for a full five weeks' stay. His chief desire was to see Shakespeare performed. He was prepared to do this the moment of his arrival, but the Bard (as for years he had referred to him) was not being played, and so on his first night in London, he settled, happily enough, for Goldsmith's *She Stoops to Conquer*. He had to wait till November 19, almost the end of his stay in London, to see the great Shakespearean actor, Edmund Kean, performing in *Othello*. Beyle was enthralled, though at the same time, always the amateur of comparative anthropology, much surprised to see that the English had an entirely different set of gestures from the French for expressing particular emotions. The excitement of enjoying Shakespeare in the poet's native setting helped distract Beyle, as he had hoped, from thoughts of Milan. Outside the theater, he did a good deal of strolling through the streets of London; observing people, housefronts, modes of dress, business, and eating; getting a sense of the spirit of the country and the peculiar pressure of class relations in this upwardly mobile mercantile society. Stendhal had zestfully resumed his familiar role as professional tourist, and this activity appears to have done at least as much as Shakespeare to pull him out of the despondency into which he had been cast by his disappointment over Métilde.

Beyle was accompanied on the trip to London by another tenant of the Hôtel de Bruxelles, Rémy Lalot, one of the three friends of the night of the fiasco in the Parisian bordello. About a week after their arrival, Beyle and Lalot were joined by Mareste, and the three were soon persuaded by an enterprising British intermediary to undertake another *partie de filles*, English style. Beyle in fact was not by this point in his life accustomed to frequenting prostitutes, but the first episode had been arranged by his friends to rouse his sunken spirits, and in this second instance, just three months later, he was, after all, a tourist looking for adventure. What drew him, in fact, to participate in the evening was not so much the sexual occasion as the idea of danger he attached to it. The women lived in an out-of-the-way neighborhood on Westminster Bridge Road, and Beyle imagined that he and his friends might be ambushed by sinister accomplices of the unknown whores, who would slit their throats for the sake of the contents of their wallets.

He arrived at the house on Westminster Bridge Road armed with two pistols and a dagger, but instead of the slatternly creatures he had expected, the three women turned out to be prim little English misses, and their tiny house was full of the accoutrements of an impoverished but terribly proper domesticity: Stendhal invokes the English word *snugness* to sum it up. Lalot wanted to pay the women and leave at once, but Beyle was delighted. When he went upstairs with a certain Miss Appleby, she shyly insisted that he put out the bedroom light, and she started with fear when he laid out his pistols and dagger on the night table. On the way over to Westminster Bridge Road, Lalot had taunted Beyle, "If you performed so brilliantly with Alexandrine in a charming house in the middle of Paris, what are you going to do here?" But in the event there was no recurrence of his earlier difficulties. For the rest of his London stay, Beyle looked forward each day to an evening of cozy retreat in the house on Westminster Bridge Road. "This was the first real and intimate consolation," he observes in *Souvenirs d'égotisme* (chap. 6), "for the unhappiness which had been poisoning all my moments of solitude." In keeping with the shrewd perspective on himself that he had attained by the time of writing in 1832, he adds the following comment: "One can readily see that I was only twenty-one in 1821. Had I been thirty-eight, as my baptismal certificate seemed to prove, I would have tried to find this consolation with the decent women in Paris who showed me sympathy." On the eve of his departure, his little British friend pleaded with him to take her back with him to France, offering to live on apples so that she would hardly cost him anything. Beyle's horror of encumbrances was evoked (he recalled how his widowed sister Pauline had threatened to attach herself to him in Milan "like a barnacle"), and he made his excuses. The episode of Miss Appleby, however, had restored his confidence in his own capacity for the simple enjoyment of experience and so had helped free him from his three-year-long obsession with Métilde.

Back in Paris, Beyle was now prepared to enter into the cultural life of the city with real enthusiasm. For all the hostility he had harbored since 1814 toward a France dominated by what he called *le parti de l'éteignoir* ("the party of the candlesnuffer," that is, the extinguishers of the light kindled by the Revolution which had flared in the national glory of the Empire), he had to recognize that exciting intellectual changes had occurred during his years of expatriation. The Romantic movement in France was in full bloom, and though its political allegiances were quite different from those of its Milanese counterpart, Beyle was soon to make himself one of its chief spokesmen. One important connection that existed between Italian and French Romanticism was the opposition of youth to age. The regime of Louis XVIII was something of a gerontocracy, a form of rule confirmed in the literary sector by the culturally conservative gerontocracy of the Académie Française. During the years of the Empire, crowds of bright young men had been drawn to the civil service by Napoleon's policy of "careers open to talents"; now, with many of the possibilities of advancement in the national bureaucracy closed, large numbers of gifted young men were attracted instead to literature. The bumbling, grudgingly constitutional monarchy of the restored Bourbons actually allowed much more freedom of expression than had existed under Napoleon's autocratic rule. (Such censorship as there was affected for the most part political rather than literary publications, and in any case, it was only in the misguided reign of Charles X, in the later 1820s, that some serious attempt was made to impose more stringent controls.) Peace and the concomitant free contact with foreign countries also encouraged a broad range of intellectual activity. Perhaps the single most important innovation in Parisian cultural life during the Restoration was the new vitality of the literary salons, which attained a centrality they had never before possessed. The testimony of Alphonse de Lamartine, one of the major Romantic poets, is instructive:

> Conversation had returned with the Restoration, together with Court, nobility, and émigrés, leisure and liberty. The constitutional regime, which provided a constant source of party controversy; the guaranteed freedom of opinion; the animation and liberty of discourse; the very novelty of this political regime, which permitted thinking and speaking out in a country that had just undergone ten years of silence—all these accelerated more than in any other era of our history that flow of ideas and that regular, lively hubbub which mark Parisian society.[1]

One of the few comparisons between France and Italy that Stendhal makes in favor of France—implicitly at the end of *Souvenirs d'égotisme*, explicitly in his journalism—is that in France alone, the homeland of Voltaire and Molière, the art of conversation is properly exercised. By the early months of 1822 he was becoming a fixture in the salons of Paris, except for the exclusive homes of the aristocratic Faubourg Saint Germain, to which he could have no access, and except for only a very few

1. Lamartine, *Histoire de la Restauration* (Paris, 1851), p. 347.

others, such as the circle around Victor Hugo (there was to be very limited and unsympathetic contact between the two writers). The most important weekly gathering frequented by Beyle, beginning in February 1822, was the literary-intellectual circle that met each Sunday afternoon in the loft-apartment of the art critic, Étienne Delécluze. The brilliance and diversity of the crowd at Delécluze's were dazzling. Regular participants included the painter, Eugène Delacroix; the leading poets of the day, Lamartine and Béranger; Sainte-Beuve, who was to become the most influential literary critic of his generation; the philosopher, Victor Cousin; the sculptor, David d'Angers, who in 1829 struck a fine medallion of Stendhal; General de La Fayette, who had been involved in 1820 in an attempted French Carbonari insurrection and who remained a leading force in the liberal opposition to the regime; the novelists Benjamin Constant, Balzac, who would later accord signal recognition to Stendhal's genius, and Prosper Mérimée, then a precocious young man not yet twenty, who was destined to become Stendhal's lifelong friend. In the heady discussions in the Delécluze loft on politics and literature, the self-styled citizen of Milan found a large measure of compensation for the more purely aesthetic splendors of La Scala which he had placed behind him.

Contemporary testimony suggests that Beyle played a brilliant role in the Delécluze Sundays, as he did at the salons of Destutt de Tracy, Mme Cabanis (widow of the physiologist whose work he had long admired, like Tracy's Ideology), Countess Beugnot, Mme Ancelot, and others. But his intellectual brilliance was joined with a madcap quality, a fondness for adopting outrageous stances—Beyle acquired the epithet of a "fat Mephistopheles"—and that tendency, only occasionally adumbrated in his earlier social behavior, deserves some comment. Mme Virginie Ancelot, who actually came to know Beyle only in 1827, transmits an account of his first appearance at her salon, which seems typical of his behavior in Paris throughout the 1820s. As an advance introduction, Beyle had sent her a copy of his life of Haydn, a work, one recalls, ascribed to one César Bombet. When he arrived at her home in the evening, he had himself announced as M. César Bombet. For the next half-hour he persisted volubly and inventively in the fiction that he was Bombet, a provisioner of caps and stockings for the army, entering into the details of the profit he made on each cap and the intricacies of competitive trade, rhapsodizing over the honor of his calling and its sublime usefulness to society.[2]

2. Pierre Jourda, *Stendhal raconté par ceux qui l'ont vu* (Paris, 1927), pp. 37–38.

Beyle had exhibited a mania for pseudonyms and a delight in role playing since adolescence, but his performances in the salons of Paris after his
return from Milan mark a critical new stage in his addiction to disguise.
The difference was made by the anguish over Métilde which he brought
back with him to Paris as a hidden wound. "The worst of misfortunes," he
remarks (*Souvenirs d'égotisme*, chap. 1), "would be . . . that these terribly
dry men, my friends, in the midst of whom I was going to live, should
detect my passion, and for a woman I hadn't had! I said that to myself in
June 1821, and I see in June 1832, for the first time, as I write, that this
fear, repeated a thousand times, has been the guiding principle of my life
for ten years. It is because of it that I have come *to be witty* [H.B.'s
emphasis]."

A large part, then, of Beyle's zany role playing is a matter of providing
himself protective cover. He was a kind man, sometimes even sentimental,
and above all acutely vulnerable; the posture he tended to assume in the
salons of Paris was aggressive, provocative, flippant, impervious. He was
prepared to be thought anything but his real self—an inclination which
might conceivably explain even his equanimity at his public disgrace in
the bordello: like Horner in *The Country Wife* (Beyle was certainly
familiar with Wycherley's comedy), he might be content to be laughed at
as a eunuch if that could keep his true identity hidden for his own good
purposes. It is surely significant that just around this time he settles on one
favorite pseudonym in his private references to himself: Dominique, a
name that suggests *domino*, a person wearing a hooded mask at a masquerade.

But apart from any need for self-protection, disguise begins to appeal
to Beyle during this period as a means of escaping a self with which, especially after his failure with Métilde, he felt sharp dissatisfaction. "I found
all faults in myself," he observes of his mood in 1821 (*Souvenirs
d'égotisme*, chap. 6), "I would have wanted to be another." The fantasy
of becoming another—in physique, temperament, cultural situation, and
personal destiny—is one he would play with till the end of his life. He
was, as we have abundantly seen, painfully self-conscious of his stocky
build, his inveterate corpulence, his coarse features, his scanty, graying
hair. In *Souvenirs d'égotisme* (chap. 5), he openly proclaims: "I would
wear a mask with pleasure, change my name with delight. *The Thousand
and One Nights*, which I adore, occupies more than a quarter of my head.
Often I think of Angelica's ring;[3] my supreme pleasure would be to

3. In Ariosto's *Orlando Furioso*, a ring which when turned around renders its
bearer invisible.

change myself into a tall blond German, and to go strolling thus through Paris." [4]

To be all men, and all women (for Angelica's ring is worn by the most provocatively tempting damsel of Ariosto's poem), to move everywhere unimpeded, undetected, with a godlike omniscience—these were pleasures that could be realized through the polymorphous perspicacity of the novelist. But what helped determine the distinctiveness of Stendhal's achievement as a novelist was the radical way he transposed his own penchant for role playing into the lives of his protagonists. In this one essential respect, Stendhal would prove to be the most modern of nineteenth-century novelists, for he would imagine Europeans after the Age of Napoleon—most centrally, in *Le Rouge et le Noir*—caught up in such a pervasive, compulsive round of role playing that the notion of a stable identity behind the roles began to seem problematic. And beyond the masks of the characters, as Victor Brombert has brilliantly shown,[5] he created through the ambiguous and fluctuating ironies of his narrators an elaborate series of masks for his own deepest sympathies and keenest enthusiasms. During the 1820s, the material of experience was slowly percolating through the alembic of the self before it would emerge as art: from the need of a wounded Beyle to avoid detection and of a defeated Beyle to escape his own aching sense of inadequacy, some of the most nuanced complexities of the nineteenth-century novel would be born.

Meanwhile, he was faced with the more mundane task of making a living. Any clandestine savings he may have drawn on in Milan were now exhausted, and his only substantial resource was the annuity of 1,600 francs from his grandfather's legacy and his always uncertain pension of 900 francs as excommissioner. Beyle still dreamed of realizing an immense sum from one of his books, as by this time Hugo, Chateaubriand, Eugène Scribe, and other French writers were beginning to do, but *De l'Amour*, published in the summer of 1822, remained almost entirely unsold—he later pretended to Mme Ancelot that the whole edition had ended up as ballast on a ship—and none of the books he wrote during this decade, including *Le Rouge et le Noir*, brought him more than 1,500 francs. Not long after his return to France, however, the opportunity was presented for him to support himself through his writing in an unexpected direction—as a journalist, chiefly for the English press.

There were several Englishmen and Irishmen among Beyle's Paris

4. The most suggestive general discussion of Stendhal's love of masks is Jean Starobinski's "Stendhal pseudonym," *L'Oeil vivant* (Paris, 1961), pp. 193-257.
5. *Stendhal et la voie oblique* (New Haven, 1954).

acquaintances in the 1820s. Indeed, another of the signal changes that had occurred in the French capital during his absence was the large influx of visitors, after two decades of hostilities, from Great Britain. (In 1821, more than 20,000 Englishmen came to France for stays of anywhere from a few weeks to a few months.) The Anglophile Beyle was readily attracted to many of the English people he now encountered in Paris. During his trip to London in 1817, he had made the acquaintance of a hard-drinking young Englishman named Edward Edwards. In 1822, he began to attend the salon of Edwards's older brother, William, who was a prominent experimental physiologist residing permanently in France (it was at Dr. Edwards's Wednesdays that Beyle came to know the great English essayist, William Hazlitt). Soon after, he became good friends with Sutton Sharpe, a bon vivant bachelor attorney, who would be his companion on a tour of England in 1826. Among Beyle's varied social contacts from the other side of the Channel was a certain Irishman named Bartholomew Stritch, who was the London editor of *The Germanic Review* and who had numerous connections in the London publishing world. In 1822, Stritch established a working relationship between Beyle and Henry Colburn, who had brought out the English version of *Rome, Naples et Florence* and who was the publisher of *The New Monthly Magazine*, *The London Magazine*, and *The Atheneum*. Through Stritch's good offices, Beyle arranged to supply articles on French cultural and political life for *The London Magazine* and *The New Monthly Magazine* —later he also did pieces for *The Atheneum*—at an annual payment of £200, or about 4,800 francs. The articles were written in French and translated for English publication, at first by Stritch, then by others. Also in 1822, Beyle began writing for *The Paris Monthly Review*, an English-language journal issued in Paris. Two years later, he began to write regular articles on current art and opera for the *Journal de Paris* and occasionally for the *Mercure de France*, the *Revue de Paris*, and other French periodicals. Between 1822 and 1829, Stendhal published over a hundred periodical pieces, many of them reviews or observations of less than 2,000 words each, all of them either unsigned or pseudonymous. His total annual income, mainly earned through his journalism, was close to 7,000 francs in 1823 and 1824, between 8,000 and 10,000 francs in his boom years of 1825 and 1826. It was not the career of letters he had imagined, but it sufficed to keep him in fashionable dress and to allow him to travel frequently, and in style.

The French originals of Stendhal's English articles have all been lost, and so the lambent play of his distinctive wit has to be glimpsed through the more deliberate movements of a four-square English prose style. Nevertheless, many of these pieces still make lively reading today, and it is easy enough to imagine Stendhal in our own time producing an utterly engaging monthly "Letter from Paris" for an urbane magazine like *The New Yorker*. He commented for his British readers on current events, political moods, and above all on new French literature. At the very moment when in France he was making himself the champion of Romanticism, he was free to express, writing for an English audience under the cloak of anonymity, his vigorous contempt for the intellectual fuzziness, the emotive effusions, the Catholic mystifications, and the aristocratic pretensions that so frequently went along with French Romantic writing. His judgments of his contemporaries are often acid, at their best witty, incisive, preeminently commonsensical in the eighteenth-century manner on which he had been raised. As a literary critic, he was very much a coolly pragmatic Don Juan in a crowd of histrionic Werthers.

Thus, he writes of Lamartine, "He . . . gave vent to his feelings in poetry, the accents of which were natural and touching, but, as soon as he wanders from the expression of his regret and tenderness, he falls into puerility" (*The New Monthly Magazine*, March 1823). And in the same article, he observes of Hugo, "His compositions are cold, antithetical and exaggerated. . . . His principal merit, in the eyes of his countrymen, is his skill in the manipulation of French versification. . . . But this quality is not sufficient to save his compositions from the charge of being supremely tiresome." The plot of Vigny's *Eloa*, an epic extravaganza about the fortunes of a tear of Christ, is summarized with great relish, and the reviewer concludes: "It will scarcely be believed, and yet such is the fact, that this incredible amalgam of absurdity and profaneness is most enthusiastically admired by a great city containing eighty thousand inhabitants and called the Fauxbourg Saint-Germain at Paris" (*The New Monthly Magazine*, December 1824). Chateaubriand, whose inflated style he had long detested, is put down with a shrewd epigram: "What M. de Chateaubriand has been all his life aiming at, is that moving kind of eloquence, which may be called *unction*, the power of impressing on those he addresses the persuasion of his sincerity; but he has never succeeded" (*The New Monthly Magazine*, September 1826). Elsewhere, unwilling to tolerate the abandonment of simple logic and quotidian reality in poetry, he takes Lamartine to task for scrambling the order of actions in the embarkation of a ship: "If M. de Lamartine is incapable of acquiring a truth so simple as the necessity of weighing anchor before setting sail, what on earth will he make of all the moral and political truths which are, as it were, the every-day current coin of conversation; the materials out of which the national stock of good sense is composed?" (*The London Magazine*, July 1825).

Through all of this journalistic commentary on the contemporary scene, Stendhal's ability to see precisely the soft spots in the greatest literary reputations of his day is altogether impressive. The most instructive case in point is that of Sir Walter Scott. Scott was the absolutely commanding figure among European novelists between 1815 and 1830, and at first, in his private writing, Stendhal expressed considerable admiration for the author of the Waverly novels. He became, however, progressively disenchanted with Scott, both because of what he felt was the political opportunism of the Scottish writer and because of many descriptive and stylistic elements in the novels that he came to see as otiose. (In 1823, Beyle received a letter from Byron objecting to a criticism of Scott made in *Rome, Naples et Florence*; in his response, the French writer firmly stood his ground.) During the 1820s, it was fashionable to set Scott on a par with Shakespeare, but Stendhal, comparing Scott's novels with the seventeenth-century classic *La Princesse de Clèves* in a French article (*Le National*, February 19, 1830), suggests, with prophetic accuracy, that by the 1970s Scott's supposed greatness would seem much diminished. He sums up his reservations about Scott in a single brief sentence that also affirms his own program for the novel: "The doublet and leather collar of the medieval serf are easier to describe than the movements of the human heart."

Stendhal, then, was repeatedly irked by the overblown style, the conservative politics, and the religiosity of the Romantic writers around him, but in their rebellion against the rigid authority of the past, he could still enthusiastically associate himself with their cause, if not with their manner of upholding it. A public act of sacrilege against Shakespeare, whom as we have seen Beyle had revered since childhood in preference to the rule-bound Racine, provided the immediate motive for his articulating a Romantic manifesto. In midsummer 1822, an English troupe, attempting to perform *Macbeth* in the original in Paris, was interrupted by a rowdy demonstration of French liberals expressing their resentment against England. Though the protest was actually political, not literary, Stendhal seized the occasion to issue a kind of declaration of independence for the French stage, setting the freedom of Shakespeare over against the rigid and anachronistic rules of the French neoclassical theater which literary conservatives felt were still binding in the nineteenth century. He published *Racine et Shakespeare* as an article, in French, in *The Paris*

Monthly Review in October 1822 and then, in expanded form, as a pamphlet the following March. Till this point, Stendhal had been known in Paris as an author of peculiarly peripheral and generally unread books, but *Racine et Shakespeare* placed him at the center of the French literary scene. His position of embattled standard-bearer was enhanced when, after Louis-Simon Auger of the Académie Française had anathematized the pernicious doctrines of the new literary sect in April 1824, Stendhal responded with a second part to *Racine et Shakespeare,* reiterating his earlier position and conducting a frontal assault on the superannuated classicism of the Académie.

The ideas proclaimed in Stendhal's manifesto were not particularly new: many were already in the air in Paris; others he had brought back with him from Italy. After two decades of futile wrestling in private with the intractable alexandrine line, he was able publicly to defend the idea of high drama in prose—a tame enough notion now but still daring in the France of 1823—and, more fundamentally, to argue for a relativistic and evolutionary view of literary norms. The power of *Racine et Shakespeare* was not in the originality of the ideas but in the vividness and polemic wit with which they were formulated. As Lamartine put it in a letter to Mareste, even as he expressed certain reservations about Stendhal's views, "He has said the word we all had on our tongue." This emphatic saying of the word for all Romantics is perhaps most memorably illustrated by the famous polemic definition of Romanticism and Classicism at the beginning of chapter 3:

> *Romanticism* is the art of presenting to peoples the literary works which, in the current state of their customs and beliefs, are susceptible of giving them the greatest possible pleasure.
> *Classicism,* on the other hand, presents the literature which gave the greatest possible pleasure to their great-grandparents.

While Beyle was deeply engaged in the battle for Romanticism in Paris and supporting himself chiefly by writing for London journals, he also found the means to maintain a connection with the third capital of his private spiritual geography, Milan. By the summer of 1822, he had moved from the Hôtel de Bruxelles to a building on the rue de Richelieu where the ground floor below his second-story rented room was occupied by the opera singer, Giuditta Pasta, then enjoying a brilliant success in Paris. He had been, as we noted earlier, a regular attendant of Mme Pasta's late evening parties; now he saw her almost daily. Their relationship was amicable, not amatory, its principal effect being to keep him in living touch with the magic art of La Scala. The most spectacular talent among opera composers of the period was Rossini, with whom Beyle had been acquainted in Milan, and with whose work Mme Pasta was closely associated as a performer. Beyle had earlier expressed certain reservations about Rossini, suggesting that at least some of his music was mechanically derivative of the always unequaled Cimarosa. The distance from Milan and the proximity to Mme Pasta seem to have allayed such doubts, and in January 1822, he published an enthusiastic article on the composer in *The Paris Monthly Review*. Encouraged by the success of this piece, which was promptly pirated by both *Blackwood's Edinburgh Magazine* and *The Galignani's Monthly Review*, Beyle proposed a book on Rossini (at first it was to be a more general work on nineteenth-century music) to the London publishers of his life of Haydn. He completed the manuscript in a few months, and the English translation, with abundant excisions made by the publisher without having consulted the author, appeared at the beginning of 1824. Meanwhile, Stendhal revised and considerably expanded his own version of the book, which appeared in French in November 1823. This time there were some sales, though not enough to exhaust the modest number of copies printed, and a rather favorable critical reception, which established Stendhal's reputation, if not as an authority, then at least as a gifted and passionate amateur of the opera.

In fact, *La Vie de Rossini* is a kind of chatty miscellany, like Beyle's earlier books on music and art, rather than a sustained study of its subject. Despite the title, it is scarcely a biography but instead a chain of episodic anecdotes about Rossini tied around lengthy synopses of the operas and abundantly adorned with digressions on the nature of Italian society, the conditions necessary for the development of the fine arts, the contrasting limitations of contemporary French society, and the inferiority of French music. By this point, through his four previous books and his journalism, Stendhal had acquired an extraordinary ease of manner and facility of production as a writer, without the necessity to borrow from predecessors. These resources, of course, hardly guaranteed a tightly written book, but without them, he would not have achieved greatness as a novelist, for his best fiction was to be written at breathtaking speed, as brilliantly sustained improvisations, and when he slowed down and took pains to revise, as a rule he faltered artistically.

The personal meaning of *La Vie de Rossini* for its author was as an affirmation of unabated fidelity to Italy, the homeland of music and passionate souls. (Significantly, shortly after reading the proofs of *Rossini*, in October 1823, he set out for a three and a half month tour of Italy. He was refused a visa to Milan because of the subversive opinions he had expressed in *Rome, Naples et Florence.*) This attachment to Italy explains the psychological necessity, if not a thematic one, in his repeated sallies here against French society and French music. In the salons of Paris and, somewhat differently, in his journalism, Stendhal was constantly wearing one mask or another, playing his endless game of *The Thousand and One Nights.* By contrast, in some of the passages on Italian music in *La Vie de Rossini*, he reveals his most intimate expectations of life, again conjuring up the dream of happiness which for him radiates from the art of Italy as he silently remembers both the joy and the pain of his years in Milan. "The fine arts are made to console," he affirms, and suddenly one hears an elegiac timbre in the voice of the forty-year-old Stendhal, the ventriloquism of the salon wit and the stridency of the controversialist and critic being momentarily stilled. "It is when the soul has regrets, it is during the first sorrows of the autumnal days of life, it is when one sees mistrust arise like a grim fantom behind every countryside hedge, that it is good to have recourse to music." [6]

Meanwhile, by the spring of 1824, Beyle unexpectedly found consolation, and more than that, reanimation, in quite another direction. Countess Clémentine Curial, the daughter of his old friend, Countess Beugnot, had, we may recall, caught his attention with her striking eyes as far back as 1814. Clémentine was married in 1808 to an army general and bore him four children. General Joseph Curial, though he showed great courage in military service was by the testimony of his own superiors, a mediocre man, and something less than an ideal husband, having the most banal twin penchant for housemaids and wifebeating. The chief advantage of the marriage for his wife may have been his long absences necessitated by field duty. A year or so before Beyle's return to France from Italy, Countess Curial took a lover, perhaps her first, principally impelled, it would seem, by motives of revenge against her husband. Henri Beyle, whose mistress she became at the age of thirty-six, was to be her first real passion.

From Beyle's point of view, the affair came about through the most curious reversal of roles. He had tended to imagine all the women to whom he had any serious emotional attachment as princesses locked high up in impregnable towers whose sheer walls he must attempt to scale at the risk of life and limb. In the case of Menti, as he came to call Clementine, it was not he but the woman who pined from afar, making him an

6. *Vie de Rossini* (ed. Abravanel and Del Litto, Aran, 1960), p. 392.

object of crystallization, not daring to confess her love for a full two years. They had begun to encounter each other at social gatherings in 1822, and Beyle, apparently still a little dazed by the aftershock of Métilde, only absently noticed that those remarkable eyes were repeatedly fixed on him. "In my stupidity I went no further. I did not ask myself: why is this young woman looking at me?—I was completely forgetting the excellent lessons of love which my Uncle Gagnon and my patron Martial Daru had long ago given me" (*Souvenirs d'égotisme*, chap. 10). But as Stendhal, writing retrospectively, certainly should have realized, there was no need of guidance from those Clausewitzes of the boudoir on how to conquer Menti, for it was she who finally made the first bold advance. Despairing over Beyle's obliviousness to all her silent hints, Menti, sometime in May 1824, approached him directly and told him that she loved him. This revelation was so astonishing to him that at first he seems to have been unsure how to respond. For on May 20 Menti writes him, in the most curious mixture of formal address and urgent passion: "Tell me, sir, how we can see each other before Monday, even for just ten minutes, because to leave for the country without having heard 'I love you' seems to be a sacrifice beyond my strength." [7] Beyle was able to produce the required *je t'aime* and to find somewhat more than ten minutes to devote to the languishing countess, for two days after this note was sent they became lovers.

If Angela Pietragrua, Beyle's last great requited love before this one, had been formidable by shrewd design, Menti was formidable by extravagant impulse, a good deal like Beyle himself. Socially, she appears to have been an eminently agreeable person—a devoted mother, a good-natured, charming hostess, often witty, much involved in literature and the arts. Some of her contemporaries claimed she was rather plain looking; others thought her beautiful: a bust of her shows an intelligent, sensitive face with gracefully feminine lines. The one thing that became clear to Beyle within a few days after the beginning of their liaison was that Menti was not only a passionate woman but a hot-tempered, jealous, mercurial one. She sought in their relationship a purity of passion so absolute that she was constantly suspecting him of indifference, or of infidelity, or of a mere fetishistic attachment to her body, to which he was giving such pleasure. Thus, she writes him in July 1824:

> I would like to spend months on end with you without being able to grant you anything; only then would I believe myself truly loved. As for the tours de force of a certain sort, I benefit by them, but I don't value them at all and

7. *Correspondance*, vol. 2, p. 783.

I swear I think it is because you have been too sublime in this respect that I have felt a little cooling-off in my own feelings. It has seemed to me that this is too vulgar a way to prove your tenderness to me.[8]

At another point in July, she writes him a considerably longer letter bristling with recriminations. He has, she complains, destroyed all prospects of happiness in her life, first cruelly fleeing her for two years, then "dismissing" her eight days after she confessed her love. He is, no doubt, eager to betray her with Mme Pasta, and Menti sarcastically urges him to return to the arms of the Italian singer since, after all, his love is the greatest disaster that could befall any woman. Her letter careens wildly in its vocative pronouns from an angry formal *vous* to an imploring intimate *tu*, beginning with a peremptory "It is I, again, sir" and reaching a peak of outraged passion with the melodramatic "You [*tu*] have been happy only when you were placing a dagger constantly in my heart."[9] This letter was written July 4. The lovers must have soon had a satisfactory reconciliation, for sometime later in the month he joined her at her country château, where she proved herself as flamboyant a mistress as his most ardent literary imaginings could have conceived. For three days, she kept him hidden in a cellar to which the only access was by a ladder that had to be set up and withdrawn each time. The countess herself, not willing to trust a confidante, brought down food and drink to her lover, even took charge of carrying away the chamberpot.[10]

Menti may have enjoyed flaunting in a letter the rhetorical hypothesis of a purely platonic relationship with Beyle, but her other surviving letters to him frankly reflect an earthy satisfaction with the physical passion they shared. Thus, on August 10, perhaps two or three weeks after the exploit in the cellar of the château, she acknowledges a note from him with the following lines: "Your little letter of Saturday has made me experience a trembling similar to the one your pretty hand gives me when it goes strolling over my old hide; you ought to lavish them on me more often." [11]

During the two years of their liaison, Menti wrote Beyle a total of two hundred fifteen letters. Before his death, he instructed Romain Colomb, his executor, to destroy the lot. The reluctantly dutiful Colomb preserved five letters and made his own summaries of others before burning the rest. From these tantalizing remnants, we can safely infer that the entire two-year period was, like these first months, a long chain of flare-ups, suspi-

8. Ibid., p. 790.
9. Ibid., pp. 790–792.
10. Auguste Cordier, *Stendhal raconté par ses amis et ses amies* (Paris, 1893), p. 36.
11. *Correspondance*, vol. 2, p. 792.

cions, accusations, ecstatic reconciliations, passionate and playful intimacies. On at least one occasion, Menti was afraid she might have contracted a venereal infection from Beyle and, berating him for his libertinism, threatened to break off with him permanently if this should prove the case. At another point, she thought she might have become pregnant by him; her resolution if this turned out to be true was no doubt just what he would have theatrically resolved in her place had he been a woman—to commit suicide. These two most Romantic lovers were so wonderfully matched that ultimately they were mismatched, too like one another in their fondness for emotional absolutes and extreme gestures to stay together very long in any semblance of stability. As Menti had been the first to kindle, she was also the first to cool.

By the end of May 1826, Beyle, who now was acutely anxious not to lose Menti, was on the point of recognizing that she no longer loved him, though he still somehow hoped that, after so many oscillations of feeling, some possibility might exist of reviving yet another time the fervid intimacy they had enjoyed together. In June, he left for England with his friend Sutton Sharpe, thinking to distract himself from his distress in a new round of tourism and perhaps also to allow some time for feelings to settle between him and Menti, with the wavering expectation she might be differently disposed when he returned. This trip to England was the longest he was to take, his stay there lasting two and a half months and including a tour of the Lake Country, Lancaster, Manchester, and Birmingham. On September 15, just before his departure from London for Paris, he apparently received a letter from Menti making it painstakingly clear that there was nothing more to hope for. What she may have conveyed to him was the fact that she had fallen in love with an officer on her husband's general staff. Whatever the precise nature of the communication, Beyle would later several times mark September 15, 1826, in his marginal notes and in *Henry Brulard* as the great day of "horrible misfortune" in his life. During the next few months, once more he was to begin describing himself, in his incorrigible English, as "*very near of* pistol."

His gloom over the end of the affair with Menti was reinforced, and no doubt ambiguously complicated, by another source of sorrow during these months. Beyle had become extremely fond of Menti's daughter Bathilde, who was by this time about thirteen. Just at the point when the lovers' relationship was pulling apart, Bathilde fell gravely ill. One scholar has suggested that Mme de Rênal's access of guilt over her adultery in *Le Rouge et le Noir* when her son Stanislaus becomes dangerously ill may be based on the countess's behavior during her daughter's sickness. Beyle, in any case, was emotionally wrung out by Bathilde's suffering (one of many traits of character that hardly accord with his "Mephistophelean" public image in this period), and after the girl died in January 1827, he was haunted by the idea of the death of children. Curiously, he imagined the elliptically reported death of Sandrino, the love child of Clélia and Fabrice, as the hidden key to *La Chartreuse de Parme*, perhaps because he may have been recalling how the death of a beloved child proved to be the bleak epilogue to his own romance with Menti.[12]

For a few days at the beginning of February 1826, Stendhal, motivated by rather special literary circumstances to which we shall presently attend, had sketched out a rough plan for a novel about a love which was, in a very literal sense, impossible. Like most of the writing projects he had till then conceived and many that he would contemplate later, it was abandoned in a fragmentary state. Now, on September 19, the day after his return from London to Paris, he immersed himself in work on the manuscript "as a remedy." The short novel, *Armance*, his first, was ready for publication within a few months. The writing of this book stands in a very different relation to his dejection over Menti from the relation of *De l'Amour* to the suffering occasioned by Métilde. The earlier book is a direct translation of his own recent experience into an idiosyncratic "geometry" of passion. As such, it is an odd work of genius outside generic frameworks and certainly beyond any contemporary readership. *Armance*, on the other hand, reflects the writer's recent romantic disappointment only obliquely, while it responds directly to certain expectations of genre and to the challenge of treating fictionally a subject currently under discussion in Parisian literary circles. As a result, it is a paler achievement than the earlier book, for the author is still trying to discover how to chart his eccentric way with the established genre. But in the gestation of this book, moving from the springboard of personal experience into the larger reaches of the contemporary social scene, Stendhal was entering into the literary medium that would allow him to express his vision of life in the most subtly compelling way. At forty-four, he was at last becoming a novelist.

---

12. The buried story of Bathilde has been ferreted out by François Michel in "Une Enfant à travers l'oeuvre de Srendhal," *Revue Hommes et Livres*, September 1947 (no. 14). See especially pp. 112–116.

XI

THE END OF THE
PARIS YEARS

(Aetat. 44–47)

ARMANCE began as a piquant literary game. The Duchess de Duras, a fashionable minor writer, had recently published two novels about "impossible" loves, one between a black woman and a white man, the other between a noble lady and a commoner. In 1825, to cap the series, she sketched out an epistolary novel which she called *Olivier, or The Secret*, about an impotent count loved by a beautiful young widow: he returns her love, even fights a duel for her, but, knowing their passion can never be consummated, finally chooses suicide. *Olivier* never actually appeared in print (the draft was discovered in the family château during the 1940s), but read aloud to a small circle of friends, it quickly attained a degree of notoriety in Paris because of its subject. A Parisian editor and man of letters with the splendid name of Hyacinthe-Joseph-Alexandre Thabaud de Latouche hastily produced a novel of his own about an impotent lover, also calling it *Olivier*, and published the book anonymously, at the end of 1825, in exactly the format in which the Duchess de Duras's two previous novels had appeared. Beyle was on friendly terms with

Latouche (who was soon to help George Sand launch her career), seeing him frequently at Delécluze's Sundays and at other literary gatherings. In mid-January 1826, he wrote a laudatory review of Latouche's *Olivier* in *The New Monthly Magazine*, attributing the novel to the Duchess de Duras—knowingly, one suspects, in order to continue the elaborate joke Latouche had initiated. A couple of weeks later, he made his first abortive attempt to write an *Olivier* of his own. In September, as we have seen, when he was confronted with the bleak finality of his loss of Menti, he went back to the novel, both because it was something with which to distract himself and because its odd subject, in ways he was hardly conscious of, offered a vehicle for his own feelings of desperation.

Stendhal's treatment of impotence in *Armance* has occasioned a great deal of critical discussion chiefly because of its virtual invisibility. Something awful seems to be plaguing the young, handsome, wealthy, aristocratic Octave de Malivert, but we are given scarcely a hint of what it might be, even the name Olivier, which would have provided the crucial clue for Parisian readers in 1827, having been altered, after some hesitation, by the author. The closest we get to a revelation of the supposed subject is near the end when Octave, engaged to the lovely, loyal Armance de Zohiloff, who adores him and whom he loves deeply and ambivalently in return, tells his fiancée that he wants to be with her always *but* —and plunges into somber silence. Poor Armance tries to coax the rest out of him, but all he can manage is the dark avowal, "I have a horrid secret that I've never confessed to anyone," followed by an explosion of convulsive movements in his facial muscles and then the entirely unexplained declaration that he is "a monster" (chap. 29). It is no wonder that contemporary reviewers found the novel merely enigmatic and bizarre.

Stendhal had showed the manuscript to Mérimée, who objected to the peculiarity of the subject, the vagueness of the execution, and to certain details that struck him as implausible. The letter to Mérimée (December 23, 1826), in which Stendhal defends his novel, offers an instructive contrast to the book itself because it reveals how explicitly and concretely he could think about the sexual subject he had rendered so obscurely. *Pudeur*, sexual reticence, was to become one of the often-noted features of all his novels, but Beyle personally was not in the least prudish: in responding to Mérimée's question about how Armance could possibly be so ecstatically happy during the brief days of her marriage with Octave, he is briskly specific about the measures an impotent man could employ to give physical satisfaction to an inexperienced young woman. The absolute suppression of such sexual *savoir-faire* and of any suggestive rendering of erotic activity in Stendhal's novels is partly a response to the demands of literary decorum and, increasingly, an element in his distinctive artistic design. In *Armance,* however, it is hard to see much artistic purposeful-ness in the extreme reticence, and one is rather startled to discover in the letter to Mérimée that Stendhal ever thought about the mechanics of Octave's honeymoon so concretely. One is led to suspect that the con-creteness is after the fact, an act of worldly bravado in reaction to the challenge by his friend Mérimée, while the novelistic conception of the subject was something else again.

Despite the incident of the *partie de filles,* which Stendhal reports about himself in *Souvenirs d'égotisme,* and despite one brief chapter devoted to sexual "fiascoes" in *De l'Amour,* there is no reason to suppose that he was especially concerned with the question of impotence. Some exegetical ingenuity has been exercised to explain Octave's impotence in psychoana-lytic terms (his excessive attachment to his mother, his apparent fear of women whom he respects) or, more recently, in the Lacanian recension of Freudian categories. Such analyses, however, end up chasing will-o'-the wisps in the novel, for what Stendhal did was to assume the hero's impo-tence as a given, never really trying to imagine what might be its etiol-ogy, and then to proceed to elaborate his fictional personages and circum-stances in ways that are at best only tenuously connected to the presumed subject. The first two-thirds of the book, in fact, can be read quite con-sistently as a novel of courtship in which the fluctuating difficulties between the two lovers stem entirely from her self-consciousness about her relative social inferiority, his moodiness and fear of being sought after because of his wealth. It is only after their engagement that one senses much need to invoke the impotence theme. The ultimate source of the problem in this novel has been shrewdly perceived by Victor Brombert: "A thinness of texture and a fundamental lack of proportion vitiate the novel, not so much because the author deprives the reader of a key to Octave's secret 'babilanism' [impotence], but because he transfers to his protagonist the private intensity of recent memories and a despondency whose sources are not rooted in the specific plight of the impotent young hero." [1]

To Henri Beyle in the autumn of 1826, despairing over his rejection by Menti, it must have been consoling to project himself into the figure of this handsome and noble young man, loved by the finest, truest woman of his acquaintance, yet forever excluded from the happiness of love by a mysterious curse. Indeed, one could argue that in imagining the novel

---

1. *Stendhal: Fiction and the Themes of Freedom* (New York, 1968), p. 53.

Stendhal in effect reversed the two terms linked by definition: impotence is conceived as a mysterious curse, but finally it is in the shadow of the Mysterious Curse, virtually independent of impotence, that Octave's life is envisaged. He is many of the things his author was beneath his buffoon's mask of salon Mephistopheles: solitary, proud, acutely vulnerable, contemptuous of the coarseness, the vulgarity, the basic venality of most men and women. His distaste for all the joys of this world looks like a rather direct mirroring of Stendhal's post-Curial depression in 1826–27, and the resolution of this fictional surrogate to destroy himself was the one reasonable way for Stendhal to act out the suicidal fantasies that had taken hold of him at this point in his life. In all this, Octave is so explicitly a Byronic figure that, at the very end, as he sails to Greece after his honeymoon, ostensibly in order to volunteer in the revolutionary cause, he thinks of Byron's early death and has a kind of hallucination of Byron witnessing all his actions. Swallowing a dose of opium and digitalis, he drifts off gently into death, loving Armance almost as much as he loves death itself, appearing at the last as the perfect reality-blurring consummation of his inventor's self-gratifying fantasies of suicide.

The artistic problems of *Armance* are compounded by the fact that the writer, in addition to this tendency to self-indulgent identification with the hero, evinces a good deal of scorn toward him. In the later novels, Stendhal would knowingly exploit a double attitude toward his heroes for the purposes of a satisfyingly complex characterization, but here the conflicting attitudes seem largely discontinuous. The novelist can rather too facilely see himself reflected in Octave as an "extraordinary soul," too good for this world, and in the next breath, without any dialectical connection between the two stances, can acidly criticize Octave's emotional extravagance, his hypersensitivity, his aristocratic snobbishness, his lack of energy. (How hostile his conscious conception of Octave could be is indicated in a letter to Jules Gaulthier [August 6, 1828], in which he brusquely describes the novel as "the story of a gentleman who resembles M. de Curial.")

Technically, this deficiency makes itself felt in the relative flatness and abruptness of the narrating voice, which is unable to bridge the discontinuous attitudes. Stendhal's later novels would work so well partly because of the constant presence of an urbane, subtle, ironic narrator who could mediate between contradictory views of the characters and set both persons and events in the luminous perspective of his own fine intelligence. In this first novel, however, there are only the barest episodic intimations of that central technical discovery.

Almost none of Stendhal's large circle of friends cared much for *Arm-*

ance, but he remained stubbornly defensive about it, insisting that the sensibilities of the day were too coarse to appreciate his novel. (It was only toward the end of his life, in the margin of *La Chartreuse de Parme*, that he would refer to his first novel as a "failed work.") Characteristically, he notes in the margin of his personal copy the opinion of one of his best Parisian friends, the exiled Neapolitan, Domenico Fiori: "M. Fiori says there is absolutely nothing good in it." To which he adds this rejoinder: "It seems to me delicate like *La Princesse de Clèves*." [2] Stendhal's aligning himself with the beautifully restrained artistry of Mme de La Fayette's seventeenth-century masterpiece illustrates both what is potentially innovative and what is actually abortive about this first novel of his. He shared with other writers of the post-Napoleonic age a new sense of history as a dynamic, possibly threatening presence, of class relations as a fragile and shifting constellation, of the subtle pressure of political institutions on private lives and individual character. (The publisher of *Armance*, rather exaggerating the hints of a portrait of society in the novel, subtitled it, for promotional purposes, "Some Scenes from a Parisian Salon in 1827," though the author's subtitle had been simply "Anecdote of the Nineteenth Century.") The prevailing notion of how to translate this new sense of history into the novel, a strategy Balzac was about to carry out with genius, was drawn from the novels of Walter Scott, and involved seeing character embedded in the richly variegated stuff of material milieu. But Stendhal, with his admiration for Mme de La Fayette, Diderot, and Laclos, was impatient with all the heavy paraphernalia of costume, implements, architecture, physiognomy, and landscape that Scott had bequeathed to the novel. The subtle truths of human nature, however profoundly determined by history, which the novel should reveal were to be detected in the movements of the mind and in the ebb and flow of speech, not in such physical trappings. This delicacy in the means of representation extended to style, which had to be chastely concise, perhaps even elliptic, avoiding all excessive specification and orotund emphasis.

The principal importance of *Armance*, then, is as a kind of manifesto of Stendhal's poetics of the novel—which may explain why he remained so stubbornly attached to this book in the face of all criticism. The trouble was that he had neither a clear psychological focus on his characters, for the reasons we have indicated, nor any sure sense of how to carry out his program for the novel technically. As a result, much of the action, instead of having the delicacy to which the author aspired, seems abrupt, jerky, or, as Henry James would have put it, insufficiently *rendered*. Thus, at the

2. *Mélanges intimes et marginalia*, vol. 2, ed. Martineau (Paris, 1936), p. 73.

end of Chapter 11, Octave's mother takes Armance aside and suddenly announces to her that there is something she has wanted to tell the girl for a long time. " 'You have an income of only a hundred *louis;* that's the worst my enemies could say against my passionate desire to have you marry my son.' " In fact, one does not readily believe that Mme de Malivert has wanted to say this for a long time because there has been no preparation for her startling revelation; it is one of several prominent improbabilities in the plot. But what concerns us more here is the way the narrator reports Armance's reaction to the revelation: "Saying these words, Mme de Malivert flung herself into Armance's arms. The moment was the most beautiful in this poor girl's life; sweet tears flooded her face." Here the chapter concludes, and though the conversation, after a presumed interval of overwrought silence, is resumed at the beginning of the next chapter, one feels that Stendhal has simply not found an adequate way of imagining Armance's response. The brevity, intended as restraint, merely produces abruptness, especially because the two short statements made about Armance at this moment are clichés of superlative feeling and action: it is the most beautiful moment of her life and her face is flooded with tears.

More generally, in *Armance,* Stendhal was struggling to find an appropriate vocabulary of analysis for the peculiar amalgam of the neoclassical and Romantic novel that he wanted to create. The Romantic hero by his nature and situation invited a language of extremes, of uniqueness, of vague yet intense emotional states, but Stendhal needed to define this figure sharply in precise and intelligible terms. The opening paragraph of Chapter 3 vividly illustrates these difficulties:

It was not only at night and alone that Octave was seized by these fits of despair. An extreme violence, an extraordinary spitefulness, marked all his actions at this time, and, doubtless, had he been only a poor law student, without family or influence, he would have been locked up as a madman. But in such a social position, he would also not have had the opportunity to acquire that elegance of manners which, giving polish to so singular a temperament, made him a creature apart, even in court society. Octave owed this extreme distinction in part to the expression of his facial features; they had strength and gentleness, not at all strength and hardness, as happens with more vulgar men who attract attention through their beauty. He possessed naturally the difficult art of conveying his thought, whatever it might be, without ever offending or at least without ever inflicting gratuitous offense, and because of this perfect measured quality in life's ordinary relations, the idea of madness was dispelled.

In the first half of the paragraph, there are several signs that Stendhal is floundering, that he has no novelistic apparatus for lifting his protagonist out of the dark swoon of Byronic stereotypes in which the character was conceived. Octave's violence is extreme; his distinction as well is extreme; his very spitefulness (*méchanceté*) is extraordinary; he has a singular temperament, is a creature apart. All that Stendhal's language manages to convey to us in the first three sentences is that the hero is not like other men, that he is unique in his perversity as in his nobility. It is the prevalence of such sentences in *Armance* that makes us feel we are asked to assume an intensity of feeling about the protagonist unsupported by any clarity in his novelistic conception. But in the second half of the passage, an unexpected perception emerges. Octave is a violent, driven man—with a perfect gentility of manners. Now he is a creature apart not merely because of the narrator's flat assertion but also because his facial expression as an attractive man, in which strength is surprisingly joined with gentleness, is interestingly distinguished from that of more ordinary good-looking men. The hostile hero's incongruous quality of *douceur* is at once a function of his class, which has trained him to behave with delicate consideration, and of his nature, which has a natural sweetness (another meaning of *douceur*) and sensitivity that stand in paradoxical contrast to his black rages. Had moments like this been more frequent in *Armance*, Octave might have begun to be a credible and engaging figure. In any case, Stendhal had made a beginning. Within three years, he would demonstrate that this play of unpredictable intelligence over character, occasionally glimpsed in his first novel, was something he could refine, expand, enliven, sustain into the lucent medium of a masterpiece.

Stendhal signed a contract for *Armance* in the spring of 1827, receiving 1,000 francs for the book. The novel appeared in mid-August, but by then, its author was far away, having left a month earlier—probably using his publisher's advance to cover expenses—for still another tour of Italy, one which was to last a full half year. He briefly visited Genoa, proceeded by water from Anzio to Naples, where he spent a month, and from there went on to extended stays in Rome and Florence. While Beyle was in Florence, he spent some time with Lamartine and, despite his impatience with much that the poet had written, found him a most agreeable person (this conjunction of severe standards of literary judgment and tolerant openness toward people was characteristic of him). On the last day of the year, Beyle arrived back in Milan for the first time since his departure in 1821. But he hardly had a chance to unpack his bags: the authorities ordered him to leave immediately, and the efforts of intercession by some of his old Milanese acquaintances were unavailing. Beyle tried to deny responsibility for the subversive *Rome, Naples et Florence*, but his authorship was too well known. The Milanese chief of police, writing to the

prefect of Vienna a few weeks later to alert him to the presence in northern Italy of this "dangerous alien," clearly enunciates the views of the
Italian authorities toward the author of "that infamous work": "Not only
has he articulated the most pernicious political principles but by slanderous
assertions he has seriously compromised the good name of several persons
residing in these provinces and in other Italian states and has even had the
insolence to discourse in the most damnable manner against the Austrian
government." Milan, for almost three decades the lodestone of his desires,
was to remain irrevocably closed to him, and in another three years, his
dossier as a political undesirable would interpose an insuperable barrier to
his professional plans elsewhere in Italy.

By the end of January 1828, Beyle was back in Paris. If he had any ves-
tigial pangs of consciousness over Menti when he set out the previous
summer, all indications are that they were dissipated during his long and
pleasurable trip. He still occasionally saw the Countess Curial socially, and
though the immediate pain of losing her had a mordancy he would never
forget, she did not become a lingering obsession like Métilde. Meanwhile,
his life in these final years of the Bourbon Restoration was increasingly
marked by a combination of social ebullience and financial flailing. It was
now that he began to frequent the salon of Mme Ancelot, who was to
record his antics as a social performer, while with two other hostesses
whom he had known rather well since the mid-1820s, Sophie Duvaucel
and Jules Gaulthier, he now attained a footing of comradely intimacy.
Sophie (who was almost engaged to his friend Sutton Sharpe) was even
solicitous about details of his wardrobe, and Jules, who had certain literary ambitions, was before long to confide in his judgment as an established
writer and by so doing provide him the impetus for a major project of his
own.

Being an established writer, however, in no way guaranteed his ability
to pay his rent and tailor's bills. The income from his journalism, which
had been relatively high in 1825 and 1826, became intermittent and uncertain. Henry Colburn, his English publisher, had broken off the arrangement between them early in 1827. After a year of negotiations, Stendhal
began again to write for Colburn in February 1828, but his correspondence in 1828 and 1829 is filled with recriminations against Colburn for
persistent nonpayment of sums owed. Just when Beyle was leaving for
his tour of Italy, the *Journal de Paris* ceased publication, and so another
significant source of revenue was cut off. In 1828, his excommissioner's
pension of 900 francs was reduced by half through legislation. Whatever
savings he may have had rapidly dwindled, disappeared entirely by the

end of 1828. Characteristically, he responds to these difficulties both melodramatically and pragmatically. On the one hand, he was once again
waving suicidal pistols over the margins of his books, and between late
August and early December 1828, he made out four different wills. On
the other, more seriously active, hand, he tried to solicit a governmental
post for himself, first as an archivist, then in several other capacities,
whether real functions or mere sinecures. These efforts were doomed to
failure until the government itself was overturned, but happily for the
impecunious Beyle, that event was not far off.

While a supplicant for financial salvation in the civil service, Stendhal
also continued energetically to pursue possibilities of supporting himself
through writing in a decidedly unsuicidal manner. In the summer of 1828,
an opportunity presented itself for the rapid production of a book that
had the potential of substantial sales. The previous year, Stendhal had collected a considerable amount of material for a second edition of *Rome,
Naples et Florence* which he was unable to use, and now the idea occurred to him to write a kind of sequel. In June 1828, his cousin Romain
Colomb, just returned from a trip to Italy, proposed a collaboration
on a new Italian travel book. This suggested to Stendhal an easy way to
utilize the material he had already accumulated. As things turned out,
Colomb was less a collaborator than a kind of research assistant for his
more gifted cousin.

Promenades dans Rome, which appeared in September 1829, was modeled on the earlier book in being organized as a series of travel-journal
entries, though in this case, since the author and his assistant were sitting
in Paris, working to some extent from notes but even more from library
research on Italy, the journal format, involving the experience in Rome of
seven travelers, was really a fictional device. *Promenades*, like its predecessor, is a charming potpourri of a book, lingering over Stendhal's cherished
ideas of Italy as the homeland of art, passion, and energy, to which is
added a new central stress on history and on how the cultural present has
evolved from the many-layered past (in a few years, the author would
actually take up archaeology as an occasional hobby). In this highly anecdotal work, particular prominence is given to the more lurid or mor-
bid Italian tales of crimes of passion, sometimes reported in gory detail,
involving ingenious varieties of poisoning, mistresses imprisoned in inaccessible convents, and so forth. Before long, Stendhal would give expression to these interests as a writer of fiction in his *Chroniques italiennes*,
and eventually, he would find a way to integrate narrative materials of
this sort into the fabric of the realistic novel in *La Chartreuse de Parme*.

Technically, the kaleidoscopic anecdotal form of *Promenades* gave Stendhal the opportunity to practice his unique gift of breathtakingly rapid narration, in which the revelation of essential character through action and speech is whipped out at us like a fencing master's rapier, almost before we realize that it is in motion. Thus, the entry dated January 27, 1828, begins with the following narrative, limned in forty words: "We were told the touching anecdote of Colonel Romanelli, who killed himself in Naples because the Duchess C. had left him. 'I could easily kill my rival,' he said to his servant, 'but that would distress the Duchess too much.'" With this agile ability to overleap the extraneous—and in literature, the extraneous often proves to be what is included chiefly because its inclusion is conventionally expected—Stendhal was ready to create the special narrative tempo that would set apart *Le Rouge et le Noir*, *La Vie de Henry Brulard*, and *La Chartreuse de Parme*.

On September 8, 1829, just as *Promenades dans Rome* was being published, Stendhal, his coffers temporarily replenished with part of the 1,500-franc payment he received for the book, set off on still another trip, to the south of France and across the Spanish border as far as Barcelona (along with Italy, the "land where the orange tree grows" of his boyhood imaginings). It is hard not to see a deliberate pattern here, for in the case of each of his last three books he had contrived to be away from Paris when the reviews appeared. Donning the aggressive flippancy of his social mask, he might claim to be indifferent to the neglect or attacks his books suffered, but his habit of absenting himself from Paris at the time of their publication suggests he may have been a good deal more sensitive to the reception of his work than he chose to admit. In this instance, the book actually received a good many favorable reviews, and as quirky a treatment of Rome as it was, it became a standard guidebook for French tourists, widely enough read to confirm Stendhal's reputation as an author, though, alas, not widely enough to transform his precarious economic situation.

If this whole imaginative plunge back into Italy helped rouse Beyle from what he fancied were suicidal broodings in the latter part of 1828, he discovered during the first half of 1829 a more immediate object of enlivening distraction from the gloom occasioned by his financial straits. Alberthe de Rubempré, then not quite twenty-five, was a cousin of Delacroix, married, like so many women of her class in this age of *mariages de convenance*, to a man from whom she was virtually estranged and from whom she would eventually be separated. According to Mérimée's testimony, she was a "very extraordinary woman," exceptionally witty, exhibiting, as her portrait suggests, a refined intellectual-looking beauty. She was full of "Romantic" caprices, adding an *h* to her given name in order to endow it with an exotic allure, and frankly addicted to spiritualism. Delacroix was to describe Alberthe at a seance, long after Beyle's death, dressed in Oriental garb, her head wrapped in a turban, summoning the spirit of "poor Henri." Around this time, she was actually having an affair with Delacroix, but he had the reputation of being a less than vigorous lover—evidently a prime consideration for Alberthe—and she appears not to have been very intensely involved with him. Beyle, Mérimée, and Mareste probably were all introduced to Alberthe by Delacroix sometime around the beginning of 1829. By February, as Beyle reveals in his marginalia, he was in love with her. For the next four months, reverting to his old style of amatory behavior, he pined for Alberthe, repeatedly asked himself whether he was making any headway with her, and was seized— no doubt with good reason—by fits of jealousy. He repeatedly complained of being unable to concentrate on correcting the proofs of *Promenades dans Rome* because of his preoccupation with her. Finally, he settled on the stratagem of making Alberthe herself jealous by pretending to pay court to Mme Ancelot—a tactic he would pass on to Julien in *Le Rouge et le Noir*. Whether this deception was really successful, as Beyle persuaded himself, or whether "Mme Azur" (Alberthe lived on rue Bleue) simply became curious, then actively enough interested in him to accord him a place among her lovers, on June 21 he achieved the "triumph" he had longed for. On that date, he notes in one of his little marginal cryptograms: *"no p by wa and hap. Ever Sanscrit."* That is, no proofreading because of [victory in this amatory] war and happiness." Sanscrit was Beyle's other private designation for Mme Azur because of her interest in spiritualism and Eastern mysticism.

From June 21 onward, it was, to judge by the hints that have come down to us, a torrid summer between the two, partaking a good deal more of what is classified in *De l'Amour* as physical love than of any crystallized intensity of imagination. Alberthe was uninhibited enough to boast in public of the athletic performance of this most unathletic-looking lover, thus finally scotching the reputation of impotence that rumor had attached to Beyle since 1822. He on his part committed a graver indiscretion by praising his mistress too warmly to his friend Mérimée. The younger man, who prided himself on his sexual knowingness, decided that Alberthe deserved investigation, and the result was a four-day affair which ended when the fastidious Mérimée was put off by the sight of Alberthe with her stockings rolled down to her ankles. Some biographers believe, on rather slender evidence, that Beyle's three-month expedition to the South in the fall of 1829 was a stratagem intended to rekindle by his absence Alberthe's erratically flickering passion. But perhaps he may have simply thought, not unreasonably, that she was a good woman to get away from for a while and that it would be easier to see how to proceed with her after a separation.

When he returned to Paris at the end of November, he discovered that there was nowhere left to proceed: he had been supplanted by his friend Mareste: (One readily sees that, between seances, Sanscrit was a women who got around.) Beyle and Alberthe renewed their liaison for a few days in January 1830, but to everyone's surprise, she was actually becoming faithful to Mareste—or at any rate, faithful in her fashion, if one credits the gossip about her activities as a sexual tease which Mérimée later reported in his letters—and she and Mareste were to remain lovers till the end of his life. Though Beyle does not seem to have been deeply wounded by the loss of Alberthe, he clearly regarded Mareste's actions as a betrayal of their friendship, and he soon found an occasion to quarrel with the man who had been his most frequent companion since 1821, and he even ceased his nine-year-long attendance at the Café Rouen in order to avoid Mareste. As for Alberthe herself, in retrospect he did not cherish any very kindly feelings toward her. At one point in *Henry Brulard*, after referring to her as Mme Azur, he is unable, or affects not to be able, to remember her real name, and in the same book, in his *catalogue raisonné* of mistresses, after describing Angela Pietragrua as a "sublime strumpet," he classifies Alberthe as an "unsublime strumpet, in the style of Mme Du Barry."

There is a crescendo movement in Beyle's life during these last months of the Restoration. After the completion of *Armance*, followed a year and a half later by *Promenades dans Rome*, he rapidly builds momentum in his newly discovered vocation as a writer of fiction. Between late 1829 and the spring of 1830, he produced three substantial stories for periodical publication, "Vanina Vanini," "Le Philtre," and "Le Coffre et le revenant." After the airless French aristocratic milieu of *Armance*, all three tales give expression to the "Hispanic" side of Stendhal's sensibility—"Le Coffre et le revenant" is actually set in Spain; "Le Philtre" has a passionate Spanish heroine; and "Vanina Vanini," the strongest of the three pieces, is the story of a young Roman noblewoman prepared to sacrifice anything for the Carbonaro she loves, even his revolutionary comrades. These tales abound in drawn daggers, disguises, midnight escapes, and other obligatory touches of dash and fire, but this flamboyant matter is conveyed in

Stendhal's astringent style, and he now demonstrates a deftness in the management of swift-paced narration hardly evident in *Armance*. At the same time, in Marseilles during his trip through the South in the fall of 1829, he conceived the idea for an ambitious new novel which he called *Julien*, and in the rhythm of sudden bursts of work that was becoming habitual, he wrote an entire first draft during his month's stay in the Mediterranean port city. A year later, the book would be published as *Le Rouge et le Noir*.

There is a similar movement of acceleration in Beyle's romantic involvements. In mid-January 1830, as we just noted, he enjoyed for the last time —vengefully? nostalgically?—the favors of Alberthe, but by January 21, he was noting the "astonishing reception" given him by Giulia Rinieri, whom he had known and liked since 1827 but whom he had never really thought of pursuing. Within a few days, he realized with growing amazement that her attachment to him was entirely serious and perhaps a little reckless. Giulia Rinieri was a patrician Sienese, at this time about twenty-nine, who was residing in Paris as the unofficial ward of Daniello Berlinghieri, the minister of the Court of Tuscany to the Court of France. Berlinghieri passed her off as his niece, but his real relation to her, avuncular at best in a somewhat ambiguous way, was as the *cavaliere servente* of her deceased mother. It is something of a puzzle why such an elegant-looking, lively woman of noble family should have remained unmarried at what was, for this period, a very advanced age. Perhaps the jealous vigilance of Berlinghieri, a little man with dangling simian arms, a pock-marked, long-nosed face like a caricature, and the charm and intelligence of a gifted diplomat, may have deterred suitors. In any case, Giulia, like Menti before, was drawn to Beyle without any encouragement on his part, gave him the first clear indication of her feelings on January 21, and by January 27 made an explicit declaration of her love.

After a lifetime of ingenious efforts to overcome the limitations of his physical appearance, Beyle was discovering that he possessed a quality of "brilliance" in women's eyes which he had not in the least imagined. As he amusingly puts it—and surely he himself was amused by all this—in a note in the margin of *Promenades dans Rome*, in his usual mixture of French and mangled English, "At last Dominique views *love as a lion terrible only at forty seven!*" To be sure, if Giulia on her part perceived a ripple of leonine splendor in Beyle, she did not deceive herself that it had anything to do with his physique. On February 3, she made him a "singular avowal of love" in the following words, which he duly noted in his marginalia: "I am perfectly aware, and have been for quite some time, that you are old and ugly"—whereupon she charmingly kissed him.

Giulia accompanied her avowals of love with an urgent request to become Beyle's mistress, but here he hesitated and, in another reversal of conventional roles, asked her for a couple of months to think things over. Getting involved with a married woman estranged from her husband was normal enough behavior for a man of the world, and had nothing dishonorable about it, but to become the lover of an unmarried woman of good family and, so it would seem, a virgin besides was quite another matter. Some skeptical analysts have questioned Giulia's motives, and her innocence, suggesting that she was on the rebound from an affair with a member of the Tuscan legation or that at the age of twenty-nine she sought out Beyle because she was nervous about getting married. A decade later, however, Beyle would explicitly note in the margin of *Chartreuse* that he had taken Giulia's virginity, a technical fact he was too experienced to have been mistaken about and which, in the privacy of a marginalium, he would have had no special motive merely to invent. If the testimony in the margin of *Chartreuse* is to be believed, then, the legation lover who was supposed to have preceded Beyle could have been at most no more than a flirtation. As for the hypothesis of fear of spinsterhood, surely the worst course that a respectable woman with marriage in mind could have chosen would have been to offer herself to an aging, impecunious French writer with a history of libertinism. The ostensibly naive assumption about Giulia finally is the most plausible one: that she was completely captivated by Beyle—age, ugliness, warts, and all—and that against all prudential considerations, she ardently desired to consummate her love. By March 22, Beyle apparently had come to the conclusion that Giulia's passion was more than a fleeting virginal infatuation, and by then, his own feelings were deeply engaged.

Their affair flowered through the spring and into the summer, as Beyle revised the manuscript, then began to correct the proofs, of *Le Rouge et le Noir*, and as Charles X's increasing defiance of parliamentary prerogatives and freedom of the press pushed the Bourbon government to the brink of disaster. On July 26 and 27, in response to royal ordinances banning the publication of all newspapers without prior authorization, workers and students began the first street demonstrations. By July 28, barricades had been set up, and there were open gun battles: Beyle, reading the *Mémorial de Sainte-Hélène* (the account of Napoleon that was Julien Sorel's private Bible), watched the gunfire from the window of his room on the rue de Richelieu. On the 29th, he went to spend the night with Giulia in order to protect her in the midst of the revolutionary violence. Such tender solicitude would continue to mark their relationship, though the rush of public events was about to separate them.

Beyle was elated to see the revolutionary tricolor flags again flying in the streets of Paris and was exhilarated to be rid at last of the detested Bourbons. He was also quick to realize that the establishment of the constitutional July Monarchy might open professional vistas for a notorious liberal like himself. As early as August 3, he was soliciting the provisional minister of the interior, Guizot, for a prefecture, and by the end of the month, he had settled on the idea of a consulate in one of the more agreeable Italian cities. His friends Mme de Tracy and Domenico Fiori both exerted their influence on his behalf, and on September 25, he received the appointment as French consul at Trieste. It was a rather out-of-the-way location, in a place he had never seen—Naples or Genoa was more what he had had in mind—but it might prove to have its attractions, and at 15,000 francs a year, it was a good deal better than hanging on in Paris without resources. He promptly began extending invitations to Mérimée, Delacroix, even to Sainte-Beuve to come stay as his guests at the consulate in Trieste. Beyle set out for his new post on November 6, not having had time to correct the last batch of proofs of *Le Rouge et le Noir*.

On the day of his departure, in an act entirely consistent with his initial hesitation and subsequent delicacy of feeling toward Giulia Rinieri, he submitted a letter to Daniello Berlinghieri asking for her hand in marriage. The three brief paragraphs of the letter are a model of candor, tact, and consideration. Beyle says he is speaking as "one honorable man to another" (*en hônnete homme à un hônnete homme*). He admits his poverty, renounces all claim to the young lady's fortune, frankly confesses, "I consider it a miracle to have been able to be loved at the age of forty-seven." He has no intention of depriving Signor Berlinghieri of his niece's devoted presence—the possessiveness of the diminutive minister is something he obviously knew he had to contend with—and to that end, he actually proposes that after marriage Giulia should continue to live six months of the year with her uncle.

Berlinghieri responded at once with an elegantly polite letter in which, as a skillful diplomat, he seemed to be saying that the decision was entirely Giulia's, that his only objection to the proposed union was the time needed for reflection before so serious a step should be taken. The polite deferral was in fact a refusal, and Giulia seems after all to have felt dependent on her guardian's approval. Three years later, she was made party to a more socially suitable match, a cousin who soon after was also attached to the Tuscan legation in Paris. The couple moved back to Italy —to Florence—in 1838, after the death of the proprietary Berlinghieri. As for Beyle, his liaison with Giulia was the least tempestuous, the least theatrical, the kindest, and the most responsible of all his loves; and despite her marriage, he and Giulia would maintain intimate relations as long as he lived.

At this moment in November 1830, as Beyle headed southward toward Italy, his life had arrived at a triple culmination, though two of these dreams on the point of realization would elude him, and the fulfillment of the third would not be definitely recognized, even by him. He had at last found a splendid woman who loved him passionately and faithfully and who was unencumbered by previous attachments—he was of course ignorant of the letter from Berlinghieri that was following him into Italy. And he had at last secured a comfortable position in a picturesque Italian city —though his recent difficulties with the Austrian authorities in Milan should have alerted him, he did not suspect the trouble that was awaiting him in Trieste. Meanwhile, a week after his departure, *Le Rouge et le Noir* was published in Paris. He was clearly aware that it was finer than anything he had previously written, but with the scant confirmation he was to get from his contemporaries, he had no sure way of knowing that what he had done, after thirty years of misdirected longings for literary greatness, was to produce one of the most boldly original masterworks of European fiction.

Stendhal had begun his career as a writer by borrowing unabashedly from the work of others. In discovering himself as a novelist, he adopted a procedure which was superficially similar but qualitatively different: in each of his novels, he took a given anecdotal kernel and elaborated it into a fictional world uniquely his own. For *Le Rouge et le Noir*, he actually drew on three anecdotes, a central one and its approximate double, and a secondary anecdote which suggested certain ways of developing one of the three principal characters. Always avid for stories in which the "Italian" qualities of energy, passion, and daring were exhibited, he had recounted in *Promenades dans Rome* the recent case of a Pyrenean cabinetmaker named Laffargue who had murdered his mistress. Then, probably not till 1829, foraging in the back issues of the sensationalistic *Gazette des Tribunaux*, where he had found the account of the Laffargue affair, he came across a more complex version of such a crime of passion, which had taken place in 1827 in his native region of Isère. Antoine Berthet, the son of a poor workman and intermittently a student of theology, had been engaged by a local family as a resident tutor and had become the lover of his pupils' hitherto virtuous mother, a woman twelve years his senior. Discharged from this post, after an interval at the theological seminary of Grenoble, he obtained another position as tutor, became involved with the daughter of the house, was once again sent packing, and, outraged, fired a pistol at his first mistress as she was kneeling in prayer in church. For this act, he was tried, sentenced, and guillotined. This sequence of events, of course, gave Stendhal the essential plot of *Le Rouge et le Noir*, which he then enriched, in order to define the character of Antoine/Julien's second mistress, with a story that was the gossip of Paris in the early months of 1830, concerning Marie de Neuville, a headstrong young aristocrat proudly indifferent to social convention who had run off to London with a lover.

As a novelist, Stendhal obviously exercised the greatest freedom not only in inventing the details to flesh out his main skeletal anecdote but also in redeploying elements of the "given" plot to suit his purposes. He displaces the story geographically to the Franche-Comté region, then rearranges its components so that he can trace Julien's progress in roughly symmetrical thirds from small town to provincial capital to Paris and, in terms of milieu, from bourgeois domicile to church institution—the seminary at Besançon—to aristocratic mansion. (It is quite possible that this tripartite social and geographical scheme was suggested to him by *Tom Jones*, a novel he by now ardently admired, in which the hero's adventures advance in perfect symmetrical units, six books each, from country manor to the road and then to London, concluding, as does *Le Rouge et le Noir*, with a return to the place of origin.) In any case, elaboration, or rather elaboration upon elaboration, is the most accurate way of describing Stendhal's method of spinning the fullness of a novel from these rudimentary elements of plot and character.

The first draft, which he wrote in a month in Marseilles during the fall of 1829, was evidently rather brief: one might guess perhaps more or less the length of *Armance*, and perhaps with some of the aspects of abruptness that characterized the earlier novel. When he began to rework this material in January 1830, he appears to have proceeded by interpolating small details, complete sentences and paragraphs, even whole episodes (some of this can be ascertained by noting the references in the published text to historical events that can be dated between February and July 1830). He continued the process of interpolation as he worked over successive batches of the proofs, which he began to receive from the printer in May. Henri Martineau has aptly likened this method of composition to the manufacture of cultured pearls, in which layer upon layer of precious material is gradually accreted around a tiny nucleus.[3] Once the process

---

3. Martineau, *L'Oeuvre de Stendhal* (Paris, 1951), p. 386.

was completed, Stendhal himself seems only sometimes to have been confident that he had produced a pearl of passing worth. More typically, he was inclined to complain, as he reread the novel several years later, that the style was still too "choppy," that he had presented only the essential matter (*le fond des choses*) without sufficient complication or development.

But in fact, these retrospective moments of self-questioning were unwarranted. For what is most astonishing about *Le Rouge et le Noir*, especially if one has been following the hesitant and circuitous progress of Stendhal's literary efforts over nearly three decades, is how, suddenly, in the work of a few months, everything comes together perfectly; how he is able to use artistically everything he has experienced and observed; how time after time in his management of style and in his insight into character, in his invention of scene, action, and gesture, he exhibits a perfect rightness of touch. The result is not only a splendid piece of fiction but also a novel in certain ways quite unlike any novel that had been written before. As with most imaginative works, an originality of vision that has its roots in the distinctive experience, psychology, and sensibility of the author is intricately intertwined with an originality of technique. Perhaps the two chief aspects of the novel in which both orders of linked originality can be seen most clearly are: Stendhal's imaginative relation to his protagonists, most especially to Julien, which is inseparable from a consideration of the kind of narrator or dramatized persona he invents to serve as his intermediary; and his less obtrusive manipulation of narrative point of view and related strategies of fictional exposition, which is inseparable from his understanding of human nature and society, from his perception of what is central and what is peripheral in experience. The issue of point of view and fictional exposition, being susceptible of concrete illustration, may profitably be considered first. In other words, in order to understand Henri Beyle's sudden leap to aristic maturity, we shall have to attend to certain innovative technical details of his craft as a novelist.

Before *Le Rouge et le Noir*, there had been a split in the handling of perspective in the novel between first-person narratives (including epistolary novels), on the one hand, and third-person narratives, on the other. The first-person narration attached us to the fictional narrator's single perspective, in some instances—especially in the epistolary novel—bringing us to the very cutting edge of one person's experience as he or she underwent it in all its emotional plenitude. By contrast, third-person narrators tended to take a magisterial overview of their personages, keeping at a distance from the subtle movements of the characters' inner life, in some cases treating the characters' consciousness and their material surroundings or their physical manifestations on more or less the same level. Jane Austen (whom Stendhal gives no evidence of having read) may have effected a partial compromise between these two traditions of narration, but it was *Le Rouge et le Noir* that signally bridged the gap between them and by so doing laid the technical groundwork for the subsequent achievements of Flaubert, Tolstoy, Henry James, and many others. For Stendhal, by virtue of all his social and amatory experience a relentlessly attentive observer and an inveterate speculator as to what others were thinking about him as he thought about them, the important thing in any scene was not how it looked but how it looked through one character's eyes or another's. This led him to build up his narrative through a shifting series of related techniques in which the narrator silently follows the train of sensory perceptions of one character, then switches to another, or, while maintaining the third person, closely mimics the interior speech of a character in *style indirect libre*, or summarizes a character's line of unspoken reasoning, or presents actual interior monologues, sometimes resembling dramatic soliloquies.[4]

Here, for example, is the very beginning of the first encounter between the young bourgeois mother, Mme de Rênal, and the future tutor of her children, Julien Sorel:

> With the vivaciousness and grace that were natural to her when she was far from the eyes of men, Mme de Rênal was going out through the French doors of the living room which opened onto the garden, when she noticed by the gate the figure of a young peasant, still almost a child, extremely pale, who had just been crying. He was in a very white shirt, and under one arm had a quite decent jacket of violet frieze.
>
> The complexion of this young peasant was so white, his eyes so gentle, that to Mme de Rênal's somewhat extravagant imagination it first occurred that this might be a young girl in disguise, who had come to lay some entreaty before His Honor the Mayor. She pitied this poor creature, halted at the gate, who evidently had not dared to raise his hand as far as the bell. [Bk. I, chap. 6]

The naturalness and transparency of Stendhal's manner are so evident that one does not immediately realize how much essential information—dramatic, psychological, social, and thematic—is conveyed in a few seem-

---

4. The classic discussion of point of view in *Le Rouge et le Noir* is Chapter 18 of Erich Auerbach's *Mimesis* (Princeton, 1953). The question has been considered intelligently though at rather ponderous length by Georges Blin in *Stendhal et les problèmes du roman* (Paris, 1954), but the best general introduction to this whole aspect of Stendhal's artistry is probably John Mitchell's elegant little study, *Stendhal: Le Rouge et le Noir* (London, 1973).

ingly casual strokes of narration. True to his strictures against the methods of Walter Scott, Stendhal makes no attempt to provide a detailed physical description of the scene or the characters or to introduce his personages formally. Mme de Rênal is characterized only in an introductory prepositional phrase, which is attached to the action she is performing at this particular moment but which nevertheless sets up an important view of her as a woman of hidden liveliness and feminine charm shyly subjected to the male-dominated bourgeois order, and in her natural unreflective grace the antithesis of the self-conscious Julien as well as of the histrionic Mathilde de la Mole. (The interweaving of expositional materials with the narrative present is itself an important technical innovation of Stendhal's.) This succinct characterization of what Mme de Rênal is like when she is by herself is of course the perception of the omniscient narrator, who then slides deftly into her point of view, emerging only momentarily in the first sentence of the second paragraph to inform us that Mme de Rênal had a "somewhat extravagant imagination" (*l'esprit un peu romanesque*).

What her eye first picks out when she catches sight of Julien is, with fidelity to the facts of visual perception from a middle distance, the whiteness of his skin. His clothing, which she then notices (after observing his youth and his tearful pallor), identifies him as a peasant, a fact seemingly contradicted by the fairness of his complexion, and this leads her to the fanciful conjecture about the young woman in disguise. The sheer efficiency with which Stendhal defines scene, character, incipient relationship, and social background is astonishing. We know that Julien, fresh from his father's sawmill, has exerted a great effort to make himself presentable; his shirt is carefully laundered, he has brought with him a very decent, or clean (*propre* can mean both) jacket, though it is, after all, only of coarse wool. We even know that it is a warm day, for he is carrying his jacket under his arm, and the rapid adverbial indications of French doors, garden, and gate are enough to let us visualize the scene as much as we need to for Stendhal's immediate dramatic purposes.

But the reader cannot fully realize until he has continued on into the novel how much more than this he is being told in these few lines. In a moment, the narrative will slip into Julien's point of view as he notices the kind expression in Mme de Rênal's eyes, her beauty, her fine clothing—he is about to step near enough to smell its "fragrance" (*parfum*)—and above all, *her* white complexion, which with his peasant's eyes he finds "dazzling." We have the first discreet hint, then, of the skin-to-skin closeness to which they will attain, but with it a nice suggestion of the class differences that separate them. We also have an appropriate intimation of the maternal aspect that this first and last love of Julien's shows him: she sees him as "almost a child," and her first words to him will be, "What do you want, my child?"

The other expositional elements in the passage are, in the light of what follows, mainly ironic. Here Julien stands below at the gate and Mme de Rênal observes him from above, in a spatial emblem of their social relationship. But as a determined climber, he is repeatedly associated with elevations: we first see him straddling the roofbeam of his father's shed, reading the *Mémorial de Sainte Hélène* (book and boy are then violently knocked off this perch by Papa Sorel); two of his most important experiences of inner assessment take place on a hilltop, watching the flight of a lonely sparrow hawk, and in a mountain cavern; Julien will ultimately realize himself in a prison one hundred eighty steps high—quite like the tower with one hundred twenty steps Henri Beyle had sketched in his journal in 1810—with a view looking out and down. Julien aspires to the boldness, the indomitable strength, the self-protective impenetrability of a Napoleon, but Mme de Rênal's first glance catches him in the full weakness of his weeping and, what is more, almost takes him for a girl. But that, too, foreshadows the course of their relationship, for it will be his spontaneous revelations of weakness, even tears, not his elaborate battle plans of seduction, that will win her for him. Finally, when we recall that the novel, after all, does set into play a whole set of associations of red—imperial military glory, violence, revolution, ritual pomp, passion, incest, *Liebestod*—against black—priesthood, hypocrisy, turpitude, Bourbon reaction, bleak death [5]—the emphasis on white in this initial scene begins to assume the function of a thematic focusing device, visually isolating two frail and lovely human faces caught in this tangled field of historical, social, and political forces. In sum, it is hard to imagine that any novelist could have managed to tell us more than all this in just a few ostensibly casual sentences. When he could write with such easy perfection, Stendhal's long literary apprenticeship was clearly over.

Le Rouge et le Noir, as even this single instance from a whole spectrum of narrative strategies may suggest, is equally impressive in the rendering of individual scenes and in sustaining through them larger architectonic designs. Stendhal, to be sure, was by no means a painstaking architect of fictional structures like Mann or Joyce: a few of the recurring patterns in the novel may have been carefully planned in advance, others

5. The possible meanings of the novel's title have been much debated. Perhaps the best discussion is Geneviève Mouillaud's carefully argued psychoanalytic interpretation in *Le Rouge et le Noir de Stendhal: le roman possible* (Paris, 1973), pp. 151–236.

probably occurred to him as he went over his draft and proofs, and a good many of these must have been intuitively woven into the individual passages in the rapid course of his composition by improvisation. As for the "rightness" of the individual scenes themselves, the suddenly accomplished technique he exhibits is finally a function of his shrewd understanding of the characters he has imagined, and that in turn is the ripe fruit of his lifelong cultivation of self-understanding and of the disciplined observation of human nature. The suppleness of the management of narrative point of view, in other words, is a consequence of the writer's experienced subtlety of perception about people.

When, for example, Julien steels himself for the second time to seize Mme de Rênal's hand in the dark of the garden, while her husband is seated four feet away inveighing against the evils of the rabble classes, we are told: "The hand that was yielded to him Julien covered with passionate kisses, or at least that is how they seemed to Mme de Rênal" (Bk. I, chap. 11). The corrective second clause, clearly from a very lucid omniscient narrator, pulls us up short, simultaneously reminds us that the perception of "passionate kisses" belongs to Mme de Rênal, that it is a worn literary cliché which has often shabbily covered more ambiguous realities, and that poor Julien at the moment is too desperately preoccupied with what he conceives to be his "duty" as a seducer to allow himself to feel any passion. These few words of narrator's comment swivel our attention around toward three different objects at once: what is going on in Mme de Rênal's mind, what is going on in Julien's mind, and the background of linguistic or literary stereotypes they both draw on to order and interpret their experience. It is a small but characteristic example of how Stendhal's narrative constantly requires little acts of critical intelligence on the part of the reader and for that very reason constantly bypasses, suppresses, or reshapes what would be the climactic actions of a more conventional piece of fiction in order to demonstrate to us that the true interest, the true human facts of the matter, lie elsewhere.

The consistent elision of the moments of sought-after sexual consummation in the novel memorably illustrates this bypassing of the conventional in the interests of intelligent perception. (Respectable novelists in this period, of course, could not permit themselves undue explicitness in sexual scenes, but Stendhal's deliberate short-circuiting of any suggestiveness in such matters remains notable.) When the virtuous Mme de Rênal finally yields to Julien's unpremeditated tears (Bk. I, chap. 14), all we are told of the fateful act itself is the following: "Several hours later, when Julien left Mme de Rênal's bedroom, one could have said, in the style of a novel, that he had nothing more to desire." Life, as most great novels tend to remind us, is not like a novel, and the phrase here turns ironically back on itself because Julien's story is to a large extent a study of the problematic nature of desire, and it is only at the end, in prison, that he discovers the meaning of desire fulfilled. A large measure of Stendhal's modernity as a novelist can be attributed to his grasp of how a protagonist can cease to know what he desires, can be alienated from his own experience by the unrelenting self-consciousness, the constant role playing, that his location in society and history seems to require of him (Beyle's own anguish of self-consciousness in the pursuit of Mélanie, Angela, Alexandrine, and Métilde had not been forgotten). Julien knows that what Mme de Rênal has just accorded him is designated "being happy" in the novels he has read, but he is far too intent on proving his worth as a superior creature to feel anything of the sort.

This elusiveness of experience at the moment of consummation is compounded in the second part of the novel when Julien encounters in Mathilde de la Mole a quixotic role player even more extravagant than himself. His first midnight scene in her bedroom (Bk. II, chap. 16), to which he has been induced to climb on a ladder in the light of the full moon, is surely one of the high points of knowing comedy in the history of the novel. Suspecting that "these people," the haughty aristocrats, have prepared an ambush for him, he climbs up to the window armed with pistol and dagger. Both Julien and Mathilde are performing solemn duties to themselves in becoming lovers, and they approach this first moment of intimacy in the moonlit room with about the same sensation of inward clenching and apprehension with which one might approach a dentist's chair. Mathilde concentrates all her attention on the supreme effort of addressing Julien as *tu*, and he, once he is assured that there are no hidden hirelings about to spring out at him, is too astounded by the sheer usage of the *tu* to notice that the tone with which she invokes this language of intimacy is manic rather than tender. Throughout the scene, they scarcely pay any attention to each other, so intent is each on following all the prescribed steps of a proper lover, so anesthetized are their real feelings by the chill suffusion of self-consciousness. "Passionate love," Stendhal observes with dry precision after the two have finally been in bed together, "was still rather a model to be imitated than a reality." For Julien, in grim pursuit of the exaltation his books have promised him, "this night . . . seemed singular rather than happy."

The British novelist Elizabeth Bowen once aptly observed that the revelation of character in the novel should be unforeseeable before the fact but must seem inevitable after. That rule of thumb is preeminently applicable to *Le Rouge et le Noir,* where the three principal characters, in rather different ways, zigzag sharply in action and feeling, yet seem more fully themselves with each sudden turn they take. Mme de Rênal, the demure Christian wife and mother, becomes a passionate mistress, then a guilt-stricken penitent, then a devotee of love supremely indifferent to the world's censure. The proud Mathilde forces herself to yield to this mere secretary of her father's, then immediately resents the power she has let him obtain over her, then delightedly wallows in the sensation of becoming Julien's "slave" when he seems to threaten her with a sword he has seized from the wall, then resents him again, and finally, through Julien's strategy of arousing her jealousy, resolves on a noble course of devotion unto death, consummating at the end her secret theatrical dream when she is privileged, like the mistress of her Renaissance ancestor, to carry off her lover's severed head.

In the case of Julien, whose consciousness dominates much of the narrative, we are allowed to follow small zigzags as well as large. At one point, for example, he feels a sudden impulse of solidarity with M. de Rênal, the man he has been cuckolding, and anger against Mme de Rênal because she has shown herself able to use feminine wiles to deceive her husband for the sake of her lover; a few hours later, he rebukes himself for the foolishness of this sentiment. The cumulative indication of such quicksilver fluctuations of consciousness in Julien, unpredictable before the fact yet convincing in their revelation, prepares us for the great reversal of the denouement: Julien's somnambulistic journey from Paris to Verrières (conveyed in a few staccato sentences) to fire the pistol at Mme de Rênal, the flood of renewed affection for her when he learns she will survive, his renunciation of the world in the unexpected happiness of his prison retreat.

There is no easy way to explain how Stendhal suddenly acquired the ability to know his fictional personages with such magisterial sureness, though his success as a psychologist of character has at least something to do with the fact that the characters, the women included, are at once splendidly heightened, gratifying fantasy-projections of himself and aspects of himself that had long been held under scrutiny in the cold light of self-analysis. One way *not* to explain the persuasiveness of the characters is to seek, as so many critics have done, especially in the case of the heroines, "real-life" models in the history of Henri Beyle. Stendhal's characters pulsate with the inward movements of his own experience, and he does sometimes lend them actual anecdotal fragments of his past, but the vivid individuality with which he endows them is hardly the result of a scissors-and-paste assemblage from persons remembered and acts performed.

Stendhal's complicated relation to Julien offers the best illustration of the double activity of fantasy and severe scrutiny that generates a sense of psychological depth in the characters. In certain respects, Julien is obviously what his author would have dreamed of being: a perfectly beautiful young man with a natural ability to charm women, especially when he is not trying to do so; a devotee of the Napoleonic ideal of hero- ism who is prepared to follow his assertion of superiority over the common herd to the utmost limits, even to his own death. Julien, like Henri Beyle, has a detested father with whom he feels no connection, but unlike Beyle, he is given sufficient hints to indulge at length in the suppo- sition that he is really the son of some nobleman and thus to play out the appealing central role in a Freudian Family Romance, even in the end being granted undisputed possession of the mother after having acted out his aggression toward her. The resonance between the lovely, maternal Mme de Rênal and the ardently desired mother, snatched away by death so early, in *Henry Brulard*, has often been noted, and the pointing of the pistol at Mme de Rênal might well be an unconscious transformation of guilt felt by the seven-year-old Henri over his mother's death in childbirth [6] or, better, of guilt fused with anger over having been "aban- doned" by the mother.

With all this, Julien remains in important ways his author's inferior. He is a peasant, not a bourgeois, which means that his ignorance about the complexities of social life is even greater than was that of the nineteen- year-old Beyle and that his constant misperceptions of people are partly determined by a feeling Beyle did not share—deep class resentment. He has committed to memory *La Nouvelle Héloïse* as well as the Vulgate, but he uses Rousseau's work only as a source book for the language of seduc- tion, believing that all novels are written by scoundrels in order to get ahead, never having glimpsed the imaginative horizons that literature can open. Julien, in short, has a decidedly limited inner world, and it is not surprising that the narrator should often condescend to him, call him "my poor little Julien," or flatly state that he is a mediocre creature. To be more precise, his notions of human nature, love, happiness, and culture are

6. The most helpful general analysis of the Family Romance as it applies to *Le Rouge et le Noir* is Marthe Robert's *Roman des origines et origines du roman* (Paris, 1972). The suggestion about the child's feelings of guilt over his mother's death, based on a careful reading of relevant passages in *Henry Brulard*, is made by Geneviève Mouillaud, op. cit., pp. 191–192.

mediocre, but his innate sensibility, which he goes to such lengths to pervert, is a fine one, and the energy of his desires, however misdirected, is extraordinary, impelling him through the tragicomic twists of the entire plot and making him fit for his heroically tragic ending.

Technically, Stendhal is able to keep in focus this figure who embodies his intimate fantasies and is yet inferior to himself [7] by presenting Julien through the mediation of an engagingly urbane Parisian narrator—a more ideal self of the author—who is often chattily sympathetic toward the protagonist but always above him, seeing his limitations and self-deceptions. Thus, when Julien sits on his lofty rock (Bk. I, chap. 13), surveying the world below him, the narrator, perched still higher, observes of his hero: "Placed as though on a high promontory, he could judge, and he dominated as it were extreme poverty and the condition of being well-off which he still called wealth." Julien, it is clear, has much to learn about society as well as about himself. His ignorance is not so much a recollection of the young Beyle's ignorance of the world as an extrapolation, an emphatic comic heightening, of it. Beyond the characterization of the hero, this worldly, conversational narrator gives Stendhal certain distinct advantages in anchoring the action in time, place, class, and politics. Though, as we have seen, the narrator may often choose to disappear into the characters, he also can exercise the option of talking all around them, eliciting the nuances of their motives and values through commentary, moving outward from the characters proper to brief or extended observations on nineteenth-century society, the role of woman, life in the provinces and life in Paris, the nature of the novel itself.

Stendhal had of course been practicing this fluently discursive voice for fifteen years in his art, music, and travel books, but there was probably one model among novelists he had specifically in mind. At the end of an 1832 letter to a Florentine friend, Count Salvagnoli, which he hoped to "plant" as a pseudonymous Italian article on his own book, he describes *Le Rouge et le Noir* as a novel that deserved a place on the bookshelf alongside "the immortal *Tom Jones*." To mention *Tom Jones* as a touchstone of excellence need not imply that his own novel was necessarily similar in kind to Fielding's, but the one formal device that most clearly connects these two novels so different in mood and theme is the presence in both of a genial expatiating narrator who casts a finely woven net of cultural, social, and political commentary over the narrated events; enriches

---

7. A similar observation, that Julien is both inferior and superior to Stendhal, has been made by G. C. Jones in describing Stendhal's stance as ironist. See *L'Ironie dans les romans de Stendhal* (Lausanne, 1966), p. 83.

our perception of the characters through a shifting play of ironies; and by all this subtly enlarges the significance of the novel's action. Stendhal virtually recognizes this particular connection with Fielding, at least as something he aspired to, when four years later he notes in the manuscript margin of *Lucien Leuwen,* his next novel, after rereading a section of *Le Rouge et le Noir:* "true but dry. One must adopt a more ornate, less dry style, witty and gay, not like the *Tom Jones* of 1750, but as the same Fielding would be in 1834." [8] The informing sensibility of *Le Rouge et le Noir* is ambivalently Romantic, the sense of history and how it impinges on private lives is eminently post-Napoleonic, but the qualities frequently exhibited by the mediating narrator hark back to the poised satiric achievements of the eighteenth century in England and France and are the very attributes of "daring, resourcefulness, liveliness, *sang-froid,* amusing wit" ascribed to Don Juan at the end of *De l'Amour.*

In this connection, it is noteworthy that the famous definition of the novel as a mirror on the road, which Stendhal introduces into the text of *Le Rouge et le Noir,* is perfectly appropriate for Fielding's novel and for the antecedent picaresque tradition, but not, at least at first glance, for his own novel, which moves mostly between salons and bedrooms and attends so often not to a traveling panorama but to the interior vision of the characters. Some critics have read this passage as a naively "reflective" theory of the relation between the novel and the world; others have argued that in context the whole statement is nonsense and so is intended to be ironically self-subverting, or that it occurs in a long parenthesis, which must somehow complicate any meaning it might have. A simpler justification for the choice of this "Fieldingesque" emblem of the mirror carried along the highway for the novel is that it enabled Stendhal to introduce a set of neatly opposed images that could suggest *symbolically,* though not literally, the very special vision of life which he was translating artistically into the form of the novel. These images are, moreover, ones we have already seen evoked at certain significant junctures in his journal and letters. Here is the crucial passage from *Le Rouge et le Noir:*

Ah, sir, a novel is a mirror carried along a highway. Sometimes it reflects back to you the azure of the sky, sometimes the muck of the quagmires on the road. And the man who carries the mirror in the basket on his back is to be accused by you of immorality! His mirror shows the muck, and you accuse the mirror! Accuse instead the highway where the quagmire is, and still more the road inspector who allows the water to stagnate and the quagmire to form. [Bk. II, chap. 19]

8. *Mélanges intimes et marginalia,* vol. 2, p. 218.

The narrator has just been talking about Mathilde's extravagant nature and, by contrast, about the more conventional young women of the day whose social habits, as he acidly puts it, "among all ages will assure such a distinguished rank to the civilization of the 19th century." The link, then, between the imagery of the highway and his Parisian subject is metaphoric but scarcely metonymic. The passive and humble idea, moreover, of the novelist as someone carrying a mirror in a back-basket is surely in some degree ironic, part of the narrator's rhetorical strategy in his argument with the imagined reader. What is important is that, because the emblematic mirror is located on a highway, it can reflect the two opposed elements which since 1811–12 Henri Beyle had used to indicate the opposed spheres of the odious commonality of mankind and the Happy Few—on the one hand, mud, quagmire, excremental filth, and on the other, the fine air of mountaintops, the clear blue of the sky. One recalls that, in his horror of what he saw in the Moscow campaign, Beyle had projected in his private writing a claustrophobic image of the base, venal, brutish mass of men as a contaminating, engulfing bog, and against that he had set a dream of the hills of Lombardy where the lucid air rung with the harmonious clarities of Cimarosa. The transition from the former realm to the latter is in essence the plot of *Le Rouge et le Noir*.

But there is this crucial difference between the twenty-nine-year-old diarist of 1812 and the masterly novelist of 1830: after seven years in Milan, after a decade in the salons of Paris, his response to the quagmire of contemporary French society is not revulsion but dispassionate curiosity, minutely attentive observation. Julien's story is also a brilliant "Chronicle of 1830," [9] as the subtitle of the novel announces, because the novelist, instead of contenting himself with reiterating the denigrating symbol of muck, shrewdly follows the nuanced ways in which personality, family relations, passion itself are distorted by the relentless self-serving, the materialism, the pretence, the pale prudential cast of mind encouraged by the constellation of crown, church, and class in France under the restored Bourbons.

In this regard, the relatively short central section describing Julien's months at the Besançon seminary is the thematic keystone of the novel: set in between the Rênal household and the Hôtel de la Mole, the seminary is the place where the pervasive hypocrisy of society can be seen writ large, where the reactionary Catholicism that flourished under

9. For the first edition, this subtitle, which he had intended to use, had to be changed to "Chronicle of the 19th Century" in order to avoid the misleading implication that the subject of the novel was the July Revolution.

Charles X can be observed as a concentrated presence. After Besançon, Julien's social ascent will be rapid, and step by step with it, his alienation from himself will be more pronounced.

At one point (Bk. II, chap. 3), Stendhal literally plunges his hero into the mire when he subjects Julien to the ordeal of equitation he recalled from his own youth: riding in the Bois de Boulogne with the young Count Norbert de la Mole, Julien tries to avoid a cabriolet, is tossed to the ground, and is covered with mud. Elsewhere, Julien wallows in the moral mire of nineteenth-century society without an explicit invocation of the metaphor. Stendhal keenly perceives that as Julien attains greater accomplishment in the way of the world, finally succeeding beyond expectation with the unpredictable Mathilde, he is inwardly floundering, like a man in a bog, either not knowing who he is or hating what he has become. "Yes, to cover with ridicule this utterly odious creature I call *myself* would amuse me" (Bk. II, chap. 27), he reflects as he mechanically carries out the strategy of deception that will win him back Mathilde; or still more bluntly, at the end of the next chapter, he exclaims to himself, "Good God! Why am I me?" Julien, frail by disposition, has exerted an enormous energy of will—hence his appeal for later readers like Nietzsche— but, finally, the relentless hypocrisy to which he has committed himself has the effect of *enervating* him: "His efforts at role playing had ended up draining all strength from his soul" (Bk. II, chap. 28). The quagmire contaminates, inexorably drags one down, and the only way Stendhal can save his hero is by extricating him violently through Mme de Rênal's letter of denunciation, Julien's attempted murder of her, his imprisonment, his elevation, literally and figuratively, above society in his condemned cell.

After Julien fires the two fatal shots, he stands in a daze, seeing nothing, then slowly "comes back to himself"—not only from the trance that has seized him ever since the revelation of the denunciatory letter but also from the self-estrangement into which he has allowed himself to be drawn from the start. In his high cell, Julien ceases to care about what others will think, is at last, in his tender hours with Mme de Rênal, entirely without affectation. "Never have I been so happy," he tells her, and when she questions this surprising assertion, he affirms, "Never, and I speak to you as I would speak to myself" (Bk. II, chap. 43).

It is, certainly from our post-Romantic perspective, an odd, even perverse resolution for Stendhal to suggest that in society as it is constituted the only ultimate sincerity, and therefore the only genuine happiness, must be attained in complete isolation from the world, at the door of death. This is the most thoroughly Romantic feature of *Le Rouge et le*

Noir, but it is intimated in these concluding chapters of the novel with delicate restraint. The music of Julien's final idyll is more Mozartian than Cimarosan, elegantly controlled, quietly plangent. As throughout the novel, indications of physical setting are minimal but tactically efficient: after his long struggle through the mud below, Julien has his tower, his view of the sky, and Stendhal wants to make us feel that it is enough.

Other French Romantic writers, beginning with Chateaubriand, had made fiction out of the impelling dream of some luminous *ailleurs*, an elsewhere of rapturous fulfillment beckoning to the hero caught in the toils of earthly existence. This dream, however, was characteristically expressed in a vague and lofty style that blurred or distorted the outlines of the real world. Stendhal, by contrast, is able to combine a steady clarity of perception with a chastely understated version of the Romantic dream. One important measure of his originality as a novelist is his ability to articulate in the formal structure of his fiction a bioptic vision that can take in both the varied scene of contemporary society with its characteristic vices and absurdities—the vast quagmire in which the hero is caught—and the glimpse of a beatitude quite beyond the social world. Henri Beyle, lifelong aspirant to literary greatness, had finally discovered how to realize his dream in a finely poised art distinctively his own.

Part Four

The Consul

Like his characters, like his ideas, like his books,
Stendhal is a penumbra of delicate mystery shading
off into a brilliance of contradictory clarities. At the
heart of things there is always a darkness.

Robert M. Adams, *Stendhal:*
Notes on a Novelist

XII

CIVITAVECCHIA

(Aetat. 48–53)

A BONE-CHILLING WIND was sweeping down from the mountains through Trieste when Henri Beyle arrived there on November 25, 1830. It was a grimly appropriate presage of things to come in his new Italian career. He had left Paris in a surge of youthful energy, fancying he was headed at last to the alluring land and to the comfortable situation of which he had so long dreamed, but the icy grip of the bora, the Adriatic northeasterly wind, at once reminded him that he was, after all, at a physically vulnerable age and that Italy might not correspond, meteorologically, politically, socially, or culturally, to his cherished ideas. From the day after his arrival, as he testified a couple of months later in a letter to Mareste, he suffered from constant cramps—he picturesquely called them "intestinal rheumatism"—which he attributed to the effects of the bora. The keen edge of disappointment may also have played a role in his physical debility, and from this point onward, his health, never altogether certain, was to be a continual source of disturbance.

For Trieste struck him as a dreary place, devoid of either aesthetic or social charm, peopled mainly by money-grubbing peasants. Even the language was something of a problem. He heard as much German spoken as

Italian, so that if he were to stay in Trieste he might have to acquire a proficiency in the tongue that had so successfully resisted his half-hearted efforts during his years of imperial service in Prussia and Austria. He marked the new year of 1831 with the following bleak summary, at the beginning of a letter to Mme Ancelot: "Alas, madame, I am dying of boredom and cold. That's the only news I can report today, January 1, 1831." He had scant companionship here from either sex. In the same letter to Mme Ancelot, he observes, with a sour note of exhibitionism and a monetary precision directed at the profit-minded Triestini, "The greatest beauties adore me for the price of a sequin (12 francs 63 centimes)." Soon he would try to divert himself with a flirtation, the object being a certain Mlle Ungher, a local singer about twenty-four years old. "But," he wrily comments in a letter to Mareste, "she is too good in mathematics; I wanted to persuade her that 48 = 25, something which was not at all conceded" (March 23, 1831).

The post at Trieste, then, apart from the security of 15,000 francs per annum that it carried with it, in any case would hardly have been to Beyle's liking, but it quickly became clear that the Hapsburg authorities viewed him as persona non grata. One wonders, in fact, how he could have imagined that he would have been an acceptable consul to the Austrians only two years after their vigilant police had expelled him from Milan as a subversive. Victor Del Litto's suggestion that Beyle's whole plan was a quixotic strategy of desperation seems the most plausible explanation.[1] With his material resources virtually exhausted, he somehow thought he could present the Austro-Hungarian empire with a fait accompli by rushing off to Trieste to take up his consulate, without even first getting a visa from the Austrian ambassador in Paris. En route, at Pavia, the visaless passport was questioned by an official, and Beyle was summoned to appear before the police at Milan (it was the last time he was to see his beloved city). The French consul general intervened, and Beyle was permitted to proceed to his destination. Meanwhile, however, the dossier on Henri Beyle, alias Stendhal, the notorious author of the pernicious *Rome, Naples et Florence*, had been duly examined in Vienna, and on November 21, just as Beyle was being detained in Milan, Metternich himself was sending instructions to his ambassador in France asking the French foreign ministry to withdraw this objectionable nominee to the consulate at Trieste. Rumors of the Austrian refusal were current by the first week of December; on December 24, Beyle received official notice that his credentials as consul had been rejected.

---

1. *La Vie de Stendhal* (Paris, 1965), p. 252.

Instead of living in clover, then, as a French diplomat in Italy, Beyle found himself a lame duck paddling through cold waters. Immediately after his arrival in Trieste, he took up the administration of the vacant consulate, hoping to establish through action his already challenged claim to the position, but after December 24, he knew that he was merely filling in until a new appointee arrived to take over. The actual transfer of authority did not occur till the end of March, but in the interim, his Parisian friends with influence in the foreign ministry had been active on his behalf. The proposal of the consulate at Civitavecchia must have been initiated immediately after the rejection of the appointment to Trieste, for Beyle already speaks of it—with something less than enthusiasm—in a January 17 letter to Mareste. He was once driven there by a storm, he recalls to Mareste, and found the little port city of the Papal States to be "an abominable hole." That was to remain his fixed epithet for Civitavecchia, richly confirmed by eleven years of highly intermittent residence there. He received official notice of his new appointment in mid-March and set out for Civitavecchia on the 31st, following a leisurely six-week route through Venice, Padua, Bologna, Florence, and Siena, assuming his new consular duties on April 18.

Beyle had wanted a post in Italy, but this was, from his point of view, the very doorsill of the meanest back entrance to an Italian bourn. (And economic injury was added to cultural insult: his consular salary in this outpost amounted to only 10,000 francs, the bottom of the diplomatic scale.) About forty-five miles northwest of Rome on the Mediterranean coast, Civitavecchia was the sole port of the Papal States and for that reason had a certain economic and perhaps even strategic importance—hence the necessity of a consulate. Beyle's appointment there could be confirmed because the papal authorities, unlike Metternich, were anxious to stay in favor with the new French regime, though they were distinctly unhappy with the dubious principles of the new consul, as the official correspondence reveals, and regretted the loss of his staunchly monarchist predecessor. Beyle immediately confirmed their suspicions by befriending the Italian republicans of the town, becoming especially close to Donato Bucci, a local antique dealer who introduced him to the absorbing pastime of amateur archaeology. The papal authorities on their part remained suspicious enough to have the French consul tailed by secret agents during some of his visits to Rome: his lifelong impulse to evade detection finally was given objective justification.

Apart from Beyle's expeditions to Etruscan and Roman ruins, in the outskirts of the town and elsewhere, and his conversations with a tiny handful of local liberals, he found little to amuse him in Civitavecchia.

Then a city of less than 7,500 inhabitants, it was—and remains today—a bleak place, clustered by the shore in crowded rows of graceless two-and three-story buildings peeling and cracking in the sun, the streets filled with assorted refuse and debris, the air suffused with the mingled odors of garbage and rotting fish, chain gangs digging away on the roads, the harbor itself dominated by the grim heavy mass of the Michaelangelo Fortress, which was used as a prison. In addition to all these amenities, the hot, humid climate of this marshy region gave Beyle's health almost as much trouble as had the bora in Trieste. It is hardly surprising that he repeatedly undertook the eight-hour coach ride to Rome and contrived to spend as much time as possible in the capital city.

The filth, the ugliness, the miasmal atmosphere of Civitavecchia, however heavily they weighed on Beyle, were secondary to his chief complaint about the port city, which he repeats again and again in his letters to his Parisian friends: the lack of intelligent company. And frequently, this sense of isolation leads him to reflect on the prospect of his own death. Thus, in a letter to his cousin Romain Colomb, he describes a fine dinner given him in a charming garden setting, then bemoans his separation from the witty society of Paris, the lack of a single subtle or interesting idea put forth during this entire evening in Civitavecchia. "Shall I die smothered by fools? There seems to be a great likelihood of it" (September 10, 1834). A few weeks later he strikes the same note more plangently in a letter to Sophie Duvaucel: "It's a year since I've seen you, since I've seen Paris. Must I live and die thus on this solitary shore? I am afraid so. In that case I shall die entirely stupefied by boredom and the noncommunication of my ideas" (October 28, 1834). To Domenico Fiori, who had helped him obtain his post, he paints a picture of himself sitting at the window of his office sixty feet above the sea, dully tossing scraps of paper down into the water. Others of a colder nature, he proposes, might be happy or at least tranquil in his place, "But my own soul is a fire that suffers if it does not blaze. I need three or four cubic feet of new ideas per day, as a steamboat needs coal" (November 1, 1834).

At Rome, Beyle did the best he could to stoke his intellectual furnace. He soon became good friends with the Count de Sainte-Aulaire, the French ambassador to Rome, and with his charming blonde wife. In a kind of pale recapitulation of the stubborn cerebral love for Alexandrine Daru he had conceived more than two decades earlier, he managed to persuade himself, by the early months of 1832, that he was in love with Louise de Sainte-Aulaire. She gently discouraged him, and they remained friends until her husband's transfer to Vienna at the beginning of 1833.

Beyle repeated this pattern in 1835, when he set his sights on Countess Giulia Cini ("Countess Sandre" in the schoolboy code of Beyle's private notations because the French equivalent of *cini*, ashes, is *cendres*) after having become a regular guest of the Cini household. Once again he got little encouragment, though this infatuation cost him a temporary estrangement from one of his best Roman friends, the aristocratic Filippo Caetani, who in fact had a liaison with Giulia Cini. Through these various weak reflexes of the veteran amorist, the figure of Giulia Rinieri, as we shall presently see, remained alluringly on the horizon of Beyle's emotional life.

Though he may have felt impelled to preserve a hidden self behind a whole repertoire of masks, Beyle's need for companionship and his repeatedly demonstrated capacity for friendship are remarkable. His friends in Rome, as we have just noted, included members of the French diplomatic corps and the local aristocracy as well as resident aliens like the Russian Alexander Turgenev (not to be confused with the later famous novelist) and the French artist Abraham Constantin. Beyle had known Constantin, a highly successful painter on enamel and porcelain, in Paris during the 1820s. The two now became intimate friends and, beginning in July 1831, shared an apartment in Rome. In 1833, Constantin left Rome for several years, but from 1839 to Beyle's final return to France, they again had common lodgings, and at this time, they worked together on a guide to Italian painting which was published in 1840 with Constantin's name alone as author.

In Rome, then, Beyle did not suffer the isolation among fools that he felt in Civitavecchia, but the papal city, for all its artistic treasures, lacked the magic of graceful culture and romance that had once beguiled him in Milan, and though it provided him agreeable companions, it could offer nothing like the brilliant exchange of ideas he now remembered nostalgically from his decade in Paris. The ironic truth was that between 1821 and 1830 "Arrigo Beyle, Milanese" had become thoroughly Parisian. Shuttling between two cultural realms, he had imperceptibly made himself a permanent exile: in France, he had longed for the passion, the energy, and the music of Italy; now in an Italy that scarcely resembled the idealized Lombardy of his youth, he felt himself withering inwardly because he was cut off from the wit, the rich verbal culture, the intellectual intensity of the Parisian salons. It was only in his second completed masterpiece, *La Chartreuse de Parme*, that he would find a way to combine these two disparate spiritual homelands.

Understandably, then, Beyle's life in Italy in the early 1830s is characterized by a certain fitfulness; he shows no sustained concentration either in his official duties or in his love interests or (at least till 1834) in his writing. Between illnesses—a wracking fever through the spring of 1831, then attacks of gout and kidney stone—and boredom, he traveled. In 1832, for example, he began the year in Naples, spent late February and the first half of March in Rome, then after three weeks in Civitavecchia was sent (this time on a mission) to Ancona, and from June to the year's end managed to get in repeated visits to Florence and Siena as well as a tour of the Abruzzi. In sum, he spent perhaps a third of the year at his Roman *pied-à-terre*, possibly as little as eight or nine weeks all told at Civitavecchia. It was not, however, the exuberant curiosity of his earlier years that impelled him to all these displacements, or at any rate, his usual addiction to tourism was combined with an uneasiness, a dread of boredom. An 1833 painting by Ducis, one of several formal portraits that Beyle commissioned during this decade, subtly catches the disquietude he was experiencing in his Italian career: his eyes seem melancholy or perhaps anxious, his lips are tensely pursed, his face is marked by stern vertical lines running down from the wings of his nose and around his mouth.

In this general mood, Beyle's frequent Italian excursions did not suffice to divert him from the loneliness and tedium of consular life, and by the middle of 1833, just two years after assuming his duties and after an additional personal disappointment to which we shall soon attend, he asked for an extended leave, the first and shortest of three he would be granted, to return to France. In late August, he set out for Paris, where he spent three months, from early September to early December. He renewed contacts with old friends of both sexes, including one attachment that had been something less than friendly for a number of years—his relationship with Clémentine Curial. Though just a year earlier, in writing his autobiographical fragment, *Souvenirs d'égotisme*, Stendhal still recalled the anguish he suffered when Menti jilted him, the pain had faded enough for them to be good friends once more, and remembering her as a kindred spirit who had given him her love freely, indeed extravagantly, he characteristically wanted to preserve some vestige of affectionate intimacy with her. He stayed as a guest of the Curials at the family château near Compiègne for several days at the beginning of November; afterward, their letters would resume a note of friendly confidentiality, and Beyle would seek out Menti on his next trip to Paris in 1836.

Meanwhile, he was busy in Paris with a round of social calls and dinner parties—including, among many others, a festive *partie de filles* arranged by the ever-lubricious Mérimée on the occasion of his own thirtieth birthday—as well as official meetings with government ministers and perhaps even an audience with Louis-Philippe. When his friend Jules Gaulthier entrusted him with the manuscript of a novel in early October, he had to apologize in a note that it was absolutely impossible for him to read anything while he was in Paris and that she would have to wait till January or February, when he could send her his comments and suggestions from Italy. This promise he would duly if somewhat tardily fulfill, but after giving advice to the amateur novelist, he was to discover that her manuscript had launched him on an ambitious undertaking of his own.

Altogether, Beyle had too good a time during these three months in Paris, for, as we have already seen from the letters written in 1834 that were quoted above, his sense of painful isolation in Civitavecchia was all the more acute after his return. Perhaps the last burst of his Parisian exuberance was visible on his steamboat trip down the Rhône to Marseilles in December, when he by chance met George Sand and Alfred de Musset, also headed for Italy on what was to prove for these ill-sorted lovers a disastrous excursion. Beyle, from what one can infer from George Sand's description, must have been in fine fettle: with his gifts of mimicry, he dramatized for Sand and Musset the dull and ridiculous Italian types they would encounter, as he warned them that by leaving Paris they were abandoning all true intellectual culture. George Sand was to a degree amused by Beyle's high jinks and perceptive enough to observe: "I don't believe he was wicked: he took too much trouble to appear so." But she was also too proper (for all the unconventionality of her love affairs) and too essentially serious to feel very comfortable with Beyle's zany behavior. At one point, slightly tipsy, he danced a jig for Sand and Musset, a moment in terpischorean history which Musset preserved for posterity in a crude but vivid drawing that shows the author of *Le Rouge et le Noir* in flapping greatcoat and fur-lined boots, his head, adorned with a top hat, jauntily cocked back as he cavorts around the table. This struck George Sand as rather undignified, and she was offended by his habit or affectation of obscenity: he certainly knew, probably in intimate detail, about her brief affair with Mérimée and apparently made the mistake of adopting a vocabulary he thought appropriate to that dubious association. He was, George Sand concluded, in what she imagined as balanced judgment, "of a cleverness more ingenious than apt. . . . with a genuine, original talent, writing badly, in a manner, however, to strike his readers and engage their lively interest." [2] Stendhal on his part left no account of his

2. George Sand, *Histoire de ma vie* (Paris, 1899), vol. 4, pp. 185–186.

personal reaction to this meeting with Sand, but he would make his views of her performance as a stylist acerbically clear in the comments he wrote in connection with his next major novel. Meanwhile, they parted company, much to Sand's relief, at Marseilles, Beyle proceeding overland to Italy while she and Musset continued by water. Literally and figuratively, their paths would continue to diverge.

Between Beyle's diplomatic furloughs to France, his tourism in Italy, and his extended stays in Rome, one may wonder whether he ever thought of his consular responsibilities in Civitavecchia. He was in fact accused both in his lifetime and afterward of conceiving his appointment as a mere sinecure while almost totally neglecting his duties. The facts of the matter are more complicated. For the reasons we have noted, life in Civitavecchia was not merely disagreeable but often quite intolerable. He was, however, a highly capable administrator, as he had demonstrated in the imperial service, a keen observer fascinated by the intricacies of politics, and a man who enjoyed the exercise of public authority, for which, alas, he found only the most circumscribed sphere in this boondocks consulate. One measure of Beyle's conception of himself as a diplomat is the fact that from late 1830 onward he repeatedly presses his Parisian friends in his letters to help him obtain the Cross of the Legion of Honor in recognition of his accomplishments as a civil servant. Perhaps he thought the decoration might aid his advancement in the foreign service, but it clearly also meant to him an official confirmation of his *métier* as a responsible bureaucrat, and when the cross was finally awarded to him in 1835 only in his capacity as a French man of letters, he was actually disappointed.

Beyle never spent much more than seven months a year at Civitavecchia, and some years, as we have seen, it was a good deal less than that. But the official correspondence he conducted as consul suggests that when he attended to his duties he performed them with scrupulous care; the rest of the time, considering the minor nature of his post, he felt that he could adequately manage his consular responsibilities by delegating authority. From his window overlooking the port, he did not, after all, spend most of his time floating down scraps of paper but observed the shipments of grain, sugar, fabric, and other commodities entering the port, noting, where appropriate, the flags under which the vessels sailed, indicating the precise quantity of the cargoes and the sort of containers in which they were carried, and dutifully reporting all this in his dispatches to his superiors. It must have seemed to him at times rather uncomfortably like his chores on the wharves of Marseilles during his youthful involvement in the import business.

Beyle clearly wanted a more challenging arena for the exercise of his diplomatic talents. He tried to broaden the scope of his work by sending back to the foreign ministry in Paris lengthy analyses of the fluctuations of political trends in the Papal States and elsewhere in Italy. These efforts, however, seem to have been viewed as mere officiousness. The French consul at Civitavecchia was expected to go on counting shipments of grain and sugar, and not to infringe on the prerogatives of the ambassador.

When an occasional crisis presented itself, Beyle handled matters with coolheaded competence, as when the French steamship *Henri IV* was wrecked on a reef off the coast some forty miles northwest of Civitavecchia in 1835 or in March 1832, when the French sent an expeditionary force to occupy Ancona—ostensibly to discourage Austrian penetration of the Papal States—and Beyle was dispatched to act as military intendant. After the Ancona mission, Ambassador Sainte-Aulaire praised Beyle in a letter to the foreign minister for his admirable performance of a "disagreeable and difficult assignment." But no demonstration of zeal and competence could really extricate Beyle from the "abominable hole" into which the foreign service had cast him. He was, after all, a literary man whose writing made him something of a political liability. He might dream from time to time of a new post in Spain (thinking once more, perhaps, of *El Cid* and the blossoming orange trees), but the foreign ministry felt it had done quite enough by saving him from poverty with a second-rate consulate in a dull little corner of Italy. Beyle's sole recourse, then, was to stay away from the job as much as possible while still executing the essential consular duties.

In this regard, however, he committed one grave tactical error, the consequences of which were to plague him through his entire Italian tenure in office. One of the diplomatic appurtenances Beyle inherited with the position in 1831 was a twenty-six-year-old consular employee named Lysimaque Caftangioglou Tavernier, born in Salonica of a Greek father and a French mother. Beyle's predecessor, Baron de Vaux, had warned him that Tavernier was not to be trusted, but the new consul was inclined to discount the advice, probably because he was suspicious of the baron's Bourbon politics and attracted by the republicanism Tavernier flaunted, and probably also because the young man was clever enough to ingratiate himself with his new superior, in whom he must have quickly recognized an eagerness to pass on the more disagreeable consular chores to someone else. By July 1831, Tavernier was ensconced as acting chancellor of the consulate, and from this point on, he took great pains to make himself progressively useful to his repeatedly absent employer. He bided his time until 1834, when Beyle proposed to the foreign ministry that Tavernier be confirmed as the authorized chancellor of the Civitavecchia consulate. Beyle no doubt imagined that with Tavernier as official chancellor he could leave even more in the hands of his subaltern while he amused himself in Rome and elsewhere: even a person of great penetration can be purblind when he thinks he is affording himself an easy way out of onerous obligations.

Tavernier's appointment as chancellor became official in May, and with his position secured, he immediately proceeded to defy Beyle's orders and to do everything in his power to undermine the consul. By the beginning of June, Beyle sent a sharp rebuke to Tavernier, who responded with a letter of resignation couched in insolent terms. A week later, Beyle was persuaded by his superiors to accept Tavernier back as chancellor, though the consul knew he was by that act condemning himself to a "labyrinth of strife." Meanwhile, Tavernier was sending smarmy letters of denunciation to the foreign ministry in which he professed his own unflagging zeal for the administration of the consulate while expressing his dismay over the appointed consul's shocking neglect of his duties and over his continual absences. These maneuvers resulted in several official rebukes to Beyle coupled with stern orders that he was henceforth not to absent himself from Civitavecchia.

Poor Henri Beyle, instead of providing himself a means of frequent escape from the abominable hole, had contrived to create his own private demon who danced around him, mocked him, provoked him, and helped keep him prisoner in this dreary post. One can easily understand how by 1835 Beyle could be toying with the idea of leaving the diplomatic service altogether to try his luck once again as a professional writer in Paris. "The animal's real calling," he confessed in a letter to Domenico Fiore in April of that year, "is to be writing a novel in a garret, for I prefer the pleasure of describing follies to that of wearing a brocaded suit worth 800 francs." Perhaps only the imminent prospect of another extended leave to the French capital kept him from weighing the alternative of resignation more seriously.

Another consequence of the consul Beyle's sense of being marooned on a solitary shore was that for a while he was led to think more frequently of marriage than he ever had done before. A new love affair might conceivably relieve his chronic boredom, but he now wanted something as simple and solid as intimate companionship, something a wife rather than a mistress could give him. During the first two years of his residence in the Papal States, his chief matrimonial prospect was still Giulia Rinieri. His proposal of marriage delivered in writing to Daniello Berlinghieri on the eve of his departure for Trieste had been politely set aside but not absolutely refused, and Beyle still nurtured hopes that his suit would be accepted. In late October 1832, Berlinghieri, who had just become Giulia's legal guardian, arrived with her in their hometown of Siena on a long furlough from his ambassadorial post in Paris. Giulia must have promptly apprised Beyle that she was in Italy, for within a week or two of her return he had made the two-day trip from Rome to Siena, where he arrived on November 7 for a visit of twelve days. By late November, he was back in Siena for another week's stay, this time as a houseguest at Berlinghieri's country villa. In January 1833, he was once again in Siena, in this instance for a full three weeks.

It is hard to know exactly what transpired between the hitherto passionate lovers during these visits, though whatever happened seems to have been rather ambiguous and not altogether satisfying from Beyle's point of view. The bothersome Berlinghieri was willing to receive the French consul as a guest, though he gave him no particular encouragement as a suitor and certainly would not have knowingly acquiesced in Beyle's enjoying Giulia's sexual favors. Lovers, of course, often contrive to avoid the scrutiny of the most vigilant eyes, and it is rather likely, though not entirely certain, that Beyle and Giulia found occasion to resume their Parisian intimacy in Siena. Beyle left one cryptic marginal note referring to "all the battles of Siena" in the late fall of 1832; it is not clear whether he means that Giulia at first resisted him sexually or simply rejected his renewed proposals of marriage. Later, he would recall the "lovely days and still lovelier nights" of his visits to Siena. By mid-December, she was writing to assure him that he should by no means abandon hope, to which he responded, exasperated by this ever-elusive hope, that he wished it were in his power to forget her. During his visit in late January and early February, he apparently witnessed Giulia's flirtation or infatuation with one Sienese gentleman and her being pursued by another who had serious matrimonial intentions. Nevertheless, a familiar confidentiality, and perhaps more, persisted between them, and when Giulia wrote at the beginning of April to inform him that she was to be married to a cousin, Giulio Martini, Beyle was wounded by this disappointment which he had every reason to expect.

Beyle took twelve days to compose an answer (April 20–21, 1833), softening his first version and making it friendlier, as we learn from a note he made on his rough draft. He still addresses Giulia as "my dear angel" and assumes her familiarity with his code of pseudonyms for her suitors and his companions, while he bemoans the fact that henceforth they can be no more than friends. He wants to hear from her in the greatest detail about her imminent marriage, and he tells her he is consoling himself with "the mademoiselles Pauline, like the one that bathed in the Seine this summer, you remember, in Alfred's letter." This enigmatic allusion has been identified by the assiduous François Michel.[3] "Alfred" is Mérimée, and the letter in question, which was written in late October 1832 and which Beyle had passed on to Giulia for her delectation, was typically scabrous: the piquant story of a certain Pauline picked up by Mérimée on a boating trip, Pauline's inadvertent tumble into the Seine, Mérimée's attempt to rape her after lying in wait and seizing her naked when she was changing clothes in the cabin, Pauline's apt comment that they would both get a good deal more pleasure out of the transaction if he waited till she was in the mood to comply willingly. The letter concludes with the smug observation that Pauline had in fact subsequently delighted Mérimée as a mistress, that he was sharing her with Sutton Sharpe and would offer her to Beyle on his next trip to Paris, and that she was remarkably adept at certain coital tricks specified here by their slang designations. All this, as François Michel notes, is hardly the most edifying reading matter to send an unmarried woman of good family, but his inference that Beyle could not have held Giulia in very high esteem if this is what he showed her seems unnecessary. They had, after all, been something more than platonic lovers for three years; a certain sensual comaraderie against a background of pleasurably shared intimacies could explain why Beyle would choose to send on to Giulia this titillating communication from Mérimée; and there is no documented indication that his initial affection and regard for her had become in any way tainted. The fact is, he urgently wanted her to become his wife. Her marriage to Martini, in any case, in June 1833, by no means cut off their relationship, indeed by no means limited it, as Beyle at first affirmed would be the case, to mere amicability.

With Giulia lost, at any rate as a matrimonial possibility, Beyle immediately began to look elsewhere for a wife. By May 13, barely a month after he received the portentous letter from Siena, he proposed marriage to a certain "Mlle Rietti" (possibly another of his code designations), about whom little is known except that she promptly refused him. Two years later, he entered into serious marital negotiations concerning a Signorina Vidau. The Vidaus, of French origin, were one of the leading families of Civitavecchia. After Beyle's death, the incorrigible Tavernier retailed the

3. *Les Amours de Sienne* (Paris, 1950).

story that the Vidau girl was a washerwoman's daughter and that the match had been broken off by a pious rich uncle scandalized by Beyle's character. In fact, as Beyle makes clear on two occasions in his correspondence during 1835, his prospective father-in-law, a man of sixty-five, had proposed moving in with the newlyweds, which was quite enough to send the consul scurrying back to the safety of his bachelor quarters. But on September 27, he could still say rather wistfully in a letter to Albert Stapfer on the occasion of the latter's wedding, "One can find moments of impatience in marriage but never the deep dark bleakness of the single state."

These, and perhaps other, more insubstantial plans of marriage came to nothing, and the lonely Beyle, now past his fiftieth year, was—despite the intermittent diversions of friends, travel, and amateur archaeology—repeatedly driven back upon himself, led to contemplate what his life had been, and, before long, to focus that contemplation in the act of writing. In total contrast to his busy activity as a novelist and journalist at the end of the 1820s, this was writing done for himself and (quite consciously) for posterity because Beyle was deeply convinced, on good grounds, that his official role as consul under the July Monarchy did not accord with the complete freedom of expression he needed as a writer. His residence in Italy, as we have seen, isolated him socially, while his political situation isolated him as a writer. He resolved not to produce anything for publication and firmly refused the repeated pleas for new material from Alphonse Levavesseur, who had published *Le Rouge et le Noir*. To be sure, he attentively followed from afar the reception of his last novel, vehemently defending it in his letters when he discovered to his dismay that some of his friends found it faintly scandalous (including, of all people, Mérimée!) or saw in Julien both a consummate scoundrel and a self-portrait of Henri Beyle. Meanwhile, he began to accumulate unfinished writing projects, zigzagging between fiction and autobiography as the spirit moved him.

During his first year of diplomatic service in Italy, he began two short stories, one of which, set in the Italian Renaissance, he completed. A couple of years later, he acquired a set of manuscripts of Renaissance tales of passion and vengeance, possibly through his antiquarian friend Bucci, and he began to think about reworking them into French. In the fall of 1832, he sketched the opening chapters of a novel, *Une Position sociale*: it was one of half a dozen novels Stendhal would begin in the last decade of his life and leave in a fragmentary state. From May 1834 to November of the following year, he was more or less steadily involved in work on a new novel, which he broke off to begin an autobiography. Both the novel, *Lucien Leuwen*, and the autobiography, *Le Vie de Henry Brulard*, would run to great length even in their unfinished state, and both would prove to be posthumous masterpieces. Stendhal in the first half of the 1830s by no means stopped writing but was forced by the vulnerability of his position and by the nature of his subjects to become for a time an invisible great writer.

The chronology of Stendhal's literary work in this period falls into two distinct stages, the first, from late 1830 to mid-1834, the second, from mid-1834 to the spring of 1836. During the first three and a half years of his consular service, there is what might be described as an intermittence in his vocation as a writer. He begins, as we have noted, three pieces of fiction and an autobiographical project as well, but none of these really holds his attention, and there is nothing he works on for more than a few days or at the most a few weeks. One might imagine that he could have taken advantage of the quiet and isolation of his post at Civitavecchia to settle down and to produce major work, devoting his mornings, let us say, to novel writing, and his afternoons to counting shipments of grain and to tending to quarantine arrangements. The fact is, however, that Stendhal was a novelist who thrived on the stimulation of social activity, whose inventive powers were liveliest when he himself was in a state of emotional excitement or well-being. He needed those three or four cubic feet per diem of new ideas, and he also needed, one suspects, the French language spoken around him as he wrote. It is surely no coincidence that the only three novels he actually completed and saw through to publication were all written in Paris (*Le Rouge et le Noir* having been given no more than its first scaffolding in Marseilles).

Beyle's life from late 1830 till May 1834, as we have seen, was marked by sharp disappointment over his diplomatic career, loneliness, boredom, repeated illness, fitful displacements, and, in these lamentable circumstances, by rather confused castings about for a mistress or a wife. When we add to all this his conviction that as long as he remained in the foreign service he could not publish his work, it is hardly surprising that he should have had neither the impelling motive nor the suitable mood for doing any sustained writing. His visit to Paris in the latter part of 1833 reinforced his sense that the sphere where he really belonged was, after all, the French capital, and this in turn sharpened his feeling of isolation after his return to Italy. Then his troubles with Lysimaque Tavernier in the spring of 1834 drove home to him still more forcefully how intolerable his diplomatic position was, even led him to think of abandoning the foreign service.

It is at this moment, in May 1834, that Stendhal's vocation as a writer again powerfully asserts itself. Once again, as in 1829–30, he was totally caught up in a writing project, and from this point until the spring of 1836, when he was granted a new leave to return to France, he was almost continually occupied with first one, then a second, ambitious book. Perhaps in his post-Parisian gloom of 1834, he felt that his writing was the one remaining resource he had for resuscitating his inner life, or at least for taking stock of it. More certainly, writing was the principal activity that linked him with the Parisian intellectual center which he had just again left behind, and as he now began to toy with the idea of quitting his diplomatic career, he could more readily imagine himself writing for publication in the not too distant future. And of course, for an improvisatory writer like Stendhal, the sudden momentum generated by an idea for just the book he was inwardly prepared to write is not to be discounted. The instant he took off with the conception of *Lucien Leuwen*, rapidly inventing out of his own stock of perceptions the scenes, incidents, and characters needed to elaborate the anecdotal kernel he had discovered, he was again in full stride as a novelist, and his three and a half years of "intermittence" were over.

This novel, reflecting an intricate process of self-exploration through mingled fiction and recollection, sits chronologically between two experiments in actual autobiography, and it may be useful to consider the latter first. Stendhal's first serious attempt at autobiography was *Souvenirs d'égotisme*, a brisk review of the decade he had just spent in Paris, which he worked on for a mere two weeks in Rome at the beginning of the summer of 1832. In willing the manuscript to Constantin, he left instructions that it was not to be published until ten years after this death. In fact, like *Henry Brulard*, it did not appear in print till the 1890s. *Souvenirs d'égotisme*, though informed by shrewd retrospective self-awareness, is a much more conventional piece of autobiographical writing than *Brulard*, which, at least in formal terms, is Stendhal's most radically innovative project.

This account of his first eighteen years, to which we had abundant recourse in considering Beyle's early life, has been compared by some commentators to the psychoanalytic process Freud would later devise: reflecting on the origins of the self, the narrative often seems to proceed through free association; it invokes a key metaphor of archaeology to explain its own gradual and imperfect discovery of forgotten and virtually lost layers of past experience; and it is particularly interested in exploring the roots of desire, a concern that at times leads to the uncovering of socially unacceptable or forbidden impulses, as in the famous passage in which Stendhal confesses the sexually possessive feelings toward his mother he remembers from early childhood.

But such analogies with the psychoanalytic enterprise should not be pushed too far, for what characterizes *Henry Brulard* most strikingly is its pervasive literary self-consciousness. That is, *La Vie de Henry Brulard* is a self-conscious autobiography—perhaps the first autobiography which is consistently that—in the same way that *Tristram Shandy*, to which Stendhal deliberately alludes here at a couple of points, is a self-conscious novel, articulating its own improvised form through a constant reflection on the arbitrariness of the generic conventions with which it must work, on the game of ambiguous signal and dubious response that has to go on between writer and reader, on the ontological chasm that separates words from the things to which they are supposed to refer.

"I cannot give the reality of events," Stendhal characteristically observes (chap. 16). "I can present no more than their *shadow*" (emphasis in the original). This incapacity derives from the nature of language, which is necessarily other than reality, and of memory, which is as tricky a medium as language, distorting experience, rescuing only tantalizing fragments of it, often preserving only a sense of recollected affect where the writer would like to recuperate situation, cause, and relation in all their minute interconnections. There are similar observations on the elusive nature of that *I* which the autobiographer is compelled to invoke with such embarrassing frequency: is it a stable entity, is there any real identity between the *I* of 1835 and the *I* of 1800, how much can the writer himself pretend to know of who he really is? Faithfully corresponding to this skeptical questioning of the self developing in time, the narrative scrambles any simple linear temporal progression, moving rapidly back and forth between the childhood years, which are the main narrated material, and various points in the more recent past, often interweaving dramatized images of the autobiographical present—the writer standing on a Roman promontory or sitting in his Civitavecchia study on a gloomy day—with imaginative reconstructions of the youthful Henri's point of view. All this is carried off as a rapid improvisation with a winning ease of manner, but Stendhal's commitment to a thoroughly unpretentious, somehow *transparent* presentation of self led him not merely to avoid the rhetorical excesses of the age but to create a literary form that anticipated such modernist prose-poets of interiority and convoluted time as Proust, Joyce, Woolf, and Faulkner and to produce a work that still seems extraordinarily fresh and convincing in our own age of self-consciousness about language, narrative, and fictions of the self.

"J. J. Rousseau," Stendhal noted on the manuscript of *Lucien Leuwen* in the fall of 1836, shortly after he had broken off work on *Henry Bru-lard*, "who clearly sensed that he wanted to *deceive*, half-charlatan, half-dupe, had to devote all his attention to *style*" (emphasis in the original). He would seem to be thinking of Rousseau the author of the *Confessions*, in which case the contrast he goes on to make would be to himself as autobiographer: "Dominique, quite inferior to J. J., but in other regards a man of probity, devotes all his attention to the substance of things [*le fond des choses*]." [4] In writing *Henry Brulard*, he is repeatedly aware that *le fond des choses* may by its nature resist incorporation in language, but his flaunting of this awareness, his invention of strategies to make the literary rendering of a life at least *seem* spontaneous, immediate, and utterly candid, make this one of the most remarkable pieces of autobiographical writing of the nineteenth century.

The work of fiction that he set aside in November 1835 in order to undertake *Brulard* is in its own way almost as remarkable. When Beyle returned to Italy at the end of 1833, after his three-month stay in Paris, he brought back with him, as we noted before, the manuscript of a novel by Jules Gaulthier, *The Lieutenant*. On May 4, 1834, he finally wrote his friend about her novel, telling her quite frankly that the manuscript needed thorough reworking and that "you must imagine you are translating a book into German." All traces, that is, of effusion and fashionable sublime style were to be rigorously removed. As Beyle succinctly put it, "the poor novelist should try to make one believe in the *burning passion* [of the protagonist] but never name it" (emphasis in the original). As soon as he sent off the letter, he himself began to experiment with rewriting the manuscript, which for the moment remained in his possession. Within a few days, he was plunged into work on what was now clearly his own novel. Since *The Lieutenant* has not survived, one can only surmise how much Stendhal took from it for the immense project that was to become *Lucien Leuwen*. It is unlikely that the Gaulthier manuscript suggested to him more than the outlines of the initial long episode of his novel (which, it has been proposed, Mme Gaulthier herself may have developed from an anecdotal hint in *Racine et Shakespeare*)—the story of a highly advantaged young cavalry officer stationed in a provincial town who, imagining himself impervious to love, becomes enamored of a local beauty. Stendhal then planned a second part in which Lucien, falsely believing he has been betrayed by the woman he loves obsessively, the

4. *Marginalia*, vol. 2, p. 287.

aristocratic young widow Bathilde de Chasteller, resigns his post in Nancy and returns to Paris, where, at the instance of his millionaire father, he attempts a political career as private secretary to the minister of the interior. The first part was written and extensively revised; the second part was finished with some lacunae, especially toward the end; a projected third part, in which the estranged lovers were to meet in Rome and at last be reconciled and marry, was never written.

Stendhal worked intently on *Lucien Leuwen* from May 1834 to mid-March of the following year, bringing the narrative to the end of Lucien's Paris experience, and for the next few months, until he put aside the manuscript, he continued to rework the material he had written. He had thought of publishing the novel, with its scathing view of contemporary French politics, in four or five years, by which time he hoped either that he would be out of the foreign service or that the July Monarchy would have fallen. In fact, Part One alone of the novel was published by Romain Colomb only in 1855, and the first editorial reconstruction of the whole book from Stendhal's manuscript did not appear until 1894. The manuscript itself, its margins densely crowded with comments and scenarios, its text heavily cross-hatched with deletions, insertions, and revisions, provides the most instructive evidence of how Stendhal conceived this novel, how he worked on it, and why he was unable to complete it.

"In *Julien* [that is, *Le Rouge et le Noir*]," he noted at the outset of his new project, contrasting it with his previous novel, "the reader's imagination is not led sufficiently by small details. But, on the other hand, grander manner, fresco compared to a miniature." [5] We shall soon pursue the concrete implications of this "miniaturist" manner in considering the technical innovations of *Lucien Leuwen*. The manuscript also reveals how the process of composition of *Lucien Leuwen* differed from that of its predecessor and of its successor. Both *Le Rouge et le Noir* and *Chartreuse* were written as sustained rapid improvisations, the former, as we have seen, in a series of accumulated layers of writing, the latter in one breathless burst of uninterrupted invention. *Leuwen*, by contrast, was much more painfully and consciously elaborated: Stendhal tried to preserve an improvisatory élan, noting in the margin that he did not allow himself to reread more than two pages of the previous day's work, fearing to break stride, and that ideas had to come to him before he actually planned them; and yet he became entangled in elaborate outlines and guiding notes, soon found himself restlessly revising what he had written. As Jean Prévost has

5. *Romans et nouvelles*, ed. Henri Martineau (Paris, 1952), vol. 2, p. 1520.

shown in detail,⁶ improvisation was in effect Stendhal's finished work, the final sudden snapping into focus of many years of assimilated experience, and when he began instead to revise, he generally became unsure of his way.

In *Lucien Leuwen*, especially in Part Two, he had in a sense written *more* than a complete novel, and how to make it right by diminishing its proportions proved more difficult than he imagined when he noted the following on the manuscript: "It's better that the manuscript I bring to Paris should be *too* long. I will only have to cut, while the Marseilles manuscript having been too short, I was compelled to create the essential material at the moment *Le Rouge* was being printed. Here, I will only have to polish the style and give it cadence after having made the cuts and some linkages. So, nothing wrong if the bound manuscript is *long*" (emphases in the original).⁷

Stendhal's ultimate difficulty in controlling and completing the large design of *Lucien Leuwen* may have been an uncertainty about what kind of novel he intended to make out of this material. Such a wavering sense of intention could well be reflected in the list of titles he considered using. In addition to the title editorially settled on by posterity (but not unambiguously by him), he thought of calling the book *The Telegraph*, *The Woods of Prémol*, *The Green Huntsman*, *The Orange of Malta*, *The Red and the White*, *The Blue and the White*, *The Magenta and the Black*. It is noteworthy that five of the seven titles stress colors. In three of these color titles, Stendhal manifestly meant to echo the title of *Le Rouge et le Noir* in order to indicate that his new novel was a "chronicle" of life under the July Monarchy by the same author who had produced the Chronicle of 1830. The colors are in part political emblems, but as in *Le Rouge et le Noir*, they are also radiating centers of associations: Stendhal liked to imagine that he could lay out his fictional materials like a chessboard, but in fact part of his greatness as a writer is his ability to surrender himself to his materials, to allow them to resonate with his own half-forgotten or unconscious experience.

He is not, we have seen, a very visual novelist, but there is a pronounced tendency in Part One of *Lucien Leuwen* to provide an emotional focus, which seems somehow meaningful but is in no way symbolic, at key junctures by defining the fictional situation in vivid colors. At the beginning, Lucien's decision to join the army is dramatically revealed, with a fine sense of the vibrating psychological nuances the act has for

6. *La Création chez Stendhal* (Paris, 1950).
7. *Romans et nouvelles*, vol. 1, p. 1563.

him, almost entirely through colors. He stands on the rich Turkish rug provided for his bedroom by his mother, in magenta trousers and a spectacular dressing gown of blue and gold, contemplating the green jacket with magenta pipings of a cavalry officer that has been spread out on his sofa. When he rides into Nancy with his regiment for the first time, his eye is caught by a parrot-green shutter in the middle of a large white facade, and he immediately thinks, "What gaudy colors these provincial scoundrels choose!" (chap. 4). Peering out from behind the parrot-green shutters is a beautiful young woman with ash-blonde hair and a disdainful look; distracted by those eyes behind the shutters, Lucien takes the first of his two humiliating spills from his saddle into the mud of Nancy. The parrot-green shutters will be kept in focus through most of Lucien's repeated circlings, literal and figurative, around the seemingly inaccessible abode of Bathilde de Chasteller, and their presence mnemonically invokes his two disgraceful falls, catches up something of the spatial and cultural distance between the Parisian hero and his provincial love, embodies without explanation a rich complex of feelings as some particular garment, object of decor, some taste or aroma so often becomes memory's metonym for a whole set of intensely felt experiences.

Lucien's social intercourse with other aristocratic women of Nancy is also focused in the occasional but strategic attention given to the colors that he notices they are wearing or to the orchestration of the colors of clothing and decor in their milieu. (Though Stendhal remains adamantly opposed to the notion of the novel as costume drama, he notes in the margin here, at once the conscientious researcher and the ironic literary critic: "Reread a few pages of Sand the vendor of fashions, and arrange the outfits." [8]) Elsewhere, the ferociously pious spinster, Mlle Bérard, whom Mme de Chasteller misguidedly hires as a companion in order to protect her own virtue, forever figures in Lucien's imagination in her bonnet of yellow lace with its faded green ribbon—a pale, shabby repetition of the shocking green shutters against the white housefront—which seems to incarnate the decayed, repellent nature of the woman herself.

It is instructive that all these experiments in defining crucial nodes of the protagonist's experience through color disappear in the second half of the book, for with Lucien's return to Paris there is a visible switch, perhaps not entirely intended by Stendhal, in novelistic perspective. Part One is firmly and delicately managed as Lucien's *Bildungsroman*. We follow the shifting rhythms of his moods, his introspection, and his reflections on

8. Ibid., p. 1519.

others as a highly inexperienced young man endowed with a great capacity for unaffected feeling and encumbered with a premature cynicism by his worldly father and his Parisian upbringing. Political oppositions between liberals and ultras (advocates of reestablishing a Bourbon regime) in this provincial town are nicely delineated, together with the tawdry careerism of the 1830s, the background of endemic proletarian unrest, brutal military repression, and aristocratic fear of renewed revolution. But Lucien's attachment to Bathilde de Chasteller is kept clearly in the foreground and subtly rendered through the miniaturist manner to which Stendhal himself refers.

Part Two, on the other hand, though it has some brilliant psychological perceptions and though it offers toward the end in the portrait of Mme Grandet, who sells herself to Lucien hoping to obtain a ministry for her husband, one of Stendhal's triumphs of characterization, is a relentlessly political novel in a very different manner from Part One. Lucien's inner development is often lost sight of; at times, he seems little more than a transparent, mobile, and not very interesting vehicle of observation through which Stendhal can guide us along the various venal byways of the contemporary political scene. For six long chapters, moreover, the narrative almost literally loses sight of Lucien while following the successive stages of his father's machinations as a parliamentary intriguer. Stendhal himself clearly indicates at least once in his marginal notes that he sensed he was getting bogged down in a morass of political details which prevented him from proceeding with the principal interest of his novel. After an enormously circumstantial account of a local election which Lucien has been sent to fix on behalf of the ministry of the interior, the novelist notes on his manuscript: "It is high time to get out of election matters and the self-interest of ambition. They have been going on since p. 14; this is 278, so there are 264 pages of election." [9]

These difficulties do not mean that the detailed political sections of *Lucien Leuwen* are devoid of interest. As totally unillusioned, shrewdly informed analysis of political life, there is scarcely anything in the nineteenth-century novel that surpasses them. But these sections are not sufficiently integrated with Lucien's story, not sufficiently translated from fictionalized exposé into an embracing fictional vision of the tenor of individual life against the background of contemporary institutions. All three of Stendhal's major novels are profoundly political but in very different ways, and *Lucien Leuwen*, the most explicitly political of the three, may

9. Ibid., p. 1568.

finally be the least satisfactory in how it encompasses politics in fiction. Maurice Bardèche has perceptively compared the three books in just this regard:

> *Le Rouge et le Noir* shows the political mechanism perceived from below, from without; only its consequences are seen. *Lucien Leuwen* places the observer inside the political machinery; it is a guided tour of the inner works: but the complete political vision is lacking—we are too close. . . . With *La Chartreuse de Parme* we are above the spectacle; we have a kind of dizzying downward view, total and terrifying.[10]

But if Part Two of *Lucien Leuwen*, however intellectually engaging its study of the mechanics of politics, frustrates for a long while the expectations raised by Part One, that is also because the account of the evolution of a passionate love that constitutes Part One is so exquisitely realized. Perhaps what is most remarkable here, at least technically, is Stendhal's ability to make the continual analysis of fluid feeling and attitude take the place of conventional narrative. There would be nothing to equal it in fiction until the later Henry James and Proust. Again and again, the word *raisonnement*—reasoning, argumentation with oneself—occurs to describe what the narrator conveys to us of the balancing of claims, the drawing of inferences, the changing of viewpoints that go on in the central characters. Again and again, the subjunctive mode is invoked as the characters reason about conditions contrary to fact or as the analytic narrator speculates as to what would have happened if the characters were other than what they are. Often the characters' attentiveness in the midst of experience to their own emotionally fraught reasonings is wound to such a pitch that the slightest external stimulus—a whispered word, the rustling sound of a skirt brushing against a billiard table—explodes on their consciousness with a terrific shock. Stendhal, so obsessively self-questioning and analytic, especially in his relations with women, through most of his adult life, had succeeded in transforming his own self-consciousness into a refined art.

Here, for example, is Lucien in a tête-à-tête with Bathilde, who is really beginning to love him but who is even less willing to accept the consequences of this fact than he is willing to permit himself the luxury of hope in his passion for her. In the midst of vehemently arguing her need to protect both her virtue and the appearance of virtue, she has just inadvertently begun a sentence with the words, "You might come to see me often," which Lucien interrupts with a kind of gasp:

10. *Stendhal romancier* (Paris, 1947), p. 417.

—Really? said Leuwen, barely breathing.

Until then, Mme de Chasteller's tone had been seemly, prudent, cold, at least in Leuwen's view. The voice with which he pronounced that word, *really*, would perhaps have eluded the most accomplished Don Juan; for Leuwen, there was no talent involved, it was the impulse of nature, naturalness itself. This simple word of Leuwen's changed everything. There was such unhappiness, such assurance of punctual obedience in this word, that Mme de Chasteller was as it were disarmed by it. She had gathered all her courage to struggle against a powerful being, and she had discovered extreme weakness. In a moment everything changed; she no longer had to fear that she might lack resolution but, quite to the contrary, that she might adopt too firm a tone, that she might seem to take advantage of the victory. She felt pity because of the unhappiness she was causing Leuwen. [chap. 32]

This same reaction, in which it is male infirmity rather than the strategies of seduction that wins a woman's heart, of course also figures prominently in *Le Rouge et le Noir*, but the method of rendering the turnabout in feeling is strikingly different. In the case of Julien and Mme de Rênal, it is all done with succinct, almost elliptical, drily ironic notation. In the case of Lucien and Mme de Chasteller, Stendhal proceeds patiently with fine brushstrokes, giving us not so much a direct report of the movement of consciousness within his protagonists as his own carefully mediated version of that movement. He was avidly rereading Fielding's *Tom Jones* and Gibbon's *Decline and Fall* while he worked on *Lucien Leuwen*, and as he dealt with the rise and fall of private passions in a realistically detailed contemporary milieu, he clearly sought to create a nineteenth-century equivalent for the supreme worldliness, the magisterial overview of ramified causality and subtle interconnection that operated in those two great English narratives.

In the technique he developed toward this end, the external gesture or event—the *really* of our passage—is reduced to the apex of an inverted pyramid, the base of which might be described as the whole moral history of the protagonists. The novelist's activity, with a truly Jamesian subtlety, moves away from linear narration to an analytic shuttling between apex and base, between action and the complex of feeling, attitude, preconception, disposition, and impulse that both generates action and gives it meaning. In the heavily laden interchange here between prospective lovers, the small vibration of tone has the power of a battle-mace wielded in a novel by Walter Scott; and it is characteristic that our passage should be symmetrically framed at the beginning by what Bathilde's tone seems to Lucien and at the end by what she fears her tone may sound like to him, while the entire radical transformation of their relationship is effected through the tone of voice in which he utters those two revelatory syllables.

The minute characterization of tone and what is behind it not only serves as a means of understanding the fluctuations of a relationship but also helps Stendhal suggest the delicate nuance of feeling in the lovers' experience of the relationship. A little earlier in the novel (chap. 18), the narrator speaks of the "noble simplicity of tone" that Lucien is able to adopt toward Bathilde, which makes possible the subtle intimacy "appropriate to two souls of the same caliber when they meet and recognize each other amidst the masks of this vile masquerade that is called the world." To which Stendhal adds a somewhat extravagant simile he has managed to justify by his own patient technique of representing the consciousness and conversation of the two lovers: "Thus angels might speak who, departed from heaven on some mission, meet by chance here below."

As in *Le Rouge et le Noir*, the technical accomplishment is coupled with what often seems an uncanny rightness of intuition about the nature of the characters. This rightness of intuition makes itself felt in incidental moments, as when Bathilde, jealous of a rival, studies her own face in a mirror, concludes she is ugly, and decides she loves Lucien all the more for having the good taste to prefer the other woman; or in climactic scenes, like the great confrontation near the end when Mme Grandet seeks Lucien out in his office at the ministry of the interior. Up to this point, she has been vividly exposed as an emotionally frigid, thoroughly vulgar opportunist, but in one of those surprising reversals that Stendhal makes utterly convincing, Mme Grandet, after having prostituted herself to Lucien (through the intervention of his father, of which he is at first unaware), falls in love with him and then is desolate at the thought that he may be abandoning her in anger. As she sits in an armchair in his office, her body heaving with convulsive sobs, Lucien on his part marvels over the performance "of these Parisian actresses," yet despite himself is touched, almost tempted to wonder whether it might be more than mere sham, and at the same time vaguely stirred with desire by the sight of this beautiful body, which he has so recently possessed, shaking spasmodically in the chair before him (chap. 67). Few novelists have caught with such sureness the wild veerings of moral character, the multilayered nature of consciousness, the endlessly deceptive guessing game that men and women are condemned to play in assuming they know one another.

Whatever the structural flaws of *Lucien Leuwen*, Stendhal had again found ways to use all his own experience profoundly, indeed, to *know* his own adult experience in this act of imaginative extrapolation from it more probingly than he could in simple retrospection. What may be most remarkable in this regard is his ability to invent a gratifying fantasy-self and a fantasy-destiny in Lucien and yet maintain a perfectly clear perspective on the moral problematics of his hero's advantaged condition. Lucien is in many ways an anti-Julien: raised in great wealth at the Parisian center of things, he is a protected creature, his career overseen by a loving father; in contrast to Julien, he is a person without affectation; and though he also feels nostalgia for the heroic ideal of the Napoleonic age, he is devoid of illusions about realizing any new form of heroism; proud and sensitive like Julien, he has nothing of Julien's histrionic nature, is free of the young provincial's anguished naiveté and his paranoia.

If Julien is an extreme enactment of the rebellious impulses Stendhal felt and prudently restrained, Lucien carries out to the extreme the inclination to compliance that his author must have detected in himself, first a republican, then a Bonapartist, and now that the occasion presented itself, the functionary of a new monarchy that he detested. "He is too malleable," Leuwen *père* observes of his son at one point to his wife, "he doesn't object to anything, and that frightens me" (chap. 42). Such pliancy in fact becomes a little frightening in a political and social system so pervasively corrupt as the one we see operating in this novel. After his spills in the mud in Part One, Lucien as an accomplice to electoral chicanery in Part Two gets a literal and moral mouthful of mud, hurled by an angry protester, and he seems scarcely to have the inner resources to extricate himself from the mire (there is no tower in this landscape), a central deficiency in the possibilities of the protagonist which may have been another basic obstacle between the author and the completion of the novel.

If Stendhal was aware of the quicksand into which such blithe conformism as Lucien's could lead, he was equally conscious of the fact that for a young man to be so supremely advantaged as was his hero might, in real moral experience, constitute a rather grave disadvantage. At first glance, it would appear that Henri Beyle had bestowed on Lucien exactly the father he himself might have dreamed of having after almost half a century of resentful brooding over Chérubin Beyle. Papa Leuwen, "the Talleyrand of the stockmarket," is extravagantly generous of purse and mind, so high a bourgeois that he is beyond the narrow prejudices of his class, witty and worldly, and above all sincerely devoted to promoting his only son's advancement in life. What more could any son want?—A little less devotion, is the answer that the novel quietly but firmly proposes. Like Vautrin in Balzac's *Le Père Goriot*, M. Leuwen presents himself as an accomplished instructor in the higher cynicism appropriate to the morals of the age, but the trouble is that the whole doctrine of cynicism goes against the grain of Lucien's nature. M. Leuwen's very perfection in worldliness elicits a sense of estrangement in his son, repeatedly prevents Lucien from feeling any spontaneous affection or natural intimacy in his father's presence. (From a psychological perspective, after all, the father can overpower the son as effectively with bountifulness and sheer poise as with main force.) Near the end, Lucien makes the essential discovery about his father's relation to him: "Yes, my father is like all fathers, something I have been unable to see till now; with infinitely greater wit and even greater feeling than another, he does not want any the less to make me happy *in his manner* and not in mine" (emphasis in the original, chap. 65). It is understandable that Lucien quickly follows this perception with an eminently Stendhalian flight into pseudonymity: taking a hotel room under an assumed name, he feels for the first time an exhilarating sense of freedom, detached from his father and the onus of his origins.

It is clear that there are certain deep affinities between Lucien and Henri Beyle, but it is equally important to keep in mind how different they are from one another. Stendhal's marginal notes reveal that at some points he consciously utilized "models"—he himself invokes that term— from his own experience, but the more general rule, again inferable from his marginal comments, is that he repeatedly rediscovered his past after the fact, transformed and yet compellingly alive, in what he had written.

As he patiently limned the love of Lucien for Bathilde de Chasteller, the one block of his own experience that kept reasserting itself was his three years of desperate love for a woman now long dead, Matilde Dembowski. "*I write upon sensations of 1819*, fresh as yesterday after fifteen years." [11] This and many similar notes on the manuscript have led some critics to talk of the novel as a fictional transcription of Beyle's experience in Milan and especially have led them to represent Mme de Chasteller as a "portrait" of Métilde. But Stendhal himself is more precise when he says that he writes about the *feelings* (which is what he means in his French English by "sensations") of 1819. What he brilliantly recapitulates in the story of Lucien and Bathilde is the emotional dynamics of his passion for Métilde, not its real lineaments. Bathilde virtually shares a given name with Beyle's Milanese love and also recalls Métilde in her fastidious concern for her virtue, her ambivalent mingling of encouragement and evasion in her treatment of her admirer, but she has none of the boldness, res-

11. *Romans et nouvelles*, vol. 1, p. 1525.

olution, and wit of her supposed model, and her social and political allegiances impose on her a very different mental horizon from Métilde's. She
is not a version of Métilde with external details camouflaged but a figure
imaginatively elaborated with its own inner coherence, of which only
some aspects are drawn from recollections of Métilde. Stendhal was not
reconstructing his own experience in *Lucien Leuwen* but rather was
exhibiting a genius for affective memory that gave both psychological
conviction and emotional weight to the new, and in certain respects different, experience he was creating in his fiction.

Perhaps still another reason for Stendhal's inability to write the projected third part of the novel was that, mining his own feelings for
Métilde, he had no appropriate stock of affective memory to inform the
grand reconciliation he planned for Lucien and Bathilde. Floundering
with his material, he began to cut and rewrite what he had already done,
and then, when the idea of *Henry Brulard* occurred to him, with its invitation to deal more directly with more primary memories, he set the novel
aside, probably with some sense of relief. He began work on the autobiography on November 23, 1835, and it occupied most of his attention,
between consular duties, bouts of illness, and traveling between Civitavecchia and Rome, for the next four months. Meanwhile, he had requested
leave from the consulate for reasons of health, and in late March 1836, he
was notified that his request had been granted. It was another six weeks
before he completed all arrangements for the administration of the consulate during his absence and finally left for Paris. This anxiously awaited
return from exile meant abandoning the two unfinished major works he
had produced during the past two years in Rome and Civitavecchia. Once
in Paris, Beyle managed to protract his diplomatic furlough to a full
three years. In Italy he had often remarked, in a slight variation of a statement we noted earlier, that his true vocation was to live in a garret in
Paris making masterpieces. That is precisely what he now proceeded to
do, without the garret.

XIII
PARIS

(Aetat. 53–55)

BEYLE RETURNED TO PARIS in the mild air of late May: it was in fact the beginning of a long Indian summer in his life. His leave from diplomatic service was to have had a duration of three months, as in 1833, but toward the end of the summer of 1836, just as this period was about to expire, a change of ministers suddenly opened up unexpected vistas of Parisian residence for the reluctant consul from Civitavecchia.

Count Mathieu Molé had previously served as foreign minister for a scant three months at the inception of the July Monarchy in 1830, and it was he who appointed Beyle to the consulate at Trieste. There was not much personal connection between the two men, and in fact Beyle, though genuinely grateful for the count's support, privately expressed some criticism of Molé's abilities and of what he perceived as frigidness in the nobleman. (He had thought of sending Molé a bust of Tiberius that he had uncovered on a dig in 1834, then, fearing the appearance of self-seeking flattery, settled for giving him a plaster cast of the original. In 1839, after Molé had definitively resigned from the foreign ministry, the writer gave him the bust itself.) Count Molé, however, was on very cordial terms with Domenico Fiori and with Sarah de Tracy, the English-born daughter-in-law of Destutt de Tracy, both of whom had energetically intervened on behalf of their friend Beyle in 1830 and were prepared to do so again. Molé once more assumed the portfolio of the foreign ministry in early September 1836; till the end of his tenure in office, in March 1839, he was willing to grant Beyle a series of extensions of the original leave.

Everything the writer had missed acutely in his last two years of isolation in Italy now seemed within hand's reach: civilized conversation, a vibrant literary milieu, French theater (and Italian opera as well), friends of both sexes, and women worthy to be loved. Beyle eagerly rejoined the Parisian salon world, where he had shone with a sometimes ambiguous brilliance during the Restoration, calling on Mme Ancelot, Mme de Tracy, and others of his old social acquaintance, frequenting with particular assiduousness the salon of the Countess de Castellane, which was now thought of as the leading one of Paris, famous for its animated literary discussions. He also discovered a newly organized formal group, the Cercle des Arts, founded by Mérimée and a few friends, where he could regularly encounter agreeable intellectual company. Like Lucien Leuwen, Beyle gravitated toward reading rooms, and as he stayed on in Paris, he came to spend more of his evenings, when he was not attending performances, dinner parties, or salons, at the *cabinet de lecture* of the Cercle des Arts on the rue de Choiseul, where he could peruse journals, write letters, and meet people for casual conversation.

The pleasure of this Parisian homecoming was enhanced by frequent opportunities to see French theater, a youthful addiction that Stendhal had not outgrown in putting behind him the ambition to become another Molière (an ambition which, in any case, as we shall see, he would soon realize more brilliantly than ever before as a novelist rather than as a dramatist). The most dazzling revelation for Beyle on the Parisian stage came in his second year in Paris, in 1838, when the great tragic actress Rachel made her debut in the Théâtre-Français at the age of eighteen. Beyle, one recalls, had been an acutely attentive observer, and sometimes a vehemently partisan one as well, of different acting styles since his early years in Paris at the beginning of the century, but no actor or actress he had seen before had inspired the kind of excitement elicited by this slender young performer. She "plays tragedy," he wrote Count Cini on January 3, 1839, some six months after Rachel's debut, "as though she were inventing what she said. . . . Mlle Rachel is the daughter of a German Jew who put on open-air farces at country fairs; she has a genius that overwhelms me with amazement every time I see her perform; it's been two hundred years since such a miracle has been seen in France."

What is especially noteworthy about this response is not Beyle's critical justness in recognizing the appearance of genius, which one might have expected, but the spontaneous and unrestrained enthusiasm he exhibits, which is a clear reflection of his striking shift in mood in exchanging the "solitary shore" of Civitavecchia for the cafés and salons and theaters of Paris. There is in his cultural passions, in his relations with women, and finally in his writing during this period an impulse or perhaps a wistful aspiration to return to the excitements of his own youth. That impulse may be most readily perceptible in his attempt during the first few months after his arrival from Italy to convert two old and intimate friendships into ardent romances.

In the course of his stay in France in 1833, as we noted, Beyle had re-established a footing of confidentiality with Clémentine Curial. Now he hastened to her again and during the summer of 1836 found as many opportunities as possible to spend time alone with her. The passionate countess, who a decade earlier had led him up and down château ladders and emotional passages from ecstasy to despair, was now forty-seven, but this did not prevent Beyle from seeing her again as "my old charmer" or from soon attesting that he felt the same urgent desire for her that he had experienced in 1824. When he visited Mérimée in early August at Laon, a day's journey to the northeast of Paris, where Mérimée was occupied with his work as government inspector of historical monuments, Beyle seemed altogether overwrought. The woman he was pursuing, Beyle confessed to his younger friend, had responded to his pleas with an exclamation of astonishment, "How can you love me at my age?" Beyle—Mérimée would remember him being on the point of tears—persisted in his suit, eliciting a couple of weeks later (August 22) the following judgment from Menti (in Colomb's summary of the destroyed letter): "that one does not rekindle a fire with ashes; that this feeling was dead and buried in 1836, and that he should be content with the place of best friend." [1] Ever intrepid in pursuing the consequences of his own emotional intensities, he was not entirely deterred even by this perfectly plain and sensible rebuff. Menti, however, remained adamant, and a month later (September 28), Beyle noted ruefully in the margin of one of his books that he had no choice but to abandon this "little recrudescence of love," though "to be near Menti without touching her pretty hands would make me feel disagreeably constrained." [2]

Nevertheless, his loyalty as a friend soon overcame his discomfort as a frustrated lover. By 1837, as we learn from Colomb's extracts of the correspondence between the two, Menti was not only paying Beyle regular

1. Auguste Cordier, *Stendhal raconté par ses amis et ses amies* (Paris, 1893), p. 36.
2. *Marginalia et mélanges intimes*, vol. 2, p. 278.

visits in his bachelor quarters, but she even asked for "the learned advice of the author of *De l'Amour*" on how to retain an uncertain lover. The countess, for all her forty-seven years, was obviously far from retiring from the field of amatory endeavor, but she was shrewd enough to realize that it might be a disastrous mistake to try turning back the emotional clock to 1824 with her dear Henri and that they would serve each other better now as confidants than as lovers.

Having renounced his passion for Menti, Beyle almost immediately undertook a new matrimonial scheme instead: as we shall see in a moment, he now chose to stress the consciousness of his age, as though after his failure in resuming the role of the ardent lover he thought he might as well resign himself to being an elderly and comfortable spouse. Eulalie-Françoise Lacuée was a widow of forty-six. Beyle had probably known both her and her father, Count Réal, since the days of the Empire, for they moved in the same circles as the Darus, and he definitely had social contact with them in the late 1820s, after Réal had returned from twelve years of exile into which he was forced by the Restoration. Beyle thought the Baroness Lacuée "heroic" for the way she stood by her father in adversity, and now that he was aware of her availability—she was a close friend of Mérimée and of Mérimée's mother, from whom she took counsel on marital matters—she struck him as a woman whose fine character would make her a perfectly suitable mate. In a letter bearing the date March 17, 1837, but which François Michel, with his usual determined sleuth work, has convincingly dated to October 1836, Beyle proposed marriage to Mme Lacuée in the following metaphoric, and protectively self-ironic, terms:

It seems to me that we both have a way still to go. This way lies more or less in the same direction, except that you will be going farther than I. Would you accept a traveling companion, a kind of majordomo, to be in charge of ordering the relays of horses and, when need be, of mounting them?

The ridiculous thing is that this courier is far past the age when one mounts a horse gracefully; his sole merit would be to spare you the trouble of having to talk with the postillions yourself. This cavalcading equerry is a bit afraid of you, or else he would have proposed the traveling association in person. The drawback, the major inconvenience, is that this association bears too fine a name, too romantic a name, which perhaps may still suit my character a little, but which exhibits a cruel discrepancy with the number of crowns I have to spend on traveling, with the number of years, etc., etc.

In a typical flourish of pseudonymity, Beyle signed the letter, "C. de Seyssel, aged fifty-three years." Since the letter is extant only in the writer's rough draft, we cannot even be entirely certain that it was actually sent. In any case, the matrimonial project, like Beyle's earlier ones, came to nothing. In December 1836, Mme Lacuée married an engineer who was a cousin of Mérimée's—so it would appear that not even the Mérimées had favored Beyle's suit. From this point on, the novelist would resign himself to his condition of bachelorhood.

But what he would never renounce, till the end of his life, was the pursuit of romance. "It is false," he wrote in a travel journal a year and a half later, "that at a certain age one should no longer love. As long as one is capable of loving a perfectly stupid or supremely theatrical woman for her delightful wit or her naiveté, one can love. And the happiness is far more in loving than in being loved." [3] Stendhal in his fifties had not broken faith with the apologia for crystallization he had articulated two decades earlier in *De l'Amour*, though one may detect in these lines a certain acerbic satire of the fond lover's self-delusions that was not present in the earlier work. If his attempt in the summer of 1836 to rekindle a fire from ashes had failed, he soon after conceived the idea, following his abortive marriage proposal, of fanning the spark of his friendship with Jules Gaulthier into the flame of romance.

She was away in the country for part of the fall of 1836, and the letters they exchanged reflect a quality of easy intimacy, affectionate mutual concern, and, on her part, a certain teasing pique about the sporadic nature of his attentiveness to her. (Earlier, while he was still in Italy, she had written him that she was surprised he had never been in love with her.) Jules obviously had taken no offense at his criticism of her novel, *The Lieutenant*; whether he revealed to her anything of *Lucien Leuwen*, the manuscript of which he had brought back with him to Paris, is unclear. This veteran amorist in search of an *amoureuse* needed no further hint than such friendly encouragement. On Christmas Day of 1836, he made his declaration of love to her.

Jules Gaulthier may have been clumsily amateurish as a novelist, but she handled this surprising turn of events with beautiful poise and exquisite tact. She gently declined the offer to change the nature of their relationship while making clear that she regarded his declaration as a high compliment. "Don't have the slightest regret over your day," she wrote him as soon as he had gone from her home, "it should count among the best of your life, and for me it is the most glorious! I feel all the sweet pleasure of a grand success: well attacked, well defended, no treaty, no defeat, nothing but glory for both camps. . . . Beyle, believe me, you are worth a

---

3. *Voyage dans le midi de la France*, ed. Henri Martineau (Paris, 1936), p. 207.

hundred thousand times more than people believe, than you yourself believe, and than I believed just two hours ago!" [4] The wit, the reasonableness, the generous sensibility of this response suggest that Beyle had chosen his woman friend well, and they continued afterward on affectionate terms. In any case, both of his attempts in 1836 to transform friendship into passion reflect a longing to experience once again the rapturous intensity of his earlier years. It was to be not in the arms of a mistress, however, but in the imaginative act of creating another fictional world that he would realize this desire.

Meanwhile, when Beyle arrived back in Paris in May 1836, he found still another woman who offered—in this case, quite willingly—the possibility of a romantic attachment: Giulia Rinieri, whose new husband had joined the Tuscan legation in Paris in the fall of 1833. There are indications that Giulia found occasion to welcome her old lover back to her bed soon after his return, but whether because of the obstacles raised by her married state and the proximity of her "uncle" Berlinghieri or perhaps even because of some lingering sense of resentment over her rejection of his marriage proposal three years earlier, Beyle's attentions in the latter part of 1836, as we have seen, were directed elsewhere. Through 1837 and the early months of 1838, Giulia was afflicted with an odd malady that involved acute pains in the pelvic area, which put her plainly *hors de combat*. For much of this period, Beyle was away on a series of excursions through France, Switzerland, the Lowland countries, and Germany, but when he was in Paris, he was a solicitous visitor of his ailing friend. One is tempted to wonder whether Giulia's complaint may have been psychosomatic, for the practitioner who miraculously cured her, by means peculiarly unspecified even in his own self-promoting published account of the case, was a notorious quack named Benech.

Whatever the medical facts of the matter, when Beyle returned to Paris in late July 1838, after almost four months of touring, he found his Sienese mistress completely restored to health, and by August 3, he could record in his usual reflex of marginal notation on such occasions: *She gives things, the amica of eleven years.* The uncertainty of Beyle's English is compounded by the illegibility of his handwriting, and perhaps the bluntness of the first clause, as one scholar has proposed, is simply due to a misreading of an initial *w* as a *th*. For his cryptic marginalia during these weeks include a record not only of sexual scores but also of certain soaring moments for which a vocabulary of "grace" and "sweetness" is

4. *Cent soixante-quatorze lettres à Stendhal*, ed. Henri Martineau (Paris, 1947), pp. 127–128.

invoked as the lover recalls leaving Giulia's humming cantilenas of Paësiello. Just at this time, however, Giulia and her husband were about to set off for Florence, where they would take up permanent residence. Berlinghieri had died in January 1838, and his protégé Martini soon found that his services were no longer required at the Tuscan legation. Giulia was vexed at the idea of leaving Paris, not only because of the interruption of her happily renewed liaison with Beyle, but also because, quite like her lover, she had become addicted to the verve and wit of Parisian life, as she wrote him from Italy in October. She hoped somehow to return to Paris; meanwhile, she asked Beyle to think of her and also held out the prospect of a reunion in Italy. In less than a year, that reunion would in fact take place.

One should not, however, conclude from these various involvements, both actual and merely intended, that Beyle was wholly preoccupied with women during this period. After his first few months back in Paris, he undertook a series of different writing projects, to which we shall presently attend, and through the second and third year of his protracted leave, tourism was a more persistent passion than either Giulia or Menti or Jules. It is rather likely that one of the initial motives for Beyle's extensive travels beginning in late May 1837 was economic. As long as he continued on leave from his consular duties, he received only half pay, which was hardly enough to support him in the Parisian style to which he was accustomed, and he had learned from the ripple of popularity set up by *Promenades dans Rome* that there was a certain market for travel books. But his deciding to gather material for a new travel book was a case of choosing to see a confluence between his economic needs and his insatiable curiosity about people, mores, architecture, art, history, and landscape. In the margin of *Voyage dans le midi de la France*, he notes, most revealingly: "The happiness of having as a vocation [*métier*] one's passion. Condition of Dominique" (entry dated March 22, 1838). In context, the passion referred to would seem to be both travel and writing about travel. For the key to the difference between Stendhal's tourism at this point and his less sustained travels in Italy in the earlier 1830s is that he now zestfully *writes* about what he sees as he travels—something he was inhibited from doing by his mood in Italy. It was worth bouncing around in bumpy coaches, braving sudden storms, staying at sometimes indifferent inns, being served tepid water for one's tea, not only to be able to observe new places and new people, but also because the condition of being a traveler—an outsider with great freedom of movement watching things and watching himself watching—gave him a special occasion for the reflective formulation of his experience in writing. Stendhal's vocation as a writer, by this ripe moment in his life, meant constant, eager concentration, beyond considerations of publication, on getting things into words.

Beyle set off on his first excursion, down the Loire Valley, accompanied by Mérimée, proceeding part of the time overland, part of the time by boat. From Nantes, by the Atlantic coast, he headed northward alone to Le Havre and Rouen. He was back in Paris in early July, but during the next twelve months, he managed to get in a trip to Grenoble, extensive travels through the south of France, and a rapid tour of Switzerland, Germany, Holland, and Belgium. He may have even paid a quick visit to London, though there is no explicit record of such a trip.

The first literary result of these travels was *Mémoires d'un touriste,* which Stendhal wrote after his return from Brittany, in the latter part of 1837, when he presumably remained in Paris for long stretches. He elaborated the book from his own travel journal, but he also included anecdotes reported to him by his friends, and as in the past, he did not hesitate to draw on the published works of others when he thought the occasion required it. The *Mémoires,* which brought the author a payment of 1,560 francs, appeared in June 1838, receiving a mixed press that included some highly favorable reviews. By this time, however, Stendhal was already on the road again, gathering material for a second travel book. But soon after his return to Paris in midsummer, he was seized by the compelling idea for a new novel, and so he abandoned the account of his southern tour in its journal state, and it would be published only posthumously as *Voyage dans le midi de la France.*

Both travel books are remarkable for their paradoxical union of youthful exuberance and the sober reflectiveness of mature age. In *Mémoires d'un touriste,* these qualities are mediated by a quasi-fictional device, as in Stendhal's previous travel books: the narrator presents himself as an iron merchant, supposedly a man in his thirties, though sometimes he patently speaks with the accents of the fifty-five-year-old author. His wit and his political views are also distinctly Stendhal's.

Thus, after reflecting on the spiritual grandness of Mme Roland, the revolutionary martyr who was always the embodiment of supreme heroism for Stendhal, the narrator observes: "After this great figure came the ladies of the Empire, who would weep in their calèches on the way back from Saint-Cloud when the Emperor found their dresses in poor taste; then the ladies of the Restoration, who went to mass at Sacré-Coeur to make their husbands prefects; finally the ladies of the *Juste Milieu* [adherents of the July Monarchy], models of naturalness and affability" (entry dated May 15, 1837). After the directness of the first two devastating vignettes, Stendhal pillories the ladies of the 1830s with a climactic turn of irony that would hardly have been lost on contemporary readers. Altogether, his nervousness about expressing his political views in print seems largely to have evaporated. The shorter fiction he wrote in this period was published either anonymously or with a newly coined pseudonym, but *Mémoires d'un touriste*, like *La Chartreuse de Parme* after it, was identified on the title page as written by "the author of *Le Rouge et le Noir*." Evidently, the prospect of a return to active diplomatic service seemed too distant at this point to make Beyle worry much about compromising himself politically, or perhaps the pressing need to supplement his meager income led him to think of political prudence as a secondary concern. If he were going to write at all for publication, he had to feel uninhibited about what he was writing.

At the other end of the register of voices in *Mémoires d'un touriste*, at moments the ironic observer gives way to a poignantly personal speaker pondering his own existential condition, as when the ironmonger, in the midst of an "anthropological" comparison between deathbed rituals in the islands of Saint-Malo and in Paris, suddenly comments: "Sad things happen as they will happen always, without our stupid institutions, in silence and solitude." To which he adjoins a moral reflection that is an item in the lifelong credo of Henri Beyle, disciple of his grandfather Gagnon and of the Enlightenment rationalists: "Since the idea of an *eternal hell* [H.B.'s emphasis] is disappearing, death is becoming once more a simple thing, as it was before the reign of Constantine." [5]

Voyage dans le midi de la France, because it has no quasi-fictional narrator, allows these different voices of Stendhal to speak even more directly. The book begins with a brief note celebrating the beauty of the women of Angoulême—their eyebrows, the traveler says, are the veritable ebony bow spoken of in *The Thousand and One Nights*—and the writer is drawn to the south of France by its brio, almost as though he were discovering in his native country a replacement for the Italy that he had mythologized since youth and that had now disappointed him. But even as he delights in these southern scenes, he often feels the tug of distant memories and accompanying thoughts of aging and death: "Now I think of the arts, of Napoleon's campaigns. This last subject is a sad one for me; I see myself fallen into an era of transition, that is to say, of mediocrity; and it will be scarcely half over before time, which moves so slowly for a

5. *Mémoires d'un touriste*, vol. 1, ed. E. Abravanel (Lausanne, 1961), p. 417.

people and so quickly for an individual, will signal to me that I must depart." [6] Within a few months, Stendhal would weave all of these preoccupations into the splendid tapestry of *La Chartreuse de Parme*—the nostalgia for Napoleonic heroism and the perception of the present as a transitional era of mediocrity; a penetrating satiric vision of European mores and politics in the age of Metternich; the contrast between naive, exuberant youth and self-conscious, often cynical middle age; the celebration of southern brio and passion; the power of love's longing to elevate the soul above the bleak flatlands of worldly calculation and deceit. The point is not only that there is a continuity of thematic concerns between the two travel books and the great fictional endeavor Stendhal would take up in the fall of 1838 but also that, as a matter of writer's craft, he was rehearsing and perfecting the range of narrative and reflective voices which he would then orchestrate so beautifully in the extraordinary improvisation that became *La Chartreuse de Parme*.

Before that moment, however, Stendhal had been engaged in two other writing projects that had thematic and, as it were, metonymic connections with the major novel he would then produce. His first idea for a book, once he settled down to work in the fall of 1836 after the initial period of his return from Italy, was a life of Napoleon. He had written some chapters on that subject, one recalls, during his Milanese period; now he began the book all over, devoting more attention this time to the details of Napoleon's origins and, after the passage of two decades, eliminating the criticism of the Emperor's vanity and overweening ambition that had been included in the earlier version, referring to him reverently as *ce grand homme*, this great man. In any case, Stendhal had little notion of how to conduct a biography. The narrative of Napoleon's life soon bogs down in minute accounts of his early campaigns, and one suspects the biographer was loath to pursue his story beyond the glory of the young Bonaparte's precocious achievements to the era of his misguided and finally self-destructive ambition. By the spring of 1837, Stendhal had abandoned this second attempt to produce a life of Napoleon, for which he had hoped to receive a handsome advance, and casting about for other sources of income from his writing, he had signed a contract to supply the *Revue des Deux Mondes* with a series of tales set in the Italian Renaissance. Two of these, *Vittoria Accoramboni* and *Les Cenci*, appeared in 1837; another two, *La Duchesse de Palliano* and Part One of *L'Abbesse de Castro*, during the following year. These, together with several other Italian

6. *Voyage*, p. 206.

novellas of Stendhal's, would be published together posthumously as the *Chroniques italiennes*.

Beyle had of course long been fascinated by the Italian Renaissance, but what gave him the immediate impetus for these stories was a collection of old tales in manuscript which he had acquired in Italy, probably in 1833, and of which he had fair copies made, at considerable expense. In presenting his own versions to the public, he frequently makes a pretense of merely transcribing into modern French the archaic language and rudimentary narrative procedures of the original. In fact, he began by paraphrasing his sources for the most part rather closely, but by the time he got to *L'Abbesse de Castro*, he was allowing himself great freedom in the novelistic elaboration of his Renaissance materials. In any event, the *Chroniques italiennes* are hardly great fiction, and their chief interest today is in their link with *Chartreuse* and in the keys they help provide to the phenomenology of Stendhal's imagination. In the notes for a preface he left among his papers, Stendhal insists on one significant phrase in order to justify his project. It is "the depths of the human heart" that are vividly revealed in this tangle of corrupt and violent despotism, unbridled impulse, macabre vengefulness, constant transgression of moral limits. "The one thing I am sure of," he observes, after briefly indicating the different styles of passionate action in Naples and Rome, "is that today England, Germany, and France are too gangrened with affectations and vanities of every possible kind to be able to provide for very long such sharp illumination of the depths of the human heart." [7] The heart has depths that we moderns rarely glimpse because of the fundamental contradiction between the polite and superficial codes of civilization, which encourage the pursuit of trivial gratifications, and the awesome capacity for unthinkable extremes of which people are capable if they have, like these figures from the Italian Renaissance, the courage to follow their own fierce impulses. This is in a sense a transposition back into the heroic key of the ghastly spectacle of humanity that Henri Beyle had seen in the retreat from Moscow, an attempt to imagine a heroic code of intransigent will untrammeled by any considerations of conventional morality.

In these tales of strangling, poisoning, conspiracy, incest, unquenchable love, and smoldering hatred, perhaps the most notable recurrent motif is that of immurement. In story after story, the beloved woman is locked up in a cell in some convent or castle and can be reached only by overcoming guards, scaling walls, traversing labyrinthine passages, uncovering secret

7. *Romans et nouvelles*, vol. 2, p. 557.

entrances. The Renaissance chronicles that Stendhal had discovered in effect gave him a dramatic correlative for the powerful sense of the inaccessibility of the longed-for woman that he had harbored since adolescence, or perhaps indeed since the early death of his mother.

The fascination with incarceration, however (which of course had already been expressed in the conclusion to *Le Rouge et le Noir*), set off still deeper reverberations in Stendhal when the prisoner was not a female object of desire but a male protagonist in whom he could imagine himself more directly. For the idea of immurement had an appealing ambiguity, suggesting at once persecution, claustrophobic isolation, and claustrophiliac solitude, protected removal from the world. Whatever the gender of the immured figures, the lurid events and distanced protagonists of the *Chroniques italiennes* did not afford him much opportunity to develop such psychological paradoxes in any interesting way; but he would soon give those paradoxes suggestive elaboration in a novel whose central image is a prison that becomes a charterhouse.

In the tales themselves, in fact, there is an odd tension between the sensationalistic situations of the narrative and Stendhal's commitment to rendering everything in cool, rapid understatement, eschewing all rhetorical excess. Here, for example, is his account of the death of the Duchess of Palliano, one of a gallery of proud, unflinching women in the *Chroniques*. Her brother has just finished preparations to murder her for betraying the family honor: "he once more arranged the kerchief over her eyes, put back the cord around her neck, and thrusting the rod through the knot, twisted it and strangled her. The whole affair was carried out, on the part of the Duchess, absolutely in the tone of an ordinary conversation." [8] The casualness of Stendhal's manner, mirroring the heroic casualness of the Duchess, is interesting but a bit too bizarre to effect a persuasive fictional realization of this horrendous moment. What Stendhal needed to do in order to create the perfect balance between his taste for extremes of character and his devotion to an astringent manner was to locate his Italian souls in a setting where his narrator-surrogate could operate on them intimately and comfortably with the full resources of a contemporary ironic intelligence. This is what first occurred to him to do in the fall of 1838, with immediate and extraordinary results.

Among the Italian tales Stendhal had brought back from Civitavecchia was a brief narrative, less than 1,200 words, entitled "Origin of the Greatness of the Farnese Family." The protagonist of this narrative is

8. Ibid., vol. 2, p. 729.

Alexander Farnese, who in 1534 became Pope Paul III. A libertine youth, he was arrested for having abducted a noblewoman to serve his pleasure, but he managed to escape prison by climbing down a rope provided him through the help of Cardinal Roderigo Borgia, the lover of Alexander's beautiful Aunt Vandozza. Afterward, the devoted aunt saw to it that her nephew was appointed cardinal, at the age of twenty-four. For much of his subsequent life, he lived with an aristocratic woman named Cleria, an arrangement which did not prevent him from being elected to the papacy at the age of sixty-seven. These personages and relations are a rather scrambled version of the historical facts, but they provided Stendhal with the situation he needed: only the ending of worldly success on the throne of St. Peter had to be radically changed to suit the novelist's special version of the Romantic ethos. Otherwise, Alexander Farnese, graced with freshness and naiveté, became Fabrice del Dongo; Cleria, assimilated into the folkloric archetype of the Compassionate Jailer's Daughter, became Clélia; while Roderigo Borgia and La Vandozza were elaborated as those supremely worldly and intelligent lovers, Count Mosca and the Duchess of Sansévérina.

On August 16, 1838, just three weeks after Stendhal's return from the Lowlands and the day after *La Duchesse de Palliano* had appeared in the *Revue des Deux Mondes*, he noted in English on his copy of the Farnese chronicle: *To make of this sketch a romanzetto*. The use of the diminutive *romanzetto* makes it clear that he initially thought of doing simply another in the series of Renaissance tales he was producing for periodic publication. On September 3, he had the first idea of turning this material into a novel, but for the moment he had other occupations: the first part of *L'Abbesse de Castro*, which he wrote in mid-September; his romance with Giulia, who left Paris on September 27; a novella in imitation of Scarron, which he began then broke off in early October; and finally, still another tour of Brittany and Normandy, which kept him away from Paris from October 12 till November 3. Meanwhile, he had also been involved through friendship in another sort of fabulating activity, which was to play an important role in transforming "Origin of the Greatness of the Farnese Family" into *La Chartreuse de Parme*.

On his previous diplomatic furlough to Paris, Beyle had become acquainted through Mérimée with the Countess de Montijo, a Spanish noblewoman residing in France with her two young daughters, Paca and Eugénie (the latter would one day become Empress of France). The two girls used to look forward all week to Beyle's Thursday evening visits, with of course not the slightest notion that this utterly charming and attentive

adult friend was a professional writer who used the name Stendhal. The
girls were allowed to stay up an hour late, and the high point of these
visits was when they would settle into Beyle's lap in an armchair by the
fireplace, and he would spellbind them with tales of his days in the Grand
Army and of the exploits of Napoleon himself. "We wept, we laughed,
we trembled, we were wild," Eugénie would later recall. "He showed us
the Emperor successively resplendent under the sun of Austerlitz, pale
under the snows of Russia, dying at Sainte-Hélène." [9] On the first two
days of September 1838, as a writer's affectionate gift to the Montijo girls,
Stendhal dictated to his amanuensis a detailed narrative of the defeat at
Waterloo, articulated from the baffled viewpoint of a young combatant
named Alexander. (In his printed copy of *Chartreuse*, the novelist would
later note at the end of the Waterloo chapter, "For you, Paca and
Eugénie.") It is by no means clear whether this Alexander was already a
conscious transposition of Alexander Farnese into the nineteenth century
or whether only two months later, when Stendhal began to work in
earnest on the novel, did the idea suddenly occur to him, perhaps because
of the shared first name of the two heroes, to modernize the Farnese
story and to link it with the fall of Napoleon, inserting the Waterloo
episode which he had already written in a larger narrative. In any case,
the contemporary setting was infinitely more congenial to him, and even
in regard to political prudence, as consul to the Papal States he could
write far more freely about the machinations of a "mythical" nineteenth-
century Pamesan court than about a reprobate who became a historical
pope, aided by a seductive aunt living in sin.

On November 4, the day after Stendhal returned from Rouen, he
began dictating *La Chartreuse de Parme* in his furnished room at 8, rue
Caumartin. Within four days, he was revising his account of Waterloo,
and had decided to change Alexander Farnese into Fabrice del Dongo. For
the next seven weeks, he virtually sequestered himself with his manuscript
and with his (no doubt exhausted) amanuensis, working ten hours a day
and more, leaving word with the concierge that anyone who called should
be told he was off hunting. It is hard to imagine a masterwork of this scale
produced with such astonishing speed. Everything seemed to come to
Stendhal in a rush as he was caught up in the momentum of his own
invention—dramatically conceived dialogue, the fluctuating movements of
long interior monologues, details of romantic action and political intrigue,
subsidiary characters, endless ramifications of the protagonists' psychol-

9. Pierre Jourda, *Stendhal raconté par ceux qui l'ont vu*, p. 121.

ogy. By November 15, he had written 270 manuscript pages; on December 2, the number had reached 640; on December 26, just 52 days after he began, he handed over to Romain Colomb the six bulky notebooks of the completed manuscript to show to a publisher. He had produced so much, in fact, that Ambroise Dupont, who published the novel, "throttled"—the word is Stendhal's—the last part out of considerations of cost, which is probably why the ending we have seems so huddled.[10]

In briefer spurts, Stendhal had improvised rapidly and brilliantly before, but he could sustain this breathless, unbroken pace in the creation of *Chartreuse* because in both form and substance it was so manifestly the novel he had been gathering resources all his life to write, the great poem he had dreamed of making since his confused youthful ambition to become what he called the Bard. There is probably no other novel that has so frequently elicited such a *rhapsodic* vocabulary from its critics, and that odd fact is actually instructive about the nature of Stendhal's achievement and the sources of the achievement in his experience of art and life.

Critic after critic has spoken of the music of *Chartreuse*, of its operatic flamboyance, or, more specifically still, of the striking effect of opera buffa that it sustains. Others, developing a remark made by the author himself, have celebrated the Correggio-like play of light and shade in the descriptive passages, the characterizations, and the larger thematic structure of the novel. The splendidly willful Duchess of Sansévérina, the supreme creation among the novel's characters, has been compared to the heroines of Shakespeare, inviting talk about the book's Shakespearean qualities. The memorable satiric scenes have been called Molièresque, and there are surely reminiscences of Molière's comedy in the eminently theatrical spectacle of Prince Ranuce-Ernest IV, that most pusillanimous of provincial potentates, who struts about in a bad imitation of Louis XIV, only to be reduced to sputtering impotent fury by the defiant nonchalance of the Duchess of Sansévérina.

La Chartreuse de Parme is, in other words, a novel that impels many readers to reach for comparisons with achievements in other genres and other media, as though it somehow overflowed the limits of what we usually think of as novelistic. Such comparisons may not take us beyond the evocation of the novel's atmosphere to an analytic understanding of the book, but they point toward the peculiar direction of Stendhal's ful-

---

10. It is not entirely clear whether the publisher insisted on substantial cuts in the already written conclusion or simply refused to let Stendhal expand the last part in correcting the galleys. In either case, the effect was the same.

filled aesthetic intention here. Ever since that revelatory evening in Novara in 1800, when he first saw *Il Matrimonio Segreto* performed, Henri Beyle had clung to the vision of a buoyant union of language and music in story as the perfect catalyst of bliss. His "soul adored Cimarosa, Mozart, and Shakespeare" was one of the inscriptions that he devised for his own tombstone. The prose of *Chartreuse* joins the qualities of lyricism and wit that are deployed in very different combinations through the works of all three of his artistic idols. Music, of course, can be no more than a loose metaphor for the verbal texture of a novel that is often so disarmingly conversational, but in one respect, it is an inevitable metaphor because music is the purest form of aesthetic experience for Stendhal, and that experience in turn he sees as the reliving of remembered happiness, which is ultimately what this novel is all about. Maurice Bardèche has beautifully phrased this distinctive character of *Chartreuse* in observing that it is not just "the novel of happiness but also the novel of the nostalgia for happiness, the novel of happiness lost and always desired anew." [11]

The novel builds from and toward peaks of rapture—figurative and also literal peaks—but the source of the rapture is an oddly removed or even receding perspective, always at a distance from the delighted observer, as Clélia is from Fabrice in his prison-tower, and finally efficacious because the delights intimated are not present but remembered. The first of the remarkable visions of landscape in the novel perfectly enunciates the complex of images and themes that will constitute Fabrice's series of tower views and the essential argument of the novel. In this case, the rhapsodic observer of the natural panorama is Countess Piatranera, soon to become the Duchess of Sansévérina. At this moment, Gina is a radiantly beautiful widow of thirty-one; her arrival at the del Dongo castle at Grianta on Lake Como has restored to her sister (Fabrice's mother), who claims to have just felt a hundred years old, "the beautiful days of youth." Gina herself, as we immediately see, shares these oscillating sensations of age: "It was with rapture that the Countess rediscovered the memories of her first youth and compared them with her present feelings." With this introduction from the narrator, she goes on to survey the Lombard landscape in an interior monologue that invokes the following terms:

In the midst of these admirably formed hills which plunge to the lake in such remarkable descents, I can preserve all the illusions of the descriptions in Tasso and Ariosto. Everything is noble and tender, everything speaks of love, nothing recalls the ugliness of civilization. . . . Beyond these hills, whose crest offers

11. *Stendhal romancier* (Paris, 1947), p. 361.

hermitages where one would want to live, the astonished eye makes out the peaks of the Alps, always covered with snow, and their severe austerity recalls just enough of life's misfortunes to heighten the present pleasure. The imagination is moved by the far-off sound of the churchbell in some little village hidden beneath the trees: these sounds made gentle by the water over which they are borne assume a tinge of sweet melancholy and resignation, seem to tell man—Life is fleeting, therefore do not show yourself so obdurate toward the happiness that presents itself; hasten to enjoy. The language of these enthralling places which have no counterpart at all in the world restored to the Countess her heart of a girl of sixteen. [chap. 2]

The *carpe diem* hedonism that announces itself in the message of the invisible bells is not quite what it seems, for the pervasive emphasis of the passage is on rapture at a remove from circumambient reality, a rapture not of the senses but of the imagination, which in turn uses the external scene to revive memories of earlier experience and of art. Through the landscape, the Countess, hardly an old woman, rediscovers within herself the fresh longings that animated her when she was half her present age. A little later, Fabrice, who at the time is all of seventeen years old, will look down in delight from the belltower, where he is hiding, and will suddenly be overwhelmed by "all the memories of his childhood" (chap. 9). The aspect of *distance* stressed in this first landscape of Gina's and in the later ones enjoyed by Fabrice is explicitly spatial but implicitly temporal as well: the observer is in a sense privileged to behold once more his or her own childhood, without of course being able to enter into it again, and that is the ultimate source of this perfectly tranquil sense of beatitude, touched with a nuance of melancholy. It is no wonder that at such a moment even the worldly Gina thinks of the happiness of withdrawing to the contemplative solitude of a hermitage, as much later her nephew, surveying from the Farnese Tower a vast panorama that also includes the peaks of the Alps, substantially transforms his prison into the Carthusian retreat he will literally enter at the novel's end.

Stendhal's own imagination at this point in his life, as we have already seen in several connections, was delicately poised between a return to vivid youth and the apprehension of encroaching age and death; and the fine dialectic between those two antithetical moments of the mature mind generates many of the most distinctive qualities of the novel. The return to youth or childhood accorded the personages of *Chartreuse* in these privileged experiences in fact goes back to certain central images from the early life of Henri Beyle. The Alpine horizon has its ultimate source in the distant snow-covered peaks that looked down on the Grenoble of his childhood, offering a cool vision of escape from the constricting family circle and bourgeois milieu which embodied all the "ugliness of civilization" for the boy. The constellation of images that we noted in the young Henri's rapture over M. Le Roy's bucolic landscape, in his visits to his uncle at Les Échelles, and when he heard the bells toll at Rolles—all of which, of course, he had recalled just two years earlier in writing *Henry Brulard*—is evident here with all its constituent elements: the mountain landscape, a source of pure water, the presence of a lovely woman, and the idea of art.

Art itself is conceived not in opposition to nature but rather to ugly civilization; in fact, nature becomes more fully itself, more fully the repository of the sweet dreams of desire, by its interfusion in the mind of the observer with the beautiful "illusions" of art. Stendhal has no Wordsworthian sense of some original union of the uncorrupted soul with nature but imagines instead an experience of pleasurable closeness to nature mediated by the early exposure to art: significantly, he defines Gina's moment of delight by invoking two great Italian poets who were two of the cherished authors of his own youth. Given this restatement of the luminous themes of Stendhal's own early life at the crucial junctures of the novel, one can see a compelling emotional logic in his decision to begin the book with the entry of Napoleon's forces, "that youthful army," into Milan. It is a kind of wittily lyric overture to the main action that recalls his own elation at the age of seventeen in discovering in Milan a city which seemed to embody all the prospects of happiness he had till then occasionally glimpsed in his reading and in his intercourse with nature and people.

But *La Chartreuse de Parme* is immensely more than a gratifying fantasy of youth revisited because youth and fulfillment are set in constant tension with age and loss, just as exalted solitude is set in tension with the most lucid insight into the pervasive corruption and the comic chicaneries of political life. Or, to restate these thematic oppositions in generic terms, the romance elements here—the hero imprisoned in the tower, the flawlessly virtuous maiden, the ennobling power of love—are played against the more characteristically novelistic elements of the book. If Fabrice is, in Jean Prévost's elegant formulation, "the imaginary child Stendhal begot upon his mistress Italy," [12] this fresh, charming, passionate young man, with his dangerous facility for beguiling women, is dialectically bracketed with the projection of another aspect of the author's self—Count Mosca, with his consummate cynicism, his moments of weariness and un-

12. *La Création chez Stendhal*, p. 353.

sureness, who is not only a sort of father to Fabrice but also a vulnerable, wary rival.

The novel is the fluctuating field of force generated between these two poles, something that has been observed, though with a more geometric figure of speech that may require modification, by F. W. J. Hemmings: "The whole novel gives the impression of being balanced at the intersection of two inclined planes: the one rising with the rising sun from the warm mists of the morning, the other dipping with the lengthening shadows of evening towards the chilly darkness of cloister and tomb. The exact point of convergence [sic] can be plotted to a hair's breadth: it is the moment when an unnamed marquis whispers to Gina . . . that Fabrice has been taken." [13] This is a good deal more than half right, but there is less symmetry, less schematism, in the novel than the figure of intersecting planes implies. One can detect in the plot a broad movement from youth to cloister and tomb, but the more interesting thing about the concrete realization here of the experience of living is how in Gina, in Mosca, and occasionally even in Fabrice, there is such a wildly oscillating sense of age.

Youth is defined as a function of energy and passion; when these are deprived of an animating object, one begins to feel ancient. Gina at thirty-one, "retiring" to the castle at Grianta, talks about herself as though her life were over; Mosca's proposal to bring her to Parma as his mistress means that "youth, or at least active life, begins again" for her (chap. 6). Mosca himself, at forty-five, feels he is tottering on the brink of old age, and only his love for Gina can give him a few years' reprieve from senescence. The seventeen-year-old Fabrice in the belltower has a momentary sensation of looking back on his life from its extreme limit. When Gina hears that Fabrice has been taken to the citadel of Parma, she announces, rather melodramatically, that she is sixty, that the young woman is dead in her. "I am a woman of thirty-seven, I am at the threshold of old age, already feeling all its afflictions, and perhaps I may even be at the edge of the grave" (chap. 16). The extravagance of these declarations becomes all the more amusing in the light of Gina's subsequent activities, for over the next two hundred pages we see her splendid in her passionate energy as she contrives Fabrice's escape, conspires against the Prince, uses her sexual power to manipulate men, and throughout fiercely insists on the prerogatives of her own proud sense of self. Age, the novel repeatedly suggests, is not a matter of simple chronology, and this consciousness of aging combined with the attachment to the intensities of

---

13. *Stendhal: A Study of His Novels* (Oxford, 1964), p. 201.

youth engenders a subtle comedy tinged with sadness. This is the sort of understanding a writer could arrive at only in his own ripe maturity, and in Stendhal's case, perhaps only at this Indian-summer moment in his life.

Altogether, *Chartreuse* is the author's most resonant orchestration of all his experience from early childhood to maturity, and precisely for that reason it defies even more than his earlier books any explanation of its major characters as elaborations of "models" from Henri Beyle's life. Some commentators, for example, have argued that Gina was inspired by her namesake, Angela (or Gina) Pietragrua, who like her was a Milanese woman with a brilliantly theatrical, controlling nature; others, properly observing the vaguely incestuous tenor of Gina's love for Fabrice, see her as a version of Stendhal's lost, beloved mother; or again, in her role as a boldly resolute conspirator conducting her own private revolution, she has been linked with Métilde, accomplice of the Carbonari. The obvious point is that Gina is all of these, and something more than the sum of her parts.

Psychologically, the most fundamental of these aspects of Gina is the maternal one, and there are occasional moments when one is vividly conscious of the transformation into a fictional situation of material from the writer's life. At one point, for example, the reluctant Fabrice, yielding to his lovely aunt's inviting manner, "In a natural impulse of rapture and despite all reasonings, took this charming woman in his arms and covered her with kisses. At that very moment, the sound of the Count's carriage was heard entering the courtyard . . ." and then Mosca immediately appears in the room (chap. 11). This recapitulates, with a precise verbal echo, the famous autobiographical moment in *Henry Brulard* (chap. 3) in which Henri "covers [his] mother with kisses" and is infuriated when his father's sudden entrance interrupts this intimacy.

But if the emotional dynamics of that early experience have been powerfully remembered in the novel, they have also been turned into something different from what they were, as the novelist, with an uncanny consequentiality, follows the momentum of each character's distinctive individuality. Gina may be a nurturing, protective mother who gives Fabrice her unqualified love, but she is also a hot-tempered, jealous mistress, a genius of self-dramatization, a fanatic adherent to the dictates of her own impulsive will. And Oedipal longing itself, which some have wanted to make the magic key to all Stendhal's writing, has been radically rechanneled here. In *Le Rouge et le Noir*, Julien, moving between two women, finally chooses the mother figure and, perhaps partly through the unconscious logic of the incest taboo, by so doing chooses death as well. For Fabrice, however, there is no real problem of choice between his two women: despite his momentary "impulse of rapture" (*transport*), he is not really drawn to his aunt, and from his first day in prison, he becomes steadfastly attached to the younger woman, Clélia. One might speculate that there is even a displacement of the sense of the forbidden from the passionate mother to the nubile daughter: Fabrice's most satisfying "consummation" with Clélia will be entirely through the experience of sight, he at his lofty cell window, she looking across from her aviary; and in a bizarre complementarity, the sense of sight will be banished from their actual trysts at the end of the novel.

It is often difficult to know with Stendhal where the dividing line lies between intuition and intention, between unconscious and conscious memory. Like most of us, he was in certain ways dominated by patterns impressed on him in early childhood; yet some of these he seems to have managed consciously to recuperate, to meditate on in the light of his many-layered experience as an adult, and in any case to transform into art in rather surprising configurations. Thus, Gilbert Durand, in a book otherwise misguided in its insistence that Stendhal's mastery can be understood only when the details of the novel are aligned with mythic archetypes, makes the suggestive comment that Fabrice's peculiar solution of his problem of the Two Women represents Stendhal's recasting of the Oedipal drama after his experience of Métilde—and perhaps one should add, after two decades of fruitful introspection following that experience, which had just recently culminated in *Lucien Leuwen* and *La Vie de Henry Brulard*. "Métilde reveals to Stendhal that there is a love other than the return to the mother, but paradoxically the image of Métilde dead and 'forever' lost assumes aspects which bring it singularly close to that of the dead mother. Through Métilde, the emancipation of love becomes possible, but through Métilde's death the realization of love recedes, fleeing toward an ideal and inaccessible horizon." [14] Whether or not Durand's conjecture about the source of Stendhal's odd orientation toward love is correct, it nicely points to the fluidity with which the novelist's imagination moved among the disparate elements of his experience early and late in order to shape this masterpiece.

A novel, of course, is not just a certain way of imagining objects of desire but also a certain way of telling a story, and in this respect, too, Stendhal, in the terrific pace of his improvisation, managed to be more happily himself than ever before. The continuities with the narrative manner of *Le Rouge et le Noir* (rather than *Lucien Leuwen*) are clear:

14. *Le Décor mythique de la Chartreuse de Parme* (Paris, 1961), p. 149.

the urbane, sometimes chatty narrator, in this case mediating between his Italian heroes and his French audience, who often intervenes ironically when his protagonists are most emotionally extravagant; the touches of flaunted fictional self-consciousness; the easy movement from narrator's commentary to interior monologue to summary of the character's reasonings to the character's point of view. The only noticeable difference is that some of these procedures are used more boldly, or are more deliberately pushed to an extreme application. Thus, though Stendhal in *Le Rouge et le Noir* repeatedly experiments with restricting the field of perception to one character's point of view, there is nothing in the earlier novel quite like the extended tour de force of the Waterloo scene here, where we experience Fabrice's radical perceptual dislocation on the battlefield as he sees the plowed ground spurting little black fragments, only belatedly realizing that shots are being fired, and repeatedly trying to establish some connection between everything he confusedly sees and the word *battle*, which until this moment has had for him only literary meanings.

Perhaps the technical aspect of *Chartreuse* in which Stendhal's increased freedom with the genre is most clearly visible is the manipulation of fictional time. He may have first learned from *Tom Jones* the basic principle that time in a novel need not be chronometrically regular, that the novelist is free to slow down time to follow each word of a dramatic exchange or to speed it up by leaping over periods of varying length. A certain amount of narrative ellipsis, especially in connection with sexual matters, is observable in *Le Rouge et le Noir*, but such procedures are used more frequently, with more startling effect, in *Chartreuse*. The narrator of Stendhal's "Italian" novel repeatedly throws us just a little off balance, communicates to us through the shrewd indirection of unexpected silences, makes judgments about his subjects by exercising his prerogative concerning what to narrate and what to leave untold.

In Chapter 6, for example, when Mosca, in direct discourse, completes the exposition of his extraordinary proposal to Gina, that she consent to a pro forma marriage with the absent Duke of Sansévérina in order to assume a social position in Parma and become Mosca's mistress there, we are given neither her actual response to the Count's words nor any narrative summary of the conclusion of their discussion and what they finally resolve to do. Instead, the narrator, interrupting the temporal flow of his narrative, steps forward to protest that he can hardly be held responsible for the "profoundly immoral actions" of the personages whose chronicler he is, actions which would not be conceivable in a country (like France,

of course) where the sole passion is "money, the instrument of vanity."
Immediately after this brief paragraph of intervention, we are told the following: "Three months after the events reported till this point, the Duchess Sansévérina-Taxis astonished the court of Parma with her easy amicability and with the noble sereneness of her mind; her house was beyond
comparison the most agreeable in town." The elision of these three
months which include a marriage, a major transition, the establishment of
a ménage, is a beautiful way of conveying the accomplished fact of
Mosca's scheme by which Gina Pietranera is whisked from Milan to
Parma, where she suddenly appears in full splendor as the Duchess
Sansévérina-Taxis. Even more, the narrative ellipsis is a subtle signal of
worldly complicity between author and reader. The "profoundly immoral
action" that Mosca and Gina have just undertaken is something to be recognized, then passed over in discreet silence without inquiring into its
crude mechanics; this is how matters are arranged in the world, at least in
countries that foster passions other than vanity, as the narrator perfectly
understands and expects his audience to understand.

Stendhal's freedom to contract time and to suppress narrative materials
is exercised both on the scale of weeks, months, years, and on the level of
the individual scene. Just a few paragraphs after the one just cited, Gina
has her first audience with Ranuce-Ernest IV, which is conveyed to us in
these words: "He received Mme Sansévérina gracefully; he said subtle and
witty things to her; but she distinctly noticed that there was nothing
excessive in the cordial reception.—Do you know why? Count Mosca said
to her on her return from the audience. It's because Milan is a bigger and
more beautiful city than Parma." For a moment, in a novelistic equivalent
of a cinematic *faux raccord*, we hardly realize that we have been tumbled
from one scene to another, that an hour or so of fictional time has passed,
that we are now in another place, and that the words "Do you know
why?" are addressed to Gina by Mosca in response to her presumably
detailed account of the audience. That account is never actually given but
only intimated in the summary of her perception, "she distinctly noticed
that there was nothing excessive. . . ." What has happened in essence is
that the Prince has been refused the dignity of scenic representation. Our
conventional expectations have been frustrated or, rather, coolly dismissed, as though the narrator were saying: one really cannot be bothered
with all the preening and posturing of this silly little man with his full-
length portraits of Louis XIV, even if that is what people are accustomed
to look for in a novel. Such attention to the ridiculous can be reserved for
certain comic climaxes later on, but for the moment, the one real interest

is not in mimetic rendering but in the analysis of motive by political intelligence, and so we proceed immediately to Mosca's exposition for Gina's benefit of the provincial sense of inferiority he detects in the Prince.

This suppression, moreover, of Gina's first scene with Ranuce-Ernest IV will form a nice symmetry with the suppression, on somewhat different grounds, of her last scene with Ranuce-Ernest V near the end of the novel: "Banished by the indignant Duchess, he dared to reappear all trembling and terribly unhappy at three minutes to ten. At ten-thirty, the Duchess climbed into her carriage and left for Bologna" (chap. 27). So much for the *bonheur* that the pathetic young Prince is granted by forcing Gina to pay her sexual debt. Again, with a gesture of worldly discretion, the narrator assumes one would not want to inquire further about the unpleasantness of this half-hour, while the precise indication of the elided thirty-three minutes (with mental subtractions made for the time required to dress, undress, and come downstairs) provides an icy reminder of how minimal the Prince's "conquest" has been.

For so long a novel, *Chartreuse* repeatedly creates a sense of extraordinary speed, partly because of its unpredictable use of such narrative ellipses. To some degree, these procedures reflect Stendhal's aesthetic loyalty to the eighteenth century and perhaps most particularly to the witty narrative art of Diderot. That loyalty makes Stendhal, for all the Romanticism of his sensibility, thoroughly impatient with the circumstantial fussiness, the lumbering or emphatic style, the explicitness, the conventional regularity that characterized much of the fashionable fiction of his own time. (He would later observe tartly in the draft of a letter to Balzac that "If *Chartreuse* were translated into French by Mme Sand, it would be a success, but would require three or four volumes to express what it now does in two" [October 28–29, 1840].) Stendhal's repeated transgressions of conventional expectations are equally a function of his overriding sense that intelligence should dominate both narrative and discourse in the novel; it is a technique that repeatedly compels us to make inferential judgments, reexamine assumptions, identify significant elements in surprising directions. These innovative transgressions, moreover, have a manifest character of ad hoc inventions that derives from the process of improvisation through which the novel was made. As he dictated, Stendhal was obviously making constant spur-of-the-moment decisions about what was essential and what was dispensable, about where and how to move from one voice to another, from one narrative point of view to another.

Shifting narrative point of view, in fact, is an even more frequent feature in *Chartreuse* than ellipsis and is equally important in producing a sense of rapidity in the novel. Even when the narrator takes time to report the successive stages of reasoning within one character at a particular juncture of the narrative, this sense is not lost, for intelligence has its own velocity in shuttling between possibilities of perception. It may be helpful to look at one last passage in order to see how this method works. Here is the opening paragraph of Chapter 6:

> We frankly admit that the Canon Borda's jealousy was not absolutely wrong; on his return from France, Fabrice seemed in the Countess's eyes like a handsome stranger' whom she had once known well. Had he spoken of love, she would have loved him; did she not already have a passionate, as it were limitless, admiration for his conduct and his person? But Fabrice embraced her with such an effusion of innocent gratitude and well-meaning friendship that she would have thought it horrendous of herself had she sought another feeling in this almost filial friendship. Basically, the Countess said to herself, a few friends who knew me in the court of Prince Eugene might still find me pretty and even young, but for him I am a respectable woman . . . and, if I must say everything without at all sparing my sense of self-esteem, an old woman. The Countess was deluding herself about the stage of life which she had attained, but not in the manner of common women. At his age, besides, she added, one tends to exaggerate the ravages of time; a man more advanced in life. . . .

The elastic sense of age which we considered at length has its technical correlative in the elasticity with which the narrator, rapidly changing strategies, follows the movement of the character living in the ambiguous rhythms of time. The chapter begins with the narrator in front of the proscenium arch ("We frankly admit . . ."), commenting on the justice of one personage's view of another. By the first clause of the next sentence ("Had he spoken of love . . ."), he is off into the analysis in the subjunctive mode of conditions contrary to fact that was used so frequently in *Lucien Leuwen* to bring forth fine points of motive and character. But the approach to character is more polyphonic here than in *Lucien Leuwen*. The narrator immediately slips with great ease into *style indirect libre*, the third-person simulation of internal speech ("did she not already have . . ."), and the proximity of this rendering of thought to the actual interior monologue in the second half of the passage is increased because Stendhal uses no quotation marks to distinguish direct speech. Having entered Gina's mind by way of *style indirect libre*, the narrator then draws back half a step ("But Fabrice embraced her with such an effusion . . . that she would have thought it horrendous . . .") to summarize her thought instead of citing it, in another of his analyses of a condition contrary to fact, one which follows the trajectory of a desire Gina fears may be forbidden. (Probably no writer understood as well as Stendhal that there can be a connection between the ostensibly logical deployment of the subjunctive mode and psychological ambivalence.) Then in a wonderfully revealing non sequitur, we move from the summary of Gina's supposed moral horror over these incestuous desires into an interior monologue in which she reflects, first apprehensively, then, after the momentary hesitation of the three suspension points, with comic exaggeration, about how old she must seem to her nephew. This invites the narrator to intervene once more ("The Countess was deluding herself . . .") with a succinct observation on Gina's pretensions to antiquity that nevertheless distinguishes her from the more common sort of women. The narrator's intervention, meanwhile, has given Gina, as it were, time for still another reflection, which emerges almost as an answer to the narrator's comment, which of course she could not have heard: Well, I am not so terribly ancient after all, although a man as young as Fabrice might be incapable of appreciating me properly; but some older man—and her monologue trails off dreamily in another set of suspension points. She is thinking, of course, of Mosca, whom she has recently met in Milan, and her very next gesture, hardly that of a senescent woman, is to pause before a mirror, then smile.

One readily sees how the southern quality of brio which Stendhal had just recently been admiring in his travel notes becomes in *Chartreuse* a pervasive mode of narration. He brings one closer to the self-contradictory movements of a convincing individual psychology than any novelist before him had done, and at the same time, the play of intelligence over consciousness and character produces a luminous, humanely understanding comedy. If there is something "Shakespearean" about *La Chartreuse de Parme*, perhaps it resides chiefly in a certain affinity with Shakespeare's last romances, where the most serious spiritual issues are engaged through fairytale situations, where aging, loss, and death are encompassed in a serene comic vision, incorporated in a world of self-delighting play.

In *Chartreuse*, Stendhal was able to achieve the fullest expression of the two seemingly contradictory sides of himself: heir to the *Philosophes* and the Ideologues, and devotee of Rousseau. An avid and by now immensely experienced observer of political institutions and of men and women in society, he succeeded in making this one of the most worldly novels ever written, endlessly subtle in its perception of motives, unfettered by conventional moral notions, and offering in the microcosm of the court of Parma a virtually definitive account of politics in an era of exhausted ideologies (in some respects, ours as well as Metternich's). But the title of the novel, after all, invokes the idea of withdrawal from the world, and in

Fabrice's incarceration in the citadel, Stendhal found a way to make that idea structurally and thematically central—not merely a kind of epilogue, like Julien's prison retreat—in the midst of his worldly comedy.

The title, in fact, has bothered many readers because the charterhouse is actually introduced into the novel only in the last three paragraphs. Herbert Morris, in a curious monograph, has argued in detail that the real charterhouse is the citadel—it is there that Fabrice realizes the monastic ideal of blissful contemplative isolation, free from the world of sinful appearance—and that the charterhouse mentioned at the end is not really a monastery at all but rather the abandoned medieval tower in the forest which earlier doubled for the Farnese Tower.[15] Morris's second conclusion seems unnecessary and excessively ingenious, but he makes a persuasive case for the identity of the citadel as Fabrice's personal charterhouse. A similar observation, that "the visible citadel and the invisible monastery combine," has recently been offered by Victor Brombert with greater interpretive subtlety: "The unreal charterhouse, barely mentioned in the last pages, was somehow present from the very start, as though to warn the reader that behind the petty court intrigues, beyond the tensions of politics and the games of lifesmanship, there existed a privileged and almost inaccessible region: the world of withdrawal, of hidden spirituality." [16]

The crucial point for the success of the book is that Fabrice's "Carthusian" withdrawal does not exist merely as an idea toward which the novelist gestures but as a series of imaginatively realized scenes at the heart of the novel. All around Fabrice the buzz of plots and counterplots continues, the jealous bickering and the terrors of the ultras and the liberals, the charade of court manners, Gina's elaborate scheme to extricate him from his prison. But Stendhal summons the full lyrical resources of his dry and sparkling prose to make us see through Fabrice's eyes from his one hundred eighty foot elevation in the tower as he rapturously takes in the tranquil Italian landscape stretching all the way to the Alps and welcomes Clélia's shy looks of love from her vantage point across from him in the aviary.

The love ethic of *Chartreuse*, like the chivalric code which it invokes at certain strategic moments, is a secular version of a religious ideal, and Stendhal, habitually self-protective about his dream of transcendent love, here gives that dream living form without ironic subversion, though in a novel suffused with irony. When just before the end, Clélia in the dark of

15. *The Masked Citadel: The Significance of the Title of Stendhal's Chartreuse de Parme* (Berkeley and Los Angeles, 1968).
16. *The Romantic Prison* (Princeton, 1978), p. 67.

her orange-house pronounces those operatically resonant words (which Stendhal later noted that he was mentally translating from the Italian), *Entre ici, ami de mon coeur*, "Enter here, friend of my heart," we know we are at a moment of real fulfillment, without any residual coyness or satiric qualification. The lover, literally, metaphorically, and mystically, is about to enter into his garden. In fifty-two breathless days of composition, Stendhal had spun out a masterpiece which would receive some immediate recognition; but he had achieved this by creating a work that also held intense personal meaning for him, in which he could probe the whole range of human and social subjects he had spent a lifetime mastering, and in which his imagination could also etch a still image of longing consummated in a setting that had beckoned to him since childhood—a land where the orange tree grows.

XIV

CIVITAVECCHIA AND PARIS

(Aetat. 56–59)

THE TEMPO of book production in nineteenth-century Paris was mercifully swift, for Stendhal's days in France were numbered. On January 24, 1839, less than a month after the completion of his manuscript, he signed a contract for *Chartreuse*, granting the publisher all profits from the novel for the next five years in return for a payment of 2,500 francs. Two weeks later, he received his first batch of proofs to correct. By March 26, he had returned the last sheets of proof, and just two days later, the first bound copies of the book were delivered to him. The publication of the novel was announced on April 6.

During this period, meanwhile, a political event had occurred which would put an end to these happy Parisian days of productivity, friendship, and good society that had already lasted almost three years—Count Molé's resignation on March 8 from his post as foreign minister. Deprived of a favorably disposed eminence in the foreign office, Beyle could hardly hope to continue his constant extensions of diplomatic furlough, and by early June, he was duly informed that the packet boats, the quarantine orders, the loads of grain, and the bales of imported textiles at Civitavecchia once more required his personal consular attention. He left Paris on the evening of June 24, making his leisurely and reluctant way across Switzerland and down through northern Italy, his progress further slowed by a renewed attack of the gout that hit him as he reached Genoa. On August 10, he arrived back at Civitavecchia and resumed the administration of his consulate.

But before Beyle's departure, during his last five months in Paris, he had turned himself into a whirlwind of literary activity, spinning off one new project after another, holding onto none. One gets the impression that he was exhilarated by what he had produced in *La Chartreuse de Parme,* and by the sheer speed of the production, and through this experience was moved to a sense of how far, in all sorts of directions, his energies as a writer of fiction might take him. His continuing contract with the *Revue des Deux Mondes* immediately led him, perhaps regrettably, in one particular direction. During three days in the latter part of February, in the midst of proofreading *Chartreuse,* he dictated the second part of *L'Abbesse de Castro;* the story appeared in print at the beginning of March. Through the last half of March, he worked on *Suora Scolastica,* a new tale of convent love, this time set in the eighteenth century. Breaking off *Suora Scolastica,* in early April he spent a week on *Trop de faveur tue,* still another novella of spirited young women immured in convents, lovers let in through garden entrances, intramural plots and counterplots. Like *Suora,* it did not hold his attention for long, and he abandoned it after having written perhaps 10,000 words. Indeed, he had scarcely begun this Renaissance tale when the idea occurred to him for a novel to be set in contemporary France, which he called first *Amiel* then *Lamiel,* after the heroine. It was an idea that was to exercise a continuing fascination over Stendhal, as we shall see, but at first it remained only a glimmering possibility of a future project. In late April, he worked very briefly on *Le Chevalier de Saint-Ismier,* which was to be a historical novel set in Spain, modeled on a seventeenth-century French adaptation of Tirso de Molina. This project was left in a still more abortive state than his two recent convent tales. On May 16, he drew up a list of principal characters for *Lamiel,* but within a few days, he was hard at work on *Féder, ou le mari d'argent,* a satirical novel about a fashionable young painter in contemporary Paris, of which he would write some 30,000 words. By then, the time had arrived to pack his bags for Italy.

All this energetic fumbling in the dark for the handle of a new fictional project is really not very surprising. Though we can easily dismiss the old

canard about Stendhal's lacking the power of invention—surely to turn a
1,200-word anecdote into a novel of over 200,000 words required prodi-
gious inventiveness and was not just a matter of "borrowing" a plot—he
was, because of his need to count on the élan of improvisation, more
dependent than most major writers on sheer serendipity. That is, he
needed to hit on an unpredictable combination of fictional circumstances
and milieus congenial to his imagination with personages that exhibited, or
could be drawn into, a close fit with his own preoccupations, his conscious and unconscious desires and fears. "Origin of the Greatness of the
Farnese Family" in its fifteenth-century setting would have been no more
than another pale Italian chronicle, while perhaps the strictly contemporary story of a naive young hero who returns from Waterloo to encounter the intricacies of political life in Austrian-dominated Italy would have
sputtered out after half a dozen chapters. What fired Stendhal's creative
powers was the idea of placing these eminently Renaissance souls in a contemporary political arena and of having a hero who was not just a conventional *ingénu* but a creature of passion fixed in a psychologically
fraught constellation between a worldly father/guide/rival and an impulsive mother/protector/seductress. The sundry historical fictions Stendhal
undertook in the early months of 1839 did not present such a happy
combination, and what he wrote of them does not go beyond the rather
flat imaginative perspective of his earlier Italian tales. *Féder*, like *Le Rose
et le Vert*, still another novel he had begun and broken off two years earlier, gives evidence of the supple narrative intelligence and especially of
the comic verve that we saw operating in his major fiction, but there is
something thematically and psychologically *directionless* about both these
long fragments, as though the protagonists did not finally engage the deepest imaginative resources of the author. *Lamiel*, on the other hand, was
to touch something more profound in him, though the materials for that
novel would in the end tantalize rather than fully excite his imagination.

Meanwhile, in the summer of 1839, Beyle was faced with the more
mundane business of accustoming himself once more to his consular duties
at Civitavecchia. The lengthy official dispatches he wrote in this last
period of his diplomatic service again reflect his determination to do the
job right, when he was doing it at all. Sensitive to the rebukes of his superiors over the by now Homeric proportions of the catalogue of his
absences from his post, he congratulates himself at the beginning of October for having spent twenty-one consecutive days in Civitavecchia without going to Rome. But the dismal little port-city was more intolerable to
him than ever: the old motif of ennui begins to reappear in his private

writing, and that condition was exacerbated by his gout and by the migraine headaches he now began to suffer. And as always, there was Lysimaque Tavernier to contend with, more insolently provoking than ever after his three years of virtual autonomy in the consulate. While Beyle was away, Tavernier had actually broken into the consul's locked study, perused his papers and even appropriated some of his shirts. When Beyle's friend Bucci confronted Tavernier over the broken lock, the chancellor coolly answered that the damage must have been done by the wind.

It is understandable, then, that Beyle, despite his moments of dutiful resolution, was soon spending as much time as ever away from Civitavecchia. Within a few weeks after his return, he had again established a *pied-à-terre* in Rome with his artist friend, Abraham Constantin, and before long he was attending dinners and balls with the Cinis, with Filippo Caetani, and others of his former Roman acquaintance. On October 10, just two months after his resumption of the consulate, he went to Rome to meet Mérimée, who had come for a month's vacation in Italy. On the 20th, the two friends set out for Naples, where they stayed as tourists till the end of Mérimée's holiday. Beyle enjoyed the warm climate of Naples, but some remarks in a letter to Fiore written at the end of his stay there suggest that he was disposed to make invidious comparisons with his fresh memories of the charms of Paris: "All the women are ugly; their physiognomy is merely the revelation of the crude sensations of the animal. Never a candid manner, which could move one, which shows a capacity for passion . . . I see nothing but the digestive creature" (November 9, 1839). Mérimée's visit obviously provided some relief for Beyle's immediate sense of isolation in being banished once more from Paris, but it was a mixed blessing, for Mérimée in the best of times was a difficult friend. The day after his departure, Beyle noted that their trip had been spoiled by Mérimée's "frightful vanity."

A more agreeable Parisian intimate, however, who could offer him consolation of another sort, was now within traveling distance. When Beyle was on his way from Paris to Civitavecchia, he had stopped briefly in Siena to see Giulia Rinieri Martini. The only written note he made of this encounter was the invocation of one of his favorite formulas: "*Battle of Siena.*" That suggests some initial resistance on Giulia's part, but the subsequent course of their relationship leads one to infer that her resistance was not exactly implacable. Soon, Giulia and her husband moved to Florence, a conveniently shorter trip from Beyle's location in the Papal States, and during his two remaining years in Italy, he would make four separate visits to Florence. In July 1840, he stayed there in a rented room for eighteen days, evidently enjoying himself enough so that he was impelled to return on August 19 and linger till mid-September. His little tic of marginal notation makes it clear that he and Giulia were sweetening the bitterness of their shared Italian "exile" with their old lovers' habits: on September 4, he notes, "She a time," on September 6, "I a time," and it is safe to assume that there were a good many other times during these weeks in Florence that were not officially recorded. The evidence suggests that Giulia was no longer a great passion for Beyle, indeed, had been something less than that even in Paris two years earlier, but she did afford him emotional intimacy and a kind of comfortable sexual companionship, and these, at least for interludes, brightened the grayness of his final tour of duty in Italy.

If Beyle took prompt steps to renew this old liaison after his arrival in Italy, he was just as eager to pick up the thread of his career as a writer, despite the distractions of his consular busywork and the discouragements of his immediate surroundings. As soon as he had settled back into his responsibilities at Civitavecchia and reestablished his social connections in Rome, he began, on October 1, 1839, to write *Lamiel*, the novel he had first conceived during the spring in Paris. He was interrupted by Mérimée's visit, but after returning to Civitavecchia on November 10, he went back to work on the novel, writing without amanuensis in his inveterate scrawl. By December 3, he had produced over 60,000 words, which took the young heroine from her peasant background in Normandy through an elopement with a callow first lover to an involvement in Paris with a pretentious, ne'er-do-well count, whose grandfather was a hatmaker. At this point, the novelist went off to Rome, and progress on the novel was suspended. In the early months of 1840, he would dictate to an amanuensis, presumably with some changes, the material he had already written in his own hand (the dictated copy has not been preserved), and he would produce additional, and alternative, episodes for the novel in 1841 and again in 1842, during the last weeks of his life. But after what he had written consecutively late in 1839, he was essentially stymied, unsure how to proceed or even, as his notes and scenarios indicate, what kind of novel to make out of *Lamiel*.

Beyle's mood away from France and the increasing problems he was experiencing with his health may have made sustained writing in any case unfeasible, though there is also reason to believe that he was troubled by ambivalences toward the subject of his novel that he could not artistically resolve. But unlike his shorter novel-fragments, there is much in *Lamiel* that is of compelling interest, and in certain ways, this uncompleted novel is a more psychologically revealing document of the condition of its author than any of his earlier fictions. After *La Chartreuse de Parme* Stendhal was particularly drawn toward the idea of the satiric novel, and it is probable that his original intention when he thought of *Lamiel* in April 1839 was to produce a contemporary equivalent of Marivaux's *Vie de Marianne* or of Lesage's *Gil Blas*, the eighteenth-century picaresque masterpiece which he makes one of Lamiel's favorite books. Lamiel's career as Stendhal actually wrote it and sketched its continuation in his outlines is very much that of a traditional *pícara*: an illegitimate child of uncertain parentage, she is adopted by a village couple; as an adolescent is taken in to be the favored companion of the local marquise; runs away with her mistress's son; establishes herself in Paris through her sexual attractiveness; and in the projected development of the novel, at last discovers true passion in the arms of a criminal at war with society and joins his band of rebel-thieves. The verve and the comic sharpness of the picaresque tradition are evident in individual scenes of *Lamiel*, but the picaresque insouciance of a Gil Blas eluded Stendhal, and one detects darker, more disturbing concerns in the episodes he completed as well as in his scenarios. Lamiel's liaison with Valbayre, the archcriminal (based on a figure actually in the news in the 1830s), was intended from the start, but it is not clear whether Stendhal at first had in mind the apocalyptic ending he indicated in a scenario written in Civitavecchia in late November 1839: Valbayre was to be captured and sentenced to death, after which Lamiel, in a grand act of vengeance, would set fire to the Palais de Justice and perish in the conflagration.

Attitudes and relations that Stendhal had dealt with in his previous novels are treated here with a new degree of harshness, of potential violence, which culminates in this projected ending where the underclass resentment against the established order first articulated in *Le Rouge et le Noir* is transformed into an image of anarchic destruction. On the personal level, the scene in which Lamiel loses her virginity exemplifies the special tonality of the novel. Having been warned by priest and foster parents about the dangers of "love," an obscure experience presented in a more alluring light by the novels she has been reading, Lamiel decides to enlighten herself by hiring a healthy young peasant to meet her in the woods and perform the act upon her for 10 francs. "Of course, I want to be your mistress," she informs the baffled young Jean, who cannot understand why this pretty girl should be proposing such a transaction.

Ah! That's different, said Jean in a businesslike manner. And then without rapture, without love, the young Norman made Lamiel his mistress.
—There's nothing else? said Lamiel.

—Nothing at all, Jean replied.
—Have you had many mistresses?
—I've had three.
—And there's nothing else?
—Not as far as I know. . . .
Lamiel sat down and watched him go off (she wiped away the blood and hardly paid attention to the pain).
Then she burst into laughter, repeating to herself:
"So, this vaunted love, that's all it amounts to!" [chap. 9]

Déniaisement, being stripped of naive illusions, is a familiar rite in picaresque novels, but there is scarcely any picaresque exuberance in Lamiel's laughter. The briskness of dialogue and elliptical narration here is continuous with Stendhal's earlier fiction (and in this instance also probably emulates something of Diderot's manner in *Jacques le fataliste et son maître*), but the parenthesis that reminds us so plainly of the ruptured hymen is quite uncharacteristic and reflects a more unsparing view of what is implied by realism than does his previous work. Lamiel has often been spoken of as a female Julien, but beyond the external similarity of being an attractive and clever young peasant on the make in Restoration society, she has none of Julien's fundamental innocence, or his crippling self-consciousness, his enervating sense of strain under the pressures of role playing. She is in these respects rather an anti-Julien and, even more, an anti-Fabrice: a completely detached intelligence, devoid of sensuality and (as the narrator tells us several times) passionate only in her curiosity, amused by the world of dupes through which she passes and at the same time coolly contemptuous of it.

In Octave, in Lucien, and in Fabrice, Stendhal had represented protagonists who feared that they were incapable of love; with Lamiel, he created a figure who is genuinely incapable of that emotion, which is one of several reasons why the planned denouement with Valbayre could not be written. At least since his involvement with Angela Pietragrua, he had recognized the possibility of a woman in whom the qualities of passion and wily calculation existed in piquant, disorienting union. In many of his Italian tales, in his portrayals of Mathilde de la Mole and of Gina, in *Le Rose et le Vert* and its 1830 fragmentary predecessor, *Mina de Vanghel*, he had experimented with a whole series of what the French critics like to call "Amazons," or what Freudians think of still more picturesquely as phallic women. Now, in imagining a seductive Lamiel—her portmanteau name suggests "soul," "girlfriend," and "honey" in French—with an icy temperament, he reached the extreme possibility of this type, where the side of passion was closed off. The details of her Norman girlhood and her flight to Paris may have been suggested to him by the history of an early mistress whom he cherished retrospectively, Mélanie Guilbert, as two scholars have recently argued at length, but it is surely misguided to think of Lamiel in any sense as a "portrait" of the mild, dependent Mélanie.[1] Lamiel, moreover, does not even come across as a *belle dame sans merci*, for what chiefly seems to have drawn Stendhal to her was the possibility of projecting one particular, and pleasurable, fantasy-version of himself into this female figure. If Julien, Lucien, and Fabrice are all in their different ways the alluring young man Henri Beyle dreamed of being, the aspect of physical attractiveness is heightened in Lamiel—because she is a woman, it is virtually her sole instrument of power—while as a creature of pure intelligent calculation, she has none of the emotional vulnerability of those more impressionable and innocent male protagonists. She has been compared to Ariosto's warrior-maiden, Bradamante, but she more essentially resembles another female figure from *Orlando Furioso*, one with whom Stendhal had explicitly fantasized a bond in *Souvenirs d'égotisme*: Angelica, who drives men to distraction with her beauty and who enjoys ultimate, mobile invulnerability because she can make herself invisible with her magic ring.

Stendhal was in the habit of splitting the imaginative projections of himself in his novels into an innocent son and a worldly father—Julien and Abbé Pirard, Leuwen father and son, Fabrice and Mosca. (This process has been keenly observed by Jean Prévost in *La Création chez Stendhal*). In *Lamiel*, however, there is an extreme, potentially explosive quality in the nature of the two projections and their relationship. Lamiel's mentor in cynicism is a local physician named Sansfin, who repeatedly addresses her in the accents of a Vautrin (in Balzac's *Illusions perdues* addressing his young disciple Lucien de Rubempré). "The world is not divided, as the simpletons think, between rich and poor, between men of virtue and villains, but quite simply, between dupes and cheats; that's the key which explains the 19th century since the fall of Napoleon" (chap. 7). But Dr. Sansfin is a hunchback, seething with sexual resentment as well as with social *ressentiment*, trying to ameliorate his deformity (like Beyle himself) through dandified attire, taking a prurient interest in Lamiel which he does not attempt to consummate (in an alternative version of Lamiel's deflowering, Stendhal has him attack the peasant boy with a knife when he learns what has happened). The writer, as we learn from his

1. André Doyon and Yves du Parc, *De Mélanie à Lamiel* (Aran, 1972).

notes, had meant Sansfin to be a superficial and satirically rendered personage, but the misshapen doctor figured more powerfully in his imagination than he consciously intended, soon threatened to take the novel away from its nominal heroine. When, for example, Sansfin teaches Lamiel how to feign consumption by crushing a small bird to death each morning so that she can through a sleight-of-hand carry fresh blood to her mouth to spit up, the novel has clearly moved away from its picaresque antecedents toward the fictional representation of the sinister, the bizarre, the pathological.

In Sansfin, Stendhal focuses the harshest of all his visions of himself as an ugly, ungainly creature with only his quick intelligence to depend on in his relations with an inimical world of women. In precisely this connection, Sansfin's spill from his horse into the mud is by far the cruelest version of this archetypal Stendhalian scene of failed equitation. He is riding on a path along a brook, where he meets a group of peasant women washing their linens in the stream. They greet him in the following gentle terms: "Watch out for your hump, Doctor, it might slip and tumble all the way down here and crush us poor washerwomen." To which he replies in kind: "You have humps often enough, the lot of you, but it isn't on your backs" (chap. 3). The exchange of insults continues until Sansfin, in an impulse of rage, gallops by the washerwomen, splattering them and their newly laundered linens with mud. Then his horse shies when a laundry-paddle is tossed at its head, and the rider himself is hurled into the mud. Infuriated, he seizes the rifle he has been carrying with him and points it at the women, but it is completely clogged with mud. Sansfin is a caricature *in extremis* of Beyle, the lifelong strategist of amatory conquest: an object of ridicule because of his physical grotesqueness, full of impotent rage against the female sex that reviles him, venomous wit his only weapon, in the end humiliated and thrust into the muck. This is hardly conscious self-portraiture, but it surely issues from the murkiest meditations of the aging author in his lonely consulate on the sexual fears and insecurity he had sought to master since adolescence. The expression of this shadowy inner world of Henri Beyle was potent but perhaps not altogether under the author's control, which was still another reason for his leaving the novel in mid-course, with Lamiel in Paris well before the point when she was to be brought back into direct contact with the ambiguous Dr. Sansfin.

Just at the moment when Stendhal was recognizing that he did not know how to continue *Lamiel*, he conceived another project, which was not exactly literary but perhaps in the final analysis was more a matter of

literary notions, however scrambled and elliptical, than of actual experience. On March 6, 1840, he began what was the most peculiar of all his
private notebooks. He entitled these thirty-three manuscript pages *Earline*,
introducing them with the following bilingual superscription:

The Last Romance
Fin *of the* Carnaval 39–40.

His fondness for verbal camouflage runs riot in these pages, which are a
series of fragmentary diary notations, often in telegraphic style, in a wild
mixture of French and English, with personages indicated not only by
pseudonyms but usually by initials or eccentric abbreviations as well. This
fantastically coded account of the diarist's unrequited passion for Earline,
an unhappy history which he dates from February 16 to March 20, is in
all likelihood Beyle's record of a renewed attachment to Countess Giulia
Cini ("Earline" being his code version of "Contessa"), whom he had
fancied once before, in 1835; but it is far from clear how the journal
should be taken. The usual view, that of Henri Martineau and other biographers, is a pathetic one: *Earline* is seen as the sad, poignant document of
Henri Beyle's last attempted love, as ailing and lonely he pursues still one
more beauty who resists him. François Michel, on the other hand, has
made the shrewd and plausible suggestion that *Earline* is rather an experiment in the literary notation of feelings more hypothetical than real, "an
intellectual diversion, a *romanzetto* in *anima viva*, one might also say a
Kriegspiel." [2]

We should not forget that the English word "romance," with which
Beyle labeled his notebook, carried for him as a speaker of French an
ambiguous second sense of *roman*, novel. This does not mean that he felt
nothing at all for Giulia Cini but that whatever flutterings of feeling he
did have were magnified and fictionally distorted by the very project of
making them figure as motives in a text called The Last Romance. That
subtitle is especially apt, for *Earline* is a recapitulation of the themes of
Beyle's career as a lover, a recapitulation verging on self-parody, and one
entirely appropriate for a moment in his life just after he had been fantas-
izing himself as the grotesque Dr. Sansfin. He pines for Earline, is vexed
by the presence of a rival, tries to perceive signs of encouragement in her
fleeting glances, properly recalls his historic "defeat" at Bècheville by
Alexandrine Daru when Earline rebuffs him, and remembers his suffering
over Métilde when he sees how completely preoccupied he has become

2. *Études stendhaliennes*, p. 190.

with his Roman lady. All the old military metaphors are invoked, for this is the last campaign of the disciple of Martial Daru, but there are symptomatic little indications in the text that the writer is a man beyond the illusions which he is exercising himself to foster: "Happiness of being with her, of having been with her, but finally Nothing, absolutely *Nothing*" (H.B.'s emphasis).[3]

Beyle returned from Rome to Civitavecchia on March 23 and, as soon as he arrived, claimed in a marginal note that Earline was no longer on his mind. Nevertheless, occasional thoughts of her apparently did touch him during the next few months, and he saw her again on subsequent visits to Rome in April and once more in June, when he evidently attempted to make a declaration of love. But he was already looking forward eagerly to his early summer trip to Florence to see Giulia Rinieri, a far more substantial, less fanciful attachment. By the beginning of 1841, he could record in his marginalia that Earline was fading from his consciousness or, a few weeks later, that he still sometimes thought of her, but "not tragically," as he once had thought of Métilde. She was, indeed, a kind of pseudo-Métilde in the concluding phase of his emotional history.

For the vision of fulfillment Stendhal was pursuing more steadfastly by this moment in his life was *roman* in the sense of novel, not romance. It was not lack of desire but uncertain health and morale and the absence of French surroundings that prevented him from sustaining concentration on a single project of fiction. For a few days beginning at the end of March 1840, as his Earline experiment was failing, he began a novel he called *Don Pardo*, in which he apparently sought to solve the problem of being physically cut off from France by setting his story in Civitavecchia. This scheme, however, did not go beyond some preliminary notes and part of one chapter. Immediately afterward, he composed a curious document he entitled "Les Privilèges du 10 Avril, 1840," which is a reversion to his old fantasy, more of omniscience than of omnipotence, drawn from *The Thousand and One Nights*. In the twenty-three articles of this "patent" (*brevet*), signed with the name "Frédéric de Stendhal," the privileged person is granted magical mobility, invulnerability, preternatural power in sex and in other spheres, both native beauty and the ability of protean self-transformation. But "Les Privilèges" is, interestingly, a fantasy of godlike knowledge and power with stipulated limits dictated by the realistic habits of the novelist and the experience-tested lover. The person is to be allowed, for example, to change into any creature he wants twenty

3. *Oeuvres intimes*, p. 1515.

times a year, but only provided that the said creature really exists. A hundred times a year he can see what is being done at a given moment by anyone he wants, but the woman he loves must be entirely excluded from the operation of this clairvoyance. "Les Privilèges" is obviously an expression of self-indulgence on the part of a Stendhal for the moment vexed both with himself and with the circumstances of his life, but in the midst of free-wheeling fantasy, it strangely points back toward his commitment to the novel, the literary form in which he was able to mingle just this sort of fantasy with a hard-edged definition of historical and psychological realities.

After April 10, Beyle made his last quixotic approaches to Earline, more happily followed by his two long visits to Giulia Rinieri Martini in Florence during the summer. In the latter part of September, he was back in Civitavecchia, but after two weeks there, he went off to Rome for a month, during which time he received a copy of the *Revue Parisienne* containing an article that deeply excited him and, of all things, that set him back to work on *La Chartreuse de Parme*. The piece in question was a long review-essay on his novel by Balzac, who proclaimed it with a grand flourish as the contemporary "masterpiece of the literature of ideas," "a book in which the sublime shines forth from one chapter to the next . . . the novel that Machiavelli would have written had he lived banished from Italy in the 19th century." [4] Until this moment, critical opinion had done little more than concede that Stendhal was a clever and "interesting" writer (the decidedly qualified praise of George Sand's retrospective estimate would be typical of the contemporary climate of opinion). Now, Balzac, who had made himself the giant of the modern French novel through his remarkable production over the past ten years, had publicly recognized the author of *Chartreuse* as his equal, and Stendhal was elated, perhaps a little overwhelmed.

Such recognition, however, should not have come as a total surprise, for there is a clear prehistory to Balzac's rhapsodic article. The two writers had known each other since Delécluze's Sundays in the 1820s, and they were on friendly if distant terms. After the Waterloo episode of *Chartreuse* appeared in the *Constitutionnel*, Balzac had written Stendhal on March 20, 1839, to say that he was altogether overcome with jealousy in the face of Stendhal's brilliance in rendering a battle scene, a success he compared to the highest artistic achievements he knew. This encouraged Stendhal to send the novel to Balzac as soon as he received the first bound

---

4. Balzac, *Études sur M. Beyle* (Geneva, 1943), pp. 16–17.

copies. He turned to Balzac in a brief note inquiring about an accurate address (March 29, 1839) as "the king of novelists of the present century," and there is reason to assume that the praise was quite sincere. There are very few comments of any sort on Balzac in Stendhal's private writing, and the enterprise represented by *La Comédie humaine* obviously reflected a rather different conception of the novel from his own, but it seems likely enough that Stendhal recognized the imaginative power of such works as *Eugénie Grandet*, *La Fille aux yeux d'or*, *Le Père Goriot*, and the first part of *Les Illusions perdues*, all of which had appeared during the past five years. (As a matter of fact, the critical establishment at this time was still inclined to condescend to Balzac as a dubious and sensationalistic writer, but Stendhal's literary judgment never depended on conventional opinion, and in any case he must have envied Balzac's popular following.) By April 5, Balzac had finished reading *Chartreuse*, and was writing Stendhal to tell him that it was "a great and beautiful book," going far beyond *Le Rouge et le Noir*, which he also admired, and that the novel "explained the soul of Italy." [5] (Six days later, Balzac happened to meet Stendhal out on a stroll and again warmly praised him for his book.) Balzac's enthusiasm did not prevent him from informing his less famous colleague in this brief letter that there were *longueurs* in the early part of the novel, that the conclusion needed development, that more physical description of the characters was required, and that it was a tactical error to place the action in a specifically named state like Parma. All these faults he hoped Stendhal would correct in a second edition of the novel—a lesson he would repeat publicly the following year in his article, adding to the catalogue of minor flaws a criticism of the brusque, careless style. If Stendhal was his equal, he wanted it implicitly clear that he, Balzac, was first among equals.

By the time Balzac wrote his review of *Chartreuse*, he had read the novel three times, and there is no question that, whatever his reservations, he adored the book. He had little sense, however, of the peculiar refraction of historical material through the novelist's personal experience that was Stendhal's way of creating fiction: he assumed, for example, that Mosca was modeled on Metternich and the Duchess of Sansévérina on the Princess of Belgiojoso, a Milanese Italian nationalist who had been forced to flee to Paris in the 1830s. Balzac was equally unattuned to Stendhal's odd mixture of lyricism and witty satire, so he could not see the point of the "overture" in 1796, of the avoidance of descriptions à la Walter Scott,

5. *Cent soixante-quatorze lettres à Stendhal*, pp. 171–173.

and of the rapid, unornamented prose. All these deficiencies of perception have been aptly summarized by Maurice Bardèche: "He had seen in *Chartreuse* an admirable novel by Balzac in which certain imperfections surprised him." [6]

Stendhal's reaction to the Balzac article is a touching revelation of what all along lay behind his coolly confident resolution to write for the readers of 1880 (a formula he invokes in his letter to Balzac) or of 1935. It might be comforting to announce that, rather than betray his idiosyncratic personal standards, he would address himself to posterity, but it was positively intoxicating to be recognized in print as a genius by a writer he was prepared to think of as the leading novelist of his own day. In the privacy of his marginalia, Stendhal expressed the elation of a lagging schoolboy who has just been told by his headmaster that he has completely surpassed the rest of the class. Responding directly to Balzac was quite another matter.

There was much to gratify him in the article, not least of which was this concluding comment on his personal situation: "It is difficult to explain how this first-class observer, this profound diplomat who, in his writings and in his spoken words, has given so much proof of the loftiness of his ideas and the breadth of his practical knowledge, should be no more than consul at Civitavecchia." Some of the corrective criticism he was willing to accept; some of it he felt obliged to resist, especially in what related to style. "I see only one rule: style cannot be too clear, too simple" (draft of October 16, 1840). This point is made even more sharply in the third draft of the letter in what is probably a polemic fabrication for Balzac's benefit to illustrate the stylistic ideal to which Stendhal adhered: "In composing *Chartreuse*, in order to hit the right tone, every morning I read two or three pages of the civil code." (October 28–29).

Stendhal's letter to Balzac is both a deeply felt artistic credo and one of his most self-conscious artifices. This, too, was a piece of writing for which he wanted to strike just the right tone, and so he wrote it over three times, beginning October 16, the day after he read the article, and he did not mail the final form of the letter till October 30. He wanted to express his gratitude to Balzac without revealing how stirred he had been by the other writer's high praise, and so he professed to be amused by what he characterized as Balzac's exaggerations: "This astonishing article, the like of which one writer has never received from another, I have read, now I dare to confess to you, with bursts of laughter" (October 28–29).

6. *Stendhal romancier*, p. 421.

He also wanted to defend his own artistic principles but at the same time show himself responsive to reasonable criticism. There is, all told, a pervasive quality of *nervousness* in the extant drafts of Stendhal's letter to Balzac that suggests how much this signal recognition meant to him.

And in fact, even as he was posting the letter, he began to go over his printed copy of *Chartreuse*, making small stylistic revisions and composing entire new episodes for insertion in the novel, or indicating in the margins further developments he intended. Just as in the case of his uncompleted novels, revision quickly proved to be a self-constructed labyrinth. The general tendency of his local stylistic changes was to add a word or a phrase or a specification of narrative detail that would smooth the effect of abruptness Balzac had detected, but the result was only to retard the rapid bounding movement of the prose which helped create the special air of Stendhal's Parma. The newly invented episodes, moreover, had no clear place in the narrative logic of the novel. Stendhal devoted most of his spare time through the last months of 1840 to this attempted reworking, but by February 9, 1841, he came to the sensible conclusion that Balzac's proposals were leading him away from the strong sense of the novel he had achieved in the white heat of improvisation, and he abandoned plans for any extensive revisions.

Even had his notions of an improved version of *Chartreuse* been better directed, it is unlikely that Stendhal would have been able to carry them out, for his shaky physical condition now began to manifest truly alarming signs. At the beginning of 1840, in the midst of revising a page of *Lamiel*, he had suffered a fainting spell, falling into the fire by which he sat as he wrote. By March 29, 1840, his migraines had become so acute that he was moved to conclude a letter to Fiori with the question, "In sum, is it worth the trouble to live?" During the next few months, as he turned from one Giulia to the other, he may possibly have enjoyed a relative remission of symptoms, but by February and early March 1841, as he was abandoning the revision of *Chartreuse* and again fiddling with *Lamiel*, the headaches with accompanying nervous tension and fatigue once more became debilitating. Then in Civitavecchia on March 15 he experienced a serious stroke.

Writing to Fiori in early April from Rome, where he had gone for medical care, Beyle lists the symptoms from which he was still suffering after the crisis of March 15: a difficulty in speaking; sudden ten-minute lapses of memory in which—agony for a writer even more than for others —he was unable to recall simple French words; sensations of suffocation; complete enervation after performing a trifling task like writing a note of three lines. He entreats Fiori to keep the news from Colomb, and at the same time, he manages to preserve the posture of poised superiority to the threat of death which he had adopted since the serious illnesses of his years in the imperial service. "I have also grappled with death," he begins his April 5th letter to Fiori. "It's the transition which is disagreeable, and that horror is the consequence of all the nonsense with which our heads were stuffed at the age of three." Five days later, in another letter to Fiori, he can report no alleviation of symptoms, and he sounds a bit grimmer at one point: "A hundred times I've given up my life, going to bed in the firm belief that I would not awake." On April 19, as he describes to Fiori the unpleasant treatment of bleedings and the artificial ulceration of one arm which he was undergoing, he bids his friend farewell, in the event this letter should prove his last, and asks him to accept lightheartedly whatever may happen. Beyle stayed in Rome from the end of March until June 10, when, neither noticeably better nor worse, he returned to Civitavecchia. At midsummer, he noted in the margin of a book, in English, "*Four months of Firodea*," that is, fear of death. It is the most poignant of his many cryptograms, intended to veil his meaning, even as it was half-revealed, not from the eyes of a political censor or a callous society but from some part of himself, as though it were possible to name and not name his most intimate terror, which as a matter of stoic principle he did not want to admit as a terror.

Beyle's physical functioning, however, seems to have improved sufficiently by this point for him to enjoy a last brief romantic interlude with a new woman. On June 19, suffering quite as much from loneliness as from the effects of his recent stroke, he had described at the end of a letter to Colomb his two dogs to whom he was deeply attached; then he added, "I am sad to have nothing to love." But within a week and a half, a charming young woman named Cecchina Lablache, wife of a Parisian painter, François Bouchot, arrived at Civitavecchia to take the waters at a nearby spa, properly provisioned with a letter of introduction to the French consul. Mme Bouchot was either involved with or being pursued by a twenty-seven-year-old painter named Henri Lehmann, who showed up in Civitavecchia in early August and did a pencil sketch of the suddenly aged Beyle, the last portrait made of him. For the moment, however, she was a lovely young woman alone in a dull seaside town, and she needed some means of amusement. She and Beyle spent hours in conversation through July, he gave her *Chartreuse* to read, and she returned the compliment with teasing signs of sexual invitation. "*Great faus two and tenth august 1841*," he wrote in English in a marginalium, "*perhaps the last of his life.*" Whether the problematic word *faus* refers to an error in failing to pursue a sexual advantage, or whether it is a way of saying, as the second clause makes more likely, that he actually enjoyed the advantage, is not entirely clear. In either case, the accommodating Mme Bouchot, as Beyle equally noted, was an "oasis in the desert of this life in Civitavecchia." [7]

At this very moment, Beyle directed a request for sick leave to the foreign ministry, citing the gravity of his symptoms and his desire to consult a Dr. Prévost in Geneva, who had successfully treated him in the past. For once the request was fully justified, and perhaps out of the confident assumption that he would soon be leaving Italy, he set off on August 12 for a two-day visit to Florence. The only record he made of this visit is a brief note about his pleasure at a musical performance, but it seems unlikely that a man in his condition would have undertaken a journey of over two hundred miles and made such a short stay for any other purpose than to say a last farewell to Giulia Rinieri, the woman who had remained his persistently loyal mistress, despite intermittences, for the past eleven years. His request for leave was granted on September 15, but he could not vacate his post until Tavernier, who had gone to Constantinople to be married, returned. In early October, still in Italy but now really on the verge of departure, Beyle went up to Florence one last time, perhaps to see Giulia again and, in a more practical direction, to make arrangements with his Florentine friend, the lawyer Vincenzo Salvagnoli, who had promised to meet the ailing consul in Marseilles and then to accompany him the rest of the way to Paris. On October 21, Beyle transferred the administration of the consulate to Tavernier and the next day left by steamboat for Marseilles by way of Leghorn and Genoa. Salvagnoli was awaiting him in Marseilles when Beyle arrived there on the 24th, but the writer, already fatigued by the voyage, had to ask for a day's respite before they proceeded north to Geneva through Lyons. They spent six days in Geneva beginning on the 31st, during which time Beyle had extensive consultations with Dr. Prévost and also had the opportunity to see his friend Constantin, who was then stopping in Geneva. On November 8, Beyle and Salvagnoli arrived in Paris and took rooms together.

Being back in the city where he had flourished as a writer and a social creature bolstered Beyle's morale, gave him a momentary sense that he was at last recovering from the partial aphasia and the other distressing consequences of his stroke. On December 8, he could write Donato Bucci

7. *Marginalia*, vol. 2, pp. 388, 389.

that his health had been noticeably better since November 20. He began attending theatrical performances and dining with his old friends, who variously noted that he seemed much older, weakened, drained of energy, and yet often was still somehow able to deploy his brilliant wit in conversation. In January 1842, he had a pleasant reunion with Mme Bouchot, now back in Paris in the company of her husband, whom Beyle found to be a clever and engaging young man. But the novelist tired easily, and through the first two months of 1842, he had to restrict his social activity carefully, and he did no writing, scarcely even any correspondence.

Toward the end of February, Beyle experienced a last illusion of remission, informing Bucci in a letter on the 25th that he was enjoying good health. Within a week or so, under the impetus of this illusion, he was once again full of ideas for writing projects. On March 9, he reread the manuscript of his uncompleted convent tale, *Suora Scolastica*, and two days later conceived the plan of producing a whole new series of Italian novellas. On the 13th, he wrote a new chapter for *Lamiel*; at the same time, he was thinking of a revised edition of *De l'Amour* and was finishing a new preface for it. Beginning on March 15, he worked daily on *Suora Scolastica*. He also pulled other fragments out of his drawer with the intention of completing them for his new series of novellas. On March 21, he actually signed a contract with the *Revue des Deux Mondes* for this second series; he was to receive a sum of 5,000 francs, 1,500 paid as an advance upon signing, for half a dozen or more stories, which he undertook to supply at the rate of one every other month.

The writing he was actually doing, however, in these weeks of March belied the confidence he sought to place in his own continuing powers. The revisions and additions he made on his unfinished manuscripts were confused, uncertain in purpose; and when he was not dictating, his handwriting was so unsteady that at times it was entirely illegible. Stendhal's dedication to his vocation as a writer was now the naked reflex of stubborn will, the physical apparatus for its enactment all but broken by the cerebral hemorrhage of the previous year. Nevertheless, he persisted to the very end. On the morning of March 22, he dictated some pages of *Suora Scolastica*. That evening, on the sidewalk of the rue Neuve-des-Capucines, not far from the entrance to the offices of the foreign ministry, he suffered a second major stroke. "I find that there is nothing ridiculous," he had written Fiori the previous April 10 in an oddly bemused tone amidst real fear after his first attack, "about dying in the street, as long as one does not do it deliberately." In a coma, Beyle was carried to his own nearby room under the direction of his cousin Romain Colomb, who had happened by just then and who attended him at his bedside. On March 23 at 2 A.M., Henri Beyle died without having regained consciousness.

He had disdained all Christian notions of immortality, and despite his conviction, which time has dramatically confirmed, that he was writing for generations to come, there is not much evidence that he had invested a great deal of emotion in the idea of a secular immortality through his writing, the "lottery ticket," as he called it, that every artist holds in the vast and risky game of eternal fame. No writer of his time seems more engagingly alive today. Impelled by a self-consciousness that was in turn shrewd, playful, subtle, anguished, ridiculous, he left in his journal and letters and autobiographies, in his marginal notes, and in the personal anecdotes of his miscellaneous books a record of his own day-to-day experience that still deeply amuses and instructs as he himself was continually amused and instructed. He seems alive, then, partly because in his love of constant notation and formulation, he saw no real division between living and writing. But in quite another way, he lives because, after all those years of talented dilettantism, he discovered how in the novel he could transform the experience of his life into a compellingly realistic art heightened by the delicate intimations of a visionary horizon. He wanted to be known to posterity as a man whose soul had adored Cimarosa, Mozart, and Shakespeare. Though he had cautious hopes for an enlightened future readership capable of appreciating him, he could hardly have guessed that one day others would adore his work in the same way he had adored the art of his three exemplars, as an abiding expression of plangent feeling, poised wit, the harmonious play of an adult mind.

INDEX